Common Yardage Cuts

Refer to this chart when purchasing fabric yardage. These are the sizes of fabric you will take home when asking for specific cuts. Be sure to measure any large templates so you don't purchase a piece of fabric too narrow for the task!

Measurements are based on 44-inch-wide fabric

1/8 yard*	4.5 inches x 44 inches
fat eighth**	18 inches x 11 inches
1/4 yard	9 inches x 44 inches
fat quarter**	18 inches x 22 inches
1/3 yard	12 inches x 44 inches
1/2 yard	18 inches x 44 inches
2/3 yard	24 inches x 44 inches
3/4 yard	27 inches x 44 inches
1 yard	36 inches x 44 inches

*This is generally the smallest cut a fabric store is willing to make.

**These are "special cuts" available in quilting supply stores; they're precut, rolled, and ready to take home. These cuts can be a real bargain, and purchasing them is a great way to build your fabric stash.

Fabric yardage into centimeters

Yardage	cm
1/8 yard	11.4 x 111.8
fat eighth	45.7 x 27.9
1/4 yard	22.9 x 111.8
fat quarter	45.7 x 55.9
1/3 yard	30.5 x 111.8
1/2 yard	45.7 x 111.8
2/3 yard	61.0 x 111.8
3/4 yard	68.6 x111.8
1 yard	91.4 x 111.8

Please Return to Jane Kendrick
if Lost. 817-232-0321

For Dummies™: Bestselling Book Series for Beginners

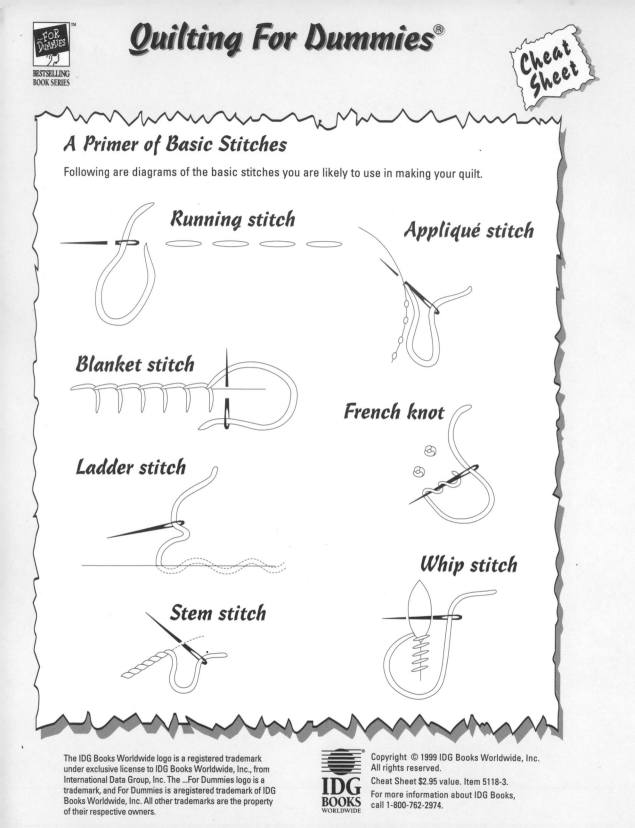

A Primer of Basic Stitches

Following are diagrams of the basic stitches you are likely to use in making your quilt.

Running stitch

Appliqué stitch

Blanket stitch

French knot

Ladder stitch

Whip stitch

Stem stitch

IDG BOOKS WORLDWIDE

Copyright © 1999 IDG Books Worldwide, Inc. All rights reserved.

Cheat Sheet $2.95 value. Item 5118-3.

For more information about IDG Books, call 1-800-762-2974.

For Dummies™: Bestselling Book Series for Beginners

Praise for Quilting For Dummies

"Cheryl Fall's book is not just for beginners. Many quilting books we are tempted to buy provide big color pictures, and as inspiring as that is, Cheryl's book has the information needed to successfully make a quilt. I was impressed with so much detailed, well-organized information presented with humor for easy reading, and can imagine the book read by those thinking of making a first quilt, as a refresher for someone coming back to quilting, or as a reference book in an experienced quilter's library."
— Eleanor Schrumm, Crafts Editor, *Woman's Day* magazine

"Welcome to the wonderful world of quilt-making! With a sense of humor (quilt-making is fun) and common sense (you really can do it), Cheryl escorts you through every realm of the quilt world — from planning your quilt (what you need and what to do with it) to displaying your quilt with pride (you really will have done it). *Quilting For Dummies* is a must-have guide as you begin your exciting journey into the wonderful world of quilting. On every page, Cheryl shares years of teaching and quilt-making experience so you learn everything you need to know (plus much more) to make a beautiful quilt."
— Jan Burns, editor, *Creative Quilting* magazine

"Quilting has become one of America's favorite activities. *Quilting For Dummies* should open this fascinating craft to even more enthusiasts!"
— Barbara Jacksier, Editor, *Country Collectibles* magazine

"Having worked with Cheryl Fall as a designer of outstanding fabric-craft projects — sewn, pieced, appliquéd, and quilted — I was anxious to see what kind of information she would present in this book. I was delighted with the scope of topics as well as the reader friendliness. Cheryl's expertise shines through, making this a sure-fire hit with quilter-wannabes. Even more experienced quilters will find helpful information. (I love her masking tape tips for easy quilting!) As a bonus, the last two sections of *Quilting For Dummies* give the reader what other quilting books don't usually think of — resources of *every* kind, from Web sites and quilting software lists to mail-order sources and quilting group information. Plus, there are fun lists of Top 10's . . . quilting inspirations, where to see quilt displays, and even novels with quilting themes!"
— Miriam Olson, Editor, *Crafts* magazine

"Written by veteran quilter Cheryl Fall, this solidly informative book approaches quilting in a non-intimidating, light-hearted way. *Quilting For Dummies* is a comforting hand-holder for the novice who will learn all there is to know. It should also appeal to long-time quilters who can dip into it to add to their quilting experience or to update their skills with the latest in materials and techniques."

— Theresa Capuana, Contributing Editor, *Home* magazine and Needlework Editor, *Woman's Day* magazine

"*Quilting For Dummies* is the perfect book for the beginning quilter. It has all the basics in an easy-to-understand format and simple projects geared for success. Even the seasoned quilter will love the humorous and down-to-earth advice in a style to keep you interested, laughing, and eager to begin a project. Although I have been sewing and quilting most of my life, I enjoyed *Quilting For Dummies* and even picked up a few new tips along the way. Quilters of all levels should include this book in their quilting library."

— Sandra L. Hatch, Editor, *Quick & Easy Quilting* and *Quilt World* magazines

 ™

References for the Rest of Us!™

BESTSELLING BOOK SERIES

Do you find that traditional reference books are overloaded with technical details and advice you'll never use? Do you postpone important life decisions because you just don't want to deal with them? Then our *...For Dummies*® business and general reference book series is for you.

...For Dummies business and general reference books are written for those frustrated and hard-working souls who know they aren't dumb, but find that the myriad of personal and business issues and the accompanying horror stories make them feel helpless. *...For Dummies* books use a lighthearted approach, a down-to-earth style, and even cartoons and humorous icons to dispel fears and build confidence. Lighthearted but not lightweight, these books are perfect survival guides to solve your everyday personal and business problems.

> *"More than a publishing phenomenon, 'Dummies' is a sign of the times."*
>
> — The New York Times

> *"...you won't go wrong buying them."*
>
> — Walter Mossberg, Wall Street Journal, on IDG Books' ...For Dummies books

> *"A world of detailed and authoritative information is packed into them..."*
>
> — U.S. News and World Report

Already, millions of satisfied readers agree. They have made *...For Dummies* the #1 introductory level computer book series and a best-selling business book series. They have written asking for more. So, if you're looking for the best and easiest way to learn about business and other general reference topics, look to *...For Dummies* to give you a helping hand.

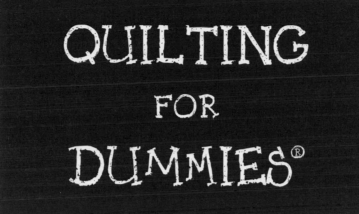

QUILTING
FOR
DUMMIES®

by Cheryl Fall

IDG Books Worldwide, Inc.
An International Data Group Company

Foster City, CA ◆ Chicago, IL ◆ Indianapolis, IN ◆ New York, NY

Quilting For Dummies®

Published by
IDG Books Worldwide, Inc.
An International Data Group Company
919 E. Hillsdale Blvd.
Suite 400
Foster City, CA 94404
www.idgbooks.com (IDG Books Worldwide Web site)
www.dummies.com (Dummies Press Web site)

Library of Congress Catalog Card No.: 99-61126

ISBN: 0-7645-5118-3

Printed in the United States of America

10 9 8 7 6 5 4

1B/QU/RQ/QQ/IN

Distributed in the United States by IDG Books Worldwide, Inc.

Distributed by CDG Books Canada Inc. for Canada; by Transworld Publishers Limited in the United Kingdom; by IDG Norge Books for Norway; by IDG Sweden Books for Sweden; by IDG Books Australia Publishing Corporation Pty. Ltd. for Australia and New Zealand; by TransQuest Publishers Pte Ltd. for Singapore, Malaysia, Thailand, Indonesia, and Hong Kong; by Gotop Information Inc. for Taiwan; by ICG Muse, Inc. for Japan; by Intersoft for South Africa; by Eyrolles for France; by International Thomson Publishing for Germany, Austria and Switzerland; by Distribuidora Cuspide for Argentina; by LR International for Brazil; by Galileo Libros for Chile; by Ediciones ZETA S.C.R. Ltda. for Peru; by WS Computer Publishing Corporation, Inc., for the Philippines; by Contemporanea de Ediciones for Venezuela; by Express Computer Distributors for the Caribbean and West Indies; by Micronesia Media Distributor, Inc. for Micronesia; by Chips Computadoras S.A. de C.V. for Mexico; by Editorial Norma de Panama S.A. for Panama; by American Bookshops for Finland.

For general information on IDG Books Worldwide's books in the U.S., please call our Consumer Customer Service department at 800-762-2974. For reseller information, including discounts and premium sales, please call our Reseller Customer Service department at 800-434-3422.

For information on where to purchase IDG Books Worldwide's books outside the U.S., please contact our International Sales department at 317-572-3993 or fax 317-572-4002.

For consumer information on foreign language translations, please contact our Customer Service department at 1-800-434-3422, fax 317-572-4002, or e-mail rights@idgbooks.com.

For information on licensing foreign or domestic rights, please phone +1-650-653-7098.

For sales inquiries and special prices for bulk quantities, please contact our Order Services department at 800-434-3422 or write to the address above.

For information on using IDG Books Worldwide's books in the classroom or for ordering examination copies, please contact our Educational Sales department at 800-434-2086 or fax 317-572-4005.

For press review copies, author interviews, or other publicity information, please contact our Public Relations department at 650-653-7000 or fax 650-653-7500.

For authorization to photocopy items for corporate, personal, or educational use, please contact Copyright Clearance Center, 222 Rosewood Drive, Danvers, MA 01923, or fax 978-750-4470.

About the Author

Cheryl Fall has been quilting for more than 15 years, but she's been sewing ever since she could hold a needle without putting out her eye. She learned to sew from her mother, grandmothers, great-grandmother, and aunts — all of whom were accomplished stitchers. Her educational background includes fine arts and architectural design studies. Possessing such a wealth of stitching and design skills and always being drawn to color and texture, it's no wonder Cheryl turned to quiltmaking!

Since beginning her professional quilting career in 1986, Cheryl has designed more than 1,000 projects for publication. She's a regular contributor to many popular quilting, women's, and craft magazines, including *Traditional Quilter, Country Living, Quilt World, Family Circle, Creative Quilting, Craftworks, Woman's World, Crafts,* and *McCall's Needlework.* She also designs projects for manufacturers such as Coats & Clark, Pellon, Singer, VIP Fabrics, and P&B Textiles. Cheryl lectures, dabbles in textile design, and makes periodic television appearances. She's the author of seven quilting-related books in addition to this one, and she's in the process of designing Web pages for her quilting and embroidery designs.

Quilting can be an all-consuming occupation, but Cheryl still finds the time to goof around with her husband, Tony, and her daughters, Rebecca and Ashley, and to scour antique stores and estate sales for vintage textiles and needlework. She also spends time tending her rose beds.

ABOUT IDG BOOKS WORLDWIDE

Welcome to the world of IDG Books Worldwide.

IDG Books Worldwide, Inc., is a subsidiary of International Data Group, the world's largest publisher of computer-related information and the leading global provider of information services on information technology. IDG was founded more than 30 years ago by Patrick J. McGovern and now employs more than 9,000 people worldwide. IDG publishes more than 290 computer publications in over 75 countries. More than 90 million people read one or more IDG publications each month.

Launched in 1990, IDG Books Worldwide is today the #1 publisher of best-selling computer books in the United States. We are proud to have received eight awards from the Computer Press Association in recognition of editorial excellence and three from Computer Currents' First Annual Readers' Choice Awards. Our best-selling ...For Dummies® series has more than 50 million copies in print with translations in 31 languages. IDG Books Worldwide, through a joint venture with IDG's Hi-Tech Beijing, became the first U.S. publisher to publish a computer book in the People's Republic of China. In record time, IDG Books Worldwide has become the first choice for millions of readers around the world who want to learn how to better manage their businesses.

Our mission is simple: Every one of our books is designed to bring extra value and skill-building instructions to the reader. Our books are written by experts who understand and care about our readers. The knowledge base of our editorial staff comes from years of experience in publishing, education, and journalism — experience we use to produce books to carry us into the new millennium. In short, we care about books, so we attract the best people. We devote special attention to details such as audience, interior design, use of icons, and illustrations. And because we use an efficient process of authoring, editing, and desktop publishing our books electronically, we can spend more time ensuring superior content and less time on the technicalities of making books.

You can count on our commitment to deliver high-quality books at competitive prices on topics you want to read about. At IDG Books Worldwide, we continue in the IDG tradition of delivering quality for more than 30 years. You'll find no better book on a subject than one from IDG Books Worldwide.

John Kilcullen
John Kilcullen
Chairman and CEO
IDG Books Worldwide, Inc.

Eighth Annual Computer Press Awards ≥1992

Ninth Annual Computer Press Awards ≥1993

Tenth Annual Computer Press Awards ≥1994

Eleventh Annual Computer Press Awards ≥1995

IDG is the world's leading IT media, research and exposition company. Founded in 1964, IDG had 1997 revenues of $2.05 billion and has more than 9,000 employees worldwide. IDG offers the widest range of media options that reach IT buyers in 75 countries representing 95% of worldwide IT spending. IDG's diverse product and services portfolio spans six key areas including print publishing, online publishing, expositions and conferences, market research, education and training, and global marketing services. More than 90 million people read one or more of IDG's 290 magazines and newspapers, including IDG's leading global brands — Computerworld, PC World, Network World, Macworld and the Channel World family of publications. IDG Books Worldwide is one of the fastest-growing computer book publishers in the world, with more than 700 titles in 36 languages. The "...For Dummies®" series alone has more than 50 million copies in print. IDG offers online users the largest network of technology-specific Web sites around the world through IDG.net (http://www.idg.net), which comprises more than 225 targeted Web sites in 55 countries worldwide. International Data Corporation (IDC) is the world's largest provider of information technology data, analysis and consulting, with research centers in over 41 countries and more than 400 research analysts worldwide. IDG World Expo is a leading producer of more than 168 globally branded conferences and expositions in 35 countries including E3 (Electronic Entertainment Expo), Macworld Expo, ComNet, Windows World Expo, ICE (Internet Commerce Expo), Agenda, DEMO, and Spotlight. IDG's training subsidiary, ExecuTrain, is the world's largest computer training company, with more than 230 locations worldwide and 785 training courses. IDG Marketing Services helps industry-leading IT companies build international brand recognition by developing global integrated marketing programs via IDG's print, online and exposition products worldwide. Further information about the company can be found at www.idg.com.   1/26/00

Dedication

In memory of Phyllis Barbieri, editor, mentor, and friend. The quilting community will miss her.

I also dedicate this book to would-be quilters the world over, and those who are learning this art. May all your quilts be terrific!

Author's Acknowledgments

I would like to thank my wonderful family. Without their support, this book may have never made it to press. I can't thank my hubby and daughters enough for all the cooking, cleaning, and laundry they did while I was putting this book together (okay, sometimes I milked it, but it sure was fun!).

My deepest gratitude to Stedman Mays, agent extraordinaire, and Holly McGuire, Kathy Cox, Wendy Hatch, and Kim Darosett at IDG books. These wonderful people helped make this book possible from concept to creation. All of you are absolutely outstanding in your profession, and are pleasures to work with.

Much of the art for this book was done by the late Phyllis Barbieri, whose help in this book was invaluable and whose loss is deeply felt. She and technical reviewer Laurette Koserowski, both from *Traditional Quilter* magazine, made a great team. Special thanks to Laurette, who persevered with her review during an incredibly difficult time, and artist Connie Rand, who stepped in and quickly completed more than a hundred illustrations so we could hold the press date for this book. I can't thank Laurette and Connie enough for their meticulous contributions. Many thanks, too, to all of the companies and individuals who contributed time or product for this book, including:

- Coats & Clark and Meta Hoge for the use of some past projects that I have done for them, as well as their terrific assortment of threads and bias tape. (Thanks too, Meta, for the occasional pep talk!)
- P&B Textiles, VIP Fabrics, Springs, RJR Fabrics, and Marcus Brothers for the delectable fabrics used in these quilts. Your catalogs offer such temptation to a fabric-phile like myself!
- Handler Textile Corporation and Pellon for their fusible products and stabilizers, which make machine appliqué a joy.
- Nolting Manufacturing for professionally machine quilting several of the larger projects in this book, saving me tons of time. Your generosity is very much appreciated.
- Fairfield Processing for the batting, pillow forms, and stuffing used in the projects.

Last but not least, I want to thank an inanimate object, which I just know has a soul hidden somewhere in its gears — my trusty, old, worn-out Kenmore sewing machine. It has seen its share of quilts pass over its throat plate; it takes a lickin' but keeps on stitchin'!

Publisher's Acknowledgments

We're proud of this book; please register your comments through our IDG Books Worldwide Online Registration Form located at http://my2cents.dummies.com.

Some of the people who helped bring this book to market include the following:

Acquisitions, Editorial, and Media Development

Project Editor: Kathleen M. Cox

Acquisitions Editor: Holly McGuire

Copy Editors: Wendy Hatch, Kim Darosett

Technical Editor: Laurette Koserowski, *Traditional Quilter* magazine

Editorial Manager: Rev Mengle

Editorial Coordinator: Maureen F. Kelly

Editorial Assistants: Paul E. Kuzmic, Jamila Pree

Acquisitions Coordinator: Jonathan Malysiak

Production

Project Coordinator: Karen York

Layout and Graphics: Linda M. Boyer, Maridee V. Ennis, Kelly Hardesty, Angela F. Hunckler, Brent Savage, Janet Seib, M. Anne Sipahimalani, Rashell Smith, Kate Snell, Michael A. Sullivan, Brian Torwelle

Proofreaders: Christine Berman, Kelli Botta, Nancy Price, Nancy L. Reinhardt, Janet M. Withers

Illustrations: Phyllis Barbieri from *Traditional Quilter* and Constance Rand from House of White Birches

Color Art: Andy Chen

Indexer: Johnna VanHoose

General and Administrative

IDG Books Worldwide, Inc.: John Kilcullen, CEO; Bill Barry, President and COO

IDG Books Consumer Reference Group

> **Business:** Kathleen A. Welton, Vice President and Publisher; Kevin Thornton, Acquisitions Manager

> **Cooking/Gardening:** Jennifer Feldman, Associate Vice President and Publisher

> **Education/Reference:** Diane Graves Steele, Vice President and Publisher; Greg Tubach, Publishing Director

> **Lifestyles:** Kathleen Nebenhaus, Vice President and Publisher; Tracy Boggier, Managing Editor

> **Pets:** Dominique De Vito, Associate Vice President and Publisher; Tracy Boggier, Managing Editor

> **Travel:** Michael Spring, Vice President and Publisher; Suzanne Jannetta, Editorial Director; Brice Gosnell, Managing Editor

IDG Books Consumer Editorial Services: Kathleen Nebenhaus, Vice President and Publisher; Kristin A. Cocks, Editorial Director; Cindy Kitchel, Editorial Director

IDG Books Consumer Production: Debbie Stailey, Production Director

IDG Books Packaging: Marc J. Mikulich, Vice President, Brand Strategy and Research

Contents at a Glance

Cartoons at a Glance

By Rich Tennant

Fax: 978-546-7747
E-mail: richtennant@the5thwave.com
World Wide Web: www.the5thwave.com

Table of Contents

· ·

Part IV: Completing the Circle: Projects to Try 167

Introduction

• •

*E*verybody loves quilts. They're soft, cozy, and comforting, and they've been around forever. Making quilts is fun and a wonderful way to express your creativity with a practical bent. And making quilts today is easier than you may have ever imagined.

The making of quilts does not require any special skills, just a general knowledge of sewing and the desire to try it! If you can sew a button or mend a hem, you can make a quilt. With just a few basic tools, a small amount of fabric, and a little time, you can create your own piece of comfort. This book shows you how.

Quiltmaking gives you a wonderful opportunity to experiment with color, design, and texture. Let your imagination guide you in choosing your fabrics and projects. Don't worry about mistakes — they add to the charm of your finished project.

And speaking of projects! The range of quilted objects you can create is limitless! Think beyond the traditional bed quilt and consider making quilted placemats or a table runner for your kitchen or to give as a hostess gift. Create quilted wallhangings as art for your walls. Stitch up a baby layette featuring a warm, soft quilt, matching quilted bonnet, and diaper tote. Whip up an eyeglass case with matching makeup bag or hanger cover as a gift for a friend. If you can imagine it, you can quilt it.

How to Use This Book

Quilting For Dummies guides even the beginningest-beginner through all the steps necessary for creating your first quilt. And I do mean your first quilt. Although most people interested in quilting have sewn a bit, you can use this book without having much more experience than having threaded a needle. Diagrams of the basic stitches you may need are included on the Cheat Sheet, so you can tear them off and post them in front of you as you work. You can start small, add experience and confidence, and eventually move on to your grand design.

If you already possess some sewing abilities, you can progress through this book somewhat faster, adding new skills and developing new techniques. Use this book in the way that makes most sense for your situation. You can read it cover to cover, or just piece through specific chapters that interest you. Think of this book as your own little quilting bee, with me as your friendly, down-to-earth mentor who presents the information you need in a way that's easy to understand and inspiring to try.

I show you how to select fabrics and materials, create a design, and then cut, piece, quilt, and finish your creation — all within the covers of this book. And to help you along, I include projects to fit any skill level. All are easy to create when you follow the illustrated and detailed step-by-step instructions.

How This Book Is Organized

For logic and ease of use, this book is organized into five parts, progressing from the most basic definition of a quilt and its parts, along with a brief glimpse of the quilt in history, and progressing through various skills and techniques that will help you create your quilt. A brief description of each of these parts follows.

Part I: Planning Your Masterpiece

You may have heard a lot about quilts, but you may not know that a quilt is not just a bedcovering, or a vest, or a placemat — to quilt is to apply a technique of stitching together layers of fabric using a decorative pattern to create a variety of beautiful and practical objects. In this part, you find out what makes a quilt a quilt and discover the wonders of fabrics, patterns, and patchwork.

Part II: Sharpening Your Sewing Skills

Quilting gives you lots of creative flexibility, but the price you pay is precision. Measuring, cutting, and pressing are crucial if you want your quilt to lay crisp and flat. This part tells you what you need to know to stay on the straight and narrow with your quilting skills. I also give you a primer on appliqué, to give you even more decorative and creative options.

Part III: Ahead at the Finish: Quilting the Pieces in Place

Ultimately, your quilt is a creatively stitched-together sandwich of fabric (the "bread") and batting (the filling). This part helps you build the Dagwood of quilt sandwiches, getting all your creative juices flowing. When you're done, you should know enough to get started on a project of your own, if you haven't already. Basting, stitching, and binding are all covered here so you can finish your masterpiece in style.

Part IV: Completing the Circle: Projects to Try

If you're anxious to start but don't have any of your own projects or designs in mind, I provide 16 projects here to get you started. I use a thimble system to rate them on degree of difficulty (that's degree of difficulty for a beginner; as you advance in this art and craft, you can achieve new and higher levels of difficulty as you strive to create precisely the effect you have in mind). One-thimble projects are the simplest; three-thimble projects are the most complex. Two-thimble projects are designed to advance your skills and increase the fun. I provide patterns for the appliqué projects, but for some you'll need to run to your trusty copier center and enlarge them to full-size. (They're reproduced here at 50 percent; my ideas are clearly bigger than this book.)

Part V: The Part of Tens

The Part of Tens is a patchwork part — a little bit of this, a little of that, and lots of information and inspiration as you become absorbed into the quilting world. Enjoy visiting some great quilt collections. Try to meet fellow quilters and shop in cyberspace. And practice timesaving techniques that give you time for more quilts (and tips for displaying them).

Let Our Icons Guide You

Sprinkled throughout this book are cute little pictures called icons that highlight important information. Here's the decoder key:

This icon points out time-tested ways to do things regardless of how your quilting or how long you've been doing it.

This bomb points out things that could wreck your project and maybe even put your love affair with quilting on hold.

This star pattern highlights a basic. Whenever you quilt, whether by hand or machine, you need to remember and apply this information — these are the eternal truths of the craft.

Quilting bees have a long history of friendship and sharing. Masters of the quilt would mentor novices and share the secrets that only years of experience can provide. This bee buzzes around those type of tips — the ones that save you years of being stung by trial and error.

 This highlights tips useful to those who are quilting by hand.

 This icon marks stuff that helps you quilt better by machine.

 Quiltspeak is a whole new language. This icon marks a translation.

On Your Fingers!

As soon as you piece your first block, I have no doubt you'll be hooked on quilting, as thousands of people all around the world are. You'll suddenly find yourself unconsciously setting aside time from your own busy schedule to collect fabric (most quilters are true fabri-holics), cut, and stitch. Little squares of fabric will unexpectedly appear in your hands each time you sit down, whether you're watching television, riding the bus, or taking some time for yourself. You'll find that quilting somehow helps you relax after a hard day. Oh, to shut yourself in your own wonderful, colorful world of fabric and thread!

Although I've attempted to include everything a beginner could want in a quilt book, keep in mind that there are as many ways of making a quilt as there are quilters, and far too many additional techniques, hints, and tidbits are available than space in this book allows. I encourage you to start building a library of quilting reference materials and a nice stash of fabric. I include some of my favorite reference works and supply sources in the Appendix to nudge you along. Happy Quilting!

Part I
Planning Your Masterpiece

Sara tells me you're an expert on the works of Michelangelo.

In this part . . .

Quilts may seem commonplace, but their artistry extends far back into human history and continues to be intertwined with our real-life experience. This part explains what makes a quilt a quilt, tempts you with the wonders of fabric, and presents the foundation for your own create-a-quilt-ivity. By the time you get through this part, you'll be on your way to being a true fabric-holic, greedily stuffing fabrics into every spare nook and cranny in anticipation of the next project.

Chapter 1

What Makes a Quilt a Quilt?

Quilts used for clothing and bedcoverings have played an important role in people's lives for centuries, providing their makers and recipients not only with warmth and comfort, but also with colorful, attractive works of art. Traditionally, quilts have also been showcases for the talents and skills of their creators.

In this chapter, I explain what a quilt is and document the quilt's rich role in the texture of human life. Quilting has been used for centuries as a practical, pleasurable, and inspirational source of art and activity.

The Quilt Sandwich

A quilt — that soft, cozy, comforting hunk of fabric and filling — in its simplest sense is a textile *sandwich;* in fact, that's how the quilt layers are traditionally described — as a sandwich. This simple sandwich is what distinguishes a quilt from any other sewn object.

All quilts — whether intended for use on a bed or as a potholder — consist of three layers: a quilt top, a filling (called batting), and a backing. The top, batting, and backing layers are held together *(quilted)* using a series of basic running stitches. The layers can also be tied together by stitching yarn, narrow ribbon, or pearl cotton through the layers at regular intervals and tying off the ends to hold the layers of the sandwich together. However you do it, your goal is to prevent the layers from shifting. You can see a cross section of a quilt in Figure 1-1.

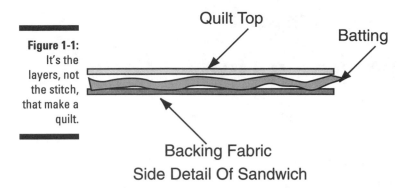

Figure 1-1:
It's the layers, not the stitch, that make a quilt.

Quilt Top

Batting

Backing Fabric

Side Detail Of Sandwich

Some folks call various types of bedcoverings quilts, but if the covering doesn't consist of three layers, it isn't really a quilt but rather a coverlet, bedspread, or throw. Although the word "quilt" is casually used to refer to a quilted bedcovering, many other objects — such as placemats, vests, and diaper bags — can be quilted.

The quilt top

The topmost layer of the quilt sandwich is the *quilt top,* which is typically made of fabric blocks that are pieced, appliquéd, or both. A *pieced* (also called *patchwork*) quilt top can be made up of tens to hundreds of small pieces of fabric, joined together by hand or machine to create a pattern or repeating design. Modern cutting and stitching techniques make the work of piecing both fun and easy to do. I discuss these techniques in Chapters 7 and 8.

Patchwork is the most popular form of quilt-making and uses basic shapes such as squares, triangles, rectangles, and hexagons to form patterns ranging from simple to complex. Various patterns can be pieced into one block, and each block is then pieced to another to create the overall quilt design. One block can be made of many pieces, or just one piece. We talk more about patchwork in Chapter 3.

Appliqué is another method of creating quilt tops. To create an appliquéd quilt top, you stitch various fabric shapes on top of a base fabric. Machine appliqué provides a variety of possibilities and is easy enough for even the rank beginner to master. Appliqué takes a bit longer to stitch than piecing, even by machine, but you can use it to create patterns that can't be pieced, such as dainty flowers with gracefully curving stems. Chapter 9 covers appliqué in more detail.

The batting

The middle layer, or filling, is cotton, wool, or polyester *batting*. Batting adds depth and dimension to the quilt as it buffers the quilt top and bottom. I talk more about batting in Chapter 2.

The backing

The bottom layer of the sandwich, the *backing*, is a large piece of plain or printed cotton that may or may not be pieced together from smaller pieces to create the proper size. I talk more about the backing in Chapter 2.

The Quilting Story

Quilts were an essential article in households of the past, not only as bedcoverings, but also as curtains to keep out drafts, and petticoats and waistcoats to keep the body warm. They were even used as armor. Old records show quilts included in a bride's dowry, and no self-respecting bride's family would allow her to marry without a certain number of quilted items in her hope chest.

Patchwork quilting evolved from the frugality of homemakers in times when fabric wasn't very plentiful. Every scrap was saved from other sewing projects, and worn out items were often recycled into patches for quilts. Necessity was truly the mother of invention, and nothing went to waste. An inventive stitcher could take the miscellaneous bits of fabric from her sewing basket and create something new for her home and family. Most patchwork quilts were intended for everyday use and were simply patched up when they became worn. If they became too worn, these tattered quilts were often used as fillers for new quilts.

Did you know?

The oldest quilted object found thus far is a rug taken from a Siberian tomb that may date from around the first century B.C.

Quilting may also have been practiced by the ancient Egyptians. Carvings at some ancient sites show objects that have a quilted appearance being used.

The oldest known quilted objects from Europe include armor and whole-cloth quilts from Sicily.

Most households also had certain quilts they used only for special occasions or when honored guests visited. Quilt-makers put their greatest efforts into these quilts, using the best quality fabric they could afford and covering them with miles and miles of beautiful quilting stitches. Many of these "best quilts" were appliquéd or elaborately pieced and were rarely used. Because these quilts were so well cared for by their makers, many of them have survived and are coveted today by collectors.

Quilt-making has also been an important social activity, both in days past and into today. The quilting bee was one of the few opportunities farm wives had for getting together and retreating from the back-breaking chores of farm life. These groups of ladies (and sometimes men) often would work on a special presentation quilt to commemorate a wedding or a birth or to express appreciation to a member of their community. These presentation quilts — which often included the signatures of the many makers, either written poetically on the blocks in permanent ink or embroidered in thread — became known as *autograph* or *album quilts*.

Autograph quilts are made in a variety of styles. Some are constructed of identical pieced blocks; others consisted of individual appliquéd blocks. Commemorative quilts in elaborate red and green appliqué were quite popular on the east coast of the United States during the 1800s and are known as the Baltimore Album style.

Granny's petticoats

Have you ever wondered what granny wore under her billowing skirts to keep warm during icy-cold winters? The answer is a quilt!

Museums featuring garment exhibits often show fine examples of quilted petticoats, corset covers, and waistcoats in their collections. Some of these items were worn strictly for warmth, but others were highly decorative or designed for supportive purposes, as in corset covers.

Quilted petticoats for everyday wear were very simple and usually made of wool, serving mainly to keep their wearers warm. The filler material in many of these old petticoats was wool wadding, but some of our more frugal grannies actually used horsehair — sounds like an itch-fest to me!

Other petticoats serving decorative purposes were elaborately quilted and were probably reserved for special occasions, or for times when skirts were pinned up to show underskirts and petticoats, depending on the fashion rules of the day. (Showing more petticoat than the rules of proper conduct allowed might have been considered scandalous!) In the 1800s, these fancy petticoats were made of silk or taffeta.

Do quilting bees still buzz?

Great-granny probably didn't get out all that much, considering the lack of transportation available to her and the fact that she may have lived out on a farm in the middle of nowhere. This is why a quilting bee was so important to her —it was one of her main means of socializing with other women and staying in touch with her community.

Although the quilting bees of days past served a very important purpose, they no longer exist in the same capacity as they once did. Society is considerably more mobile now, and a quilting bee is no longer a necessity. But before you panic, consider what has replaced it — the quilting guild.

Most quilters today are members of, or have attended some form of, a quilting guild. Most guilds meet monthly or bimonthly for a few hours and share news of quilting, show off finished projects and work on projects-in-progress. Some also work on community service projects, such as quilts for the homeless or house-bound, quilts and layettes for premature babies, and memorial quilts for AIDS victims and their families, to name just a few of the wonderful causes guilds often support.

Many guilds also have special programs that bring in top teachers from all over the country. Almost all host a yearly quilt show, which gives you an excellent opportunity to check out what other quilters in your area are working on! To find out what types of events are being planned by your local guild, contact their program chairperson.

Finding a quilting guild is easy. Simply ask at the local quilting supply store or fabric retailer. Or check with the local library. Be sure to find out what their "visitation" policy is ahead of time. Some allow one or two visits before requiring membership (which usually has a very minimal fee), or may charge a per-visit fee (a buck or two).

Don't think you have the time for a guild, but like to spend hours surfing the Web? Consider a cyber-guild! The Internet is full of great places for quilters to interact with each other without ever leaving their homes! To help you find sites for quilters on the Net, I've included a listing of great Web sites for quilters in Chapter 17.

The Quilt Story Continues

Quilts today, while continuing to add warmth to a household, are no longer a necessity, but rather a means of self-expression — a glorious work of art in fabric!

Patchwork is no longer simply a form of frugality, but rather another form of art. Although quilts are still sometimes made from fabric scraps, the maker is more likely to use the scraps to recreate the charming look of old quilts or to commemorate a life or an event, rather than out of necessity.

Quilt-making today is a hobby enjoyed by men and women alike (though women with their needle-nimble fingers still predominate). Machine techniques have replaced tedious hand-piecing and appliqué, but modern quilt-makers still take inspiration from quilts of days past, adapting those designs and techniques to today's lifestyles.

Chapter 2
The Pièce de Résistance: Fabric

*F*abric is to the quilter what paint is to the artist. So you want your fabrics to be beautiful, durable, and to work well together. Fortunately, fabrics suitable for quilting are very easy to find. Most fabric stores have entire sections devoted to quilting fabrics. Here you'll find fabrics in every color of the rainbow — enough to dazzle the mind!

You can also find stores that cater specifically to the needs of quilters (these are great places to find all those fun gadgets described in Chapter 6 that quilters enjoy). Look in the Yellow Pages under fabrics or quilting, and you're bound to find several promising listings for your area.

Even though you can easily be dazzled by the swirl of colors and patterns when you visit one of these fabric fantasies or page through a glossy catalog from one of the mail-order houses described in the Appendix, reading the following sections can help you keep a level head long enough to choose the right fabrics for all the layers of your quilt. (And then, feeling proud of your carefully made decisions, you can get impulsive and buy six yards of that sale-priced zebra fun fur that you'll never use.)

Use Cotton for Your Quilt Top

I recommend using only 100 percent cotton fabric for quilting. Cotton handles beautifully, as it is light but sturdy and cool to the touch. Cotton also holds a crease well, making it ideal for those turned-under edges of hand appliqué (I discuss appliqué in Chapter 9).

Cotton is also easy to sew through by hand or machine and can be somewhat forgiving if you make a slight mistake, as it can often be stretched into shape. If you end up ripping out stitches, the cotton fibers will obligingly work themselves back into position when moistened, and the needle holes will magically disappear! It also washes well, can take a lot of love (have you ever watched a child drag around his favorite blankie?), and is durable enough to stand the tests of time. In fact, nearly all antique quilts are made of cotton, with the exception of a few wool quilts.

You can use other fibers when necessary to add special effects to quilts, but be sure to use them only as accents. A little bit of gold tissue-lamé in a holiday quilt is a nice touch and adds sparkle. But if you do choose a special-occasion fabric for use in your quilts, be sure to check the care label on the end of the bolt (you know, the cardboard thingy the fabric is wrapped on in the stores) to make sure that you don't include dry-clean-only fabrics in a quilt meant to be laundered at home. Otherwise, you run the risk of having your special fabric shrink and buckle, ruining the entire project — now *that* would be a real bummer!

Recognizing quality

Although cotton is *the* choice for quilters, not all cottons are created equal. Remember the old cliché, "you get what you pay for" when buying cotton fabrics.

The fabrics in most quilting departments of fabric stores and those found in shops devoted to the art of quilting usually are just fine, but you often come across tables loaded with bolts of bargain fabrics, sometimes priced as low as a few dollars per yard. Although you can certainly find bargains, and when you do, you should definitely jump on them in a fabric-buying frenzy, some so-called "bargain fabrics" aren't all they're cracked up to be.

 Some fabrics feel like good choices because of the *sizing* applied to them during the manufacturing process. Sizing is the stuff manufacturers use to stiffen the fabric before wrapping it on the bolt. Its purpose is to make the fabric easier to handle in the manufacturing process, make it look nice, and keep it from slipping off the bolt. But after you wash some of these bargain fabrics, they turn into limp noodles that aren't suitable for quilting, and resemble cheesecloth!

Always check the thread count against a quality piece of fabric when in doubt. This can be difficult because the thread count is rarely, if ever, listed on the sticker at the end of the bolt. You'll have to "eyeball" this one!

Remember, the more threads per inch, the better suited the fabric is for quilting — 90 threads per inch is a good number; higher is better! Counting threads is a daunting task. I don't really expect you to physically count them; "eyeballing" the thread count is the easiest way to do it — this isn't rocket science. But do compare a bargain fabric to a more expensive piece of fabric. The store personnel won't mind too much if you drag around a bolt of good quality fabric to compare with the bargain fabric — they might look at you funny, but that's about it.

Don't buy anything that resembles glorified (meaning colorfully printed and well-stiffened) cheesecloth — the stuff so thin with threads so far apart that you can strain cottage cheese through it. Some manufacturers try to reduce the cost of their textiles by reducing the thread count and adding heavy doses of sizing. Also avoid anything with polyester (see the sidebar, "Avoiding the two evil sisters, Poly and Ester").

Avoiding the two evil sisters, Poly and Ester

Fabric pack rats tend to purchase fabrics on impulse. These impulse purchases often come from the bargain bin or remnant section, and their fiber contents are questionable. Always try to avoid polyester fabrics. They slip and slide as you stitch and are a poor choice for quilts. However, determining a fabric's fiber content can be tricky at times. Here are a few pointers for differentiating between a polyester and cotton fabric:

✔ **Read all about it.** First and easiest of all, if the fabric is still on its original bolt (ask if in doubt), read the fiber content printed on the end of the bolt.

✔ **Get in touch with your feelings.** Polyester is slippery! Rub a double layer of fabric between your fingers. Does it slide easily, or does it "grip" the other layer? A fabric that's 100 percent polyester has no "grip," but a poly-cotton blend sometimes has a slight bit of grip. Cotton will often "grip" the opposing layer. Polyester fabrics and poly-cotton blends also tend to have higher lusters (meaning the fabrics reflect light or have a bit of a sheen to them) than 100 percent cotton fabrics. Avoid them both. Fold a piece and "finger press" it by running your nail along the fold. Does it hold a crease well? Cotton tends to hold a nice sharp crease. Polyester and blends have a weak crease.

✔ **Burn it, baby!** Okay, this isn't an acceptable tip while shopping, but it's a great way to determine a hand-me-down chunk of fabric's fiber content. The technique is very simple: Cut off a small section of fabric and hold it over a piece of waxed paper with tweezers. Ignite the fabric with a match or cigarette lighter. Polyester fabric burns, melts, and shrinks away from the flame. It also has a "sweet" smell, gives off black smoke, and leaves behind a hard bead on the waxed paper. Cotton, on the other hand, leaves behind a fine ash when it burns and may smell like burning leaves or wood.

The best advice of all: If in doubt, don't buy it. Find something else.

Staying in style

When searching for fabrics to use in a particular project, keep in mind the look you want to achieve. Is the project a casual country quilt or a more formal Victorian quilt? A simple pieced block can take on many different moods depending on the style of fabric you choose. Soft pastels in tiny prints can give a project a feminine feel, while deep, muted browns, rusts, and blues may give the quilt a country flavor.

For a high-end, "decorator-put-together" look, choose coordinates for your quilt. Coordinates are just what they sound like — a group of fabrics that go together, or "coordinate" with one another. They can be as diverse as having a large-scale floral with a wide matching stripe, or a softly-shaded, sweet little calico with matching solids and tiny little prints. Most fabric stores display coordinated fabrics together, making it easier to pick and choose the fabrics that best fit your style.

Table 2-1 can guide you in your fabric selections.

Table 2-1	Fit Your Fabric to Your Style
Quilt Style	*Fabric Suggestions*
Victorian or Feminine	Realistic florals mixed with small- to medium-scale coordinates
Cottage	Bright pastels in small- to medium-scale prints with solid off-white
Lodge	Medium- to large-scale deep, woodsy-colored solids and plaids, all in shades of brown, green, rust, red, ochre, tan, navy, and sometimes black
Country	Muted, dusty-toned prints in all scales plus solids *or* two-color schemes such as red with white or blue with off-white
Scrappy	Go crazy, pal! Anything goes here!
Traditional Amish	Deep jewel-tone solids and black; no prints
Contemporary	Colorful novelty prints, especially geometrics
Juvenile	Bright crayon colors in solids and prints

Pay close attention to the *color values* of the fabrics you select (see Figure 2-1). For the best results, gather an assortment of light-, medium-, and dark-valued prints for your projects — your projects need some contrast so they won't look washed-out from a distance.

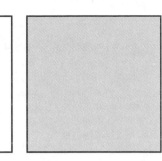

Figure 2-1:
Light-,
medium-,
and dark-
value
fabrics.

An assortment of values is essential to a well-designed quilt. If you choose, for instance, all medium-value fabrics, your quilt won't look like much from a distance. It'll just look like a lump of fabric with batting in between the layers! Having different values in your quilt adds contrast — light-value fabrics will recede, dark-value fabrics will pop out prominently, and medium-value fabrics hold the whole thing together.

Some fabric stores carry a nifty little tool called a "value finder." This is simply a little rectangle (about 2 inches x 4 inches) made of transparent red plastic that, when held over printed fabrics, allows you to see the "color value" of the fabrics, without the clutter of the print getting in your way! It's small enough to fit in your purse or pocket and can be handy to keep with you.

In addition to value, scale is also very important, as you can see in Figure 2-2.

Figure 2-2:
Small-,
medium-,
and large-
scale prints.

Just as with values, the smaller scale, lighter colored prints will recede, and large-scale prints can be real eye poppers! But do try to avoid having more than one or two large-scale prints in your quilt, as they can get pretty busy-looking and are hard on your eyes when cutting, stitching, and quilting.

Storing your stash

Collecting fabrics is half the fun of quilting. Sooner or later, though, you'll need to organize those haphazard piles you stuffed in the closet and under the bed so you can find just the right piece quickly and easily. Here are some helpful hints for organizing your stash:

✔ Purchase clear plastic shoebox-size storage boxes. Assign each box a color or group of sub-colors and label the boxes. Arrange your labeled boxes in a pretty armoire or hutch that has doors to hide the contents; then you can place it anywhere in your home.

✔ Stacking, four-drawer units on rollers are great for quilters who migrate from room to room, looking for a place to work. Use one unit for fabrics and another for threads, notions, and tools. You can find these in most office-supply stores and anywhere you find items for home organization. They're reasonably priced and quite handy!

✔ Store your fabrics under your bed in cardboard or clear plastic under-the-bed storage bins.

✔ Buy an inexpensive shelf at a home center and set it up in an unused corner of the house or garage. Better yet, set up a work table and storage areas and claim the garage for yourself.

✔ Take over the guest dresser. Guests seem to prefer living out of their suitcases anyway, so why not organize your stash in the drawers? You can use shoeboxes or cardboard strips as dividers to help keep the stacks tidy.

✔ Take over the guest closet. (This almost always follows taking over the guest dresser.)

✔ Take over the entire guest room. Send the guests to a hotel.

Measuring up

Quilting fabrics are available by the yard in 44- and 45-inch widths; you can also find them at quilting supply stores pre-cut and sold in tidy little bundles called *fat quarters*.

A fat quarter isn't cut from the bolt of cloth as a 9-inch x 44-inch strip of fabric. Instead, the store cuts a $^1/_2$ yard from the bolt and then cuts this 18-inch x 44-inch piece in half down the center crease, giving you an 18-inch x 22-inch piece of fabric. This makes it easier to cut larger-sized quilt pieces from the fabric, rather than limiting yourself to templates or patches 9 inches or smaller.

Purchasing fat quarters is a good way to go if you only need a small amount of a particular color for your project: You save time, because you don't have to wait for the store personnel to cut the fabric from the bolt for you, and you get more useable fabric for your money because of the way the pieces are cut. It's also a great way to build your fabric stash, because fat quarters are often cut from fabrics that are being discontinued, and they are often greatly discounted by the store.

TIP

Prewashing means project protection

Always prewash all your fabric. Keep in mind that a 12-inch square of 100 percent cotton fabric can shrink, sometimes as much as $\frac{1}{4}$ inch both horizontally and vertically, and that different fabrics can shrink at different rates. One fabric may not shrink at all, but another may shrink considerably. Shrinkage after you launder your finished project can have disastrous effects. Imagine, after all your effort in making a quilt, that you wash it and find that the pretty blue print in the center of the block has shrunk, puckering each and every block in such a way that the it's unrecognizable — it can happen!

Prewashing also removes the sizing from the fabrics. This makes it easier to handle or machine quilt, as the sizing won't get gummy or sticky from the moisture in your hands (remember playing with starch in grade school?). It also removes excess dye that can bleed onto other fabrics and spoil the color. (Unless, of course, you want that pretty red print to bleed and turn the entire quilt pink — hey, some folks do strange things.)

To prewash fabric, simply machine-wash it on a normal (regular, everyday washing) setting with mild detergent. Tumble dry until the fabric is only slightly damp, and then press it using a dry iron (no steam) on the "cotton" setting. Fold the fabric neatly until you're ready to use it.

I recommend washing your fabrics as soon as you bring them home — that way, when you pull them out to work on a project two days, two months or even two years later, you won't have to stare at the hunk of fabric, wondering if you've prewashed it. Washing fabric as soon as you get it home eliminates any doubt!

Quilters often inherit fabrics from other *fabriholics* or win them at quilting raffles; whether these fabrics have been prewashed is a mystery. When in doubt, wash them. Large chunks can go directly into the washing machine, but smaller pieces tend to be "eaten" by the machine.

To wash the smaller pieces, fill a sink or basin with room-temperature water and a bit of mild soap. As shown in the figure in this sidebar, slip the fabric into the water, swish it around for a few seconds, and then rinse well. Dry the fabric flat on a terry towel and press the fabric when it's just slightly damp.

(continued)

(continued)

If you notice that a particular fabric *crocks* (a technical term meaning that the color bleeds) when washing, continue washing and rinsing the fabric until it no longer loses dye. If the fabric continues to crock, discard it and replace it with something more colorfast. Imagine putting hours of work into a red and white quilt, only to discover after washing your quilt that the red fabric bled into the white fabric, turning the whole quilt pink!

When purchasing *yard goods* (another name for fabric sold on the bolt), always ask that your fabrics be cut *on the grain* — especially when you buy plaids. This eliminates wasted fabric when cutting pieces that require *cutting on the true grain*. (For more information on fabric grain, see Chapter 3.)

Hit a Homer with Your Batting

The batting, or filler (remember the sandwich?) for your quilt is just as important to the look of the finished quilt as the fabric. You need to decide if you want a flatter, old-fashioned-looking quilt, a soft and comfy but low-profile quilt, or a thick, lofty, jump-right-in-and-snuggle type of quilt. Each look requires a different type of batting.

Many varieties of batting are on the market, and each gives a different look to a quilt. Battings are available in several different fibers, the most common being polyester, cotton/polyester blend, cotton, and wool (yes, poly and ester are safe for batting). You face lots of choices, but answering a few simple questions about your project can narrow the field and help you pick the right batting for your needs:

✔ Are you hand or machine quilting or tying the quilt?

✔ How much effort are you putting into the quilting?

✔ Do you plan on heavily quilting the project or just stitching enough to hold the quilt layers together?

✔ What is the quilt's intended final use?

✔ Will the quilt be laundered often?

✔ What size is the quilt?

Always read the manufacturer's recommendations printed on the wrapper or the batting bolt label when choosing your batting. This information not only lists suggestions for using the product, but also provides laundering instructions and any special handling tips, such as prewashing the product before working with it.

The following sections help you sort through all the options and find the best batting for your quilted pieces.

Prepackaged or by the yard?

You can buy batting prepackaged or by the yard. Your choice will depend on your needs. Price-wise, there's not much difference.

Prepackaged batting is handy — it's already cut to standard bed sizes, shrink-wrapped, and easy to take home. But, if your project is smaller, you'll bring home more batting than you actually need. Too much batting isn't bad, of course — you just have batting to stash away, ready for the next small project!

Batting by-the-yard is the same stuff as prepackaged batting, but you have the option of purchasing only what you need. The downside is that the batting has not been shrink-wrapped, so it's bulky to bring home and to store. Also, this type of batting averages only 45 inches wide, making it unsuitable for larger projects because you would need to piece the batting together. Batting by-the-yard is available only in polyester, to the best of my knowledge.

Prepackaged batting also gets bulky and more difficult to store after you remove it from the package. To tame this wild beast, carefully remove the batting from the package and unroll only the amount necessary for your project. Cut off only what you need. Then quickly reroll the batting and put it back in its bag before it has a chance to expand.

Table 2-2 lists standard sizes for pre-packaged batting.

Table 2-2	Standard Sizes for Prepackaged Quilt Batting
Quilt Size	*Batting Dimensions*
Craft / Crib size	45 inches x 60 inches
Twin size	72 inches x 90 inches
Full /Double size	81 inches x 96 inches
Queen size	90 inches x 108 inches
King size	120 inches x 120 inches

With any batting choice, always try to unwrap and unfold it a few days before using it. Let it breathe! This allows the batting to expand and relax after spending months or even years in its tightly packaged form.

Cotton and other batting fibers

Cotton batting can shrink nearly 5 percent when washed. Although the "crinkled" effect achieved after this shrinkage can give your quilt a wonderful antique look, you must use closely spaced stitching intervals so the fibers don't migrate with use and laundering. Quilting through 100 percent cotton is like quilting through warm butter.

The only downside to cotton batting is that, if you do not use closely spaced intervals when quilting, the batting bunches to all the corners, nooks, and crannies during use and laundering. Trust me on this one — you'll have lots of batting in your corners, but nothing where you need it most!

A minor downside is that some cotton battings require prewashing (a step I prefer to eliminate).

Some experienced quilters — the ones who don't mind spending an entire year working on one quilt — often prefer cotton. They like the old-fashioned look, or they want to stay true to traditions (polyester batting is a new-fangled invention!). And they don't mind their batting in bunches.

Cotton/polyester blend

Like cotton batting, cotton/polyester blends can shrink, but not as much. Some won't shrink at all. In fact, if the batting does shrink any, you probably won't notice it much. Cotton/polyester batting can be quilted at slightly larger stitching intervals than 100 percent cotton batting because the polyester content helps keep the fibers from migrating during use or laundering.

Many of the blended battings will also give your quilt a very traditional look and feel, but without the hassle of cotton. Refer to the package for additional information.

Polyester

Polyester battings launder well with no shrinkage and can be quilted at larger stitching intervals. Quilting at wider intervals means you'll have the quilt finished quicker, freeing up more time for additional quilting projects! For this reason, polyester batting is the most popular choice.

Polyester is the only fiber available for *high-loft battings* — the battings you'd choose for a really thick (think sleeping-bag-thick) quilt. Because hand or machine quilting a high-loft batting is difficult at best, use high-loft battings for tied quilts (the ones held together with fancy knots of yarn or ribbon).

You're probably wondering why polyester is fine for batting, but not for fabric. Well, I really don't have much of an answer for you on this one. What it comes down to is time (you can finish the project faster because the quilting intervals are larger), and the fact that very little fiber migrates during use or laundering.

Silk

I don't recommend silk batting for bed quilts or wallhangings. Why not? First, silk batting is very expensive and often difficult to find. Second, it's usually not made in sizes large enough to accommodate a bed-size project, and if it were, the cost would be quite prohibitive!

This batting is best suited for quilted garments. Textile artists who specialize in unique, one-of-a-kind garments like to work with silk batting because it drapes well and is lightweight. However, unless you have money to burn, silk is not really not suited to the average quilter's budget.

Wool

Wool batting is very easy to needle through, but its fibers tend to migrate, and it requires closely spaced quilting (short stitching intervals). Wool batting also tends to *beard,* or lose fibers, through the quilt top easier than some of the other battings. Many experienced quilters who prefer this type of batting encase their wool batts in layers of lightweight cloth to help prevent this problem.

Because wool batting washed in warm water and tumble dried can shrink substantially, hand-washing and drying flat or professional dry cleaning are usually the recommended forms of laundering. This means that wool batting probably isn't the best choice for a young child's bed quilt, a set of placemats, or other projects requiring frequent laundering.

Do you need special treatment?

As you read batting packages, you may notice that some battings have undergone special treatments or have certain finishes.

For example, some battings are *needle-punched* or have *bonded* or *glazed* finishes:

✔ Needle-punching helps hold the fibers together to prevent shifting and helps the batting maintain its loft through years of use and abuse.

✔ With a bonded or glazed finish (such as Glazene), the batt is coated with a light resin coating that holds the outermost fibers of the batting together, helping to prevent *bearding* (losing fibers through the quilt top) and fiber migration. The glazing process allows the needle to penetrate more smoothly and cuts down on needle drag (the pull of the needle against the fabric). These battings are appropriate for pretty much everything!

Consider these features when determining your batting requirements.

Batting 1000

Use Table 2-3 to help you determine which brand of batting is best for your needs, depending on the look that you're trying to achieve.

Table 2-3	Batting Choices		
Brand Name	*Fiber Content*	*Thickness*	*Notes*
Old-Fashioned Antique Look (Low Loft)			
Soft Touch Fairfield Processing	100% cotton, bleached	1/8"	45-inch x 60-inch and 90-inch x 108-inch only; very low loft, excellent drape. Quilt at a minimum of 2-inch–4-inch intervals.

Brand Name	Fiber Content	Thickness	Notes
Poly-fil Cotton Classic Fairfield Processing	80% Cotton 20% Poly	1/8" and 3/16"	Flat, antique look, glazed to hold fibers together, can be quilted at a minimum of 3-inch–5-inch intervals.
Mountain Mist Bleached Cotton, Stearns	100% Cotton	2/16"	Low-loft; easy to needle; quilt at a minimum of 1/4-inch – 1/2-inch intervals.
Mountain Mist Blue Ribbon Stearns	100% Cotton	3/16"	Antique appearance; quilt at a minimum of 2-inch intervals.
Mountain Mist Quilt-light Stearns	100% Polyester	1/8" – 3/16"	Glazene finish allows for fine stitches. Holds up well in the wash.
Morning Glory Old Fashion	100% Cotton		Needle-punched natural cotton with scrim; easy to needle.
HTC Fleece Handler Textile Corp.	100% Polyester	1/16"	45 inches wide by-the-yard; best for smaller projects.
Traditional Look			
Poly-fil Low-Loft Fairfield Processing	100% Polyester	1/4" – 3/8"	Lightweight, easy to handle, washes well; another favorite of mine; quilt at a minimum of 2-inch – 4-inch intervals.
Poly-fil Ultra-Loft Fairfield Processing	100% Polyester	3/16"– 1/4"	Dense structure for warmth; recommend machine quilting only; washes very well; quilt at minimum of 3-inch – 5-inch intervals.
Poly-fil Traditional, Fairfield Processing	100% Polyester	1/8" – 3/16"	Easy to needle, washes well; quilt at a minimum of 3-inch – 5-inch intervals.
Mountain Mist Polyester	100% Polyester	1/4" – 3/8"	Easy to handle, great for quilts, small projects, and garments; washes well, nice drape.
Morning Glory Glory Bee I. Carpenter Co.	100% Polyester	1/4"	Lightweight, wash carefully; quilt at a minimum of 2-inch intervals.

(continued)

Table 2-3 (continued)

Brand Name	Fiber Content	Thickness	Notes
Super Fluff! Trad'l weight, Buffalo Batt & Felt Corp	100% Polyester	1/4″ – 3/8″	Resin-bonded, wash carefully, best used for machine quilting; quilt at a minimum of 2-inch intervals.
High-Loft and Tied Quilts			
Poly-fil Extra-loft, Fairfield Processing	100% Polyester	3/8″ – 1/2″	Full and airy, wash gently and dry flat when possible.
Poly-fil Hi-Loft Fairfield Processing	100% Polyester	5/8″ – 3/4″	Very lofty, great for crafts; wash gently and dry flat when possible.
Mountain Mist Fatt Batt, Stearns	100% Polyester	3/8″	Glazene finish prevents fiber migration; excellent choice for tied quilts; if you prefer to machine or hand quilt, can be quilted at up to 4-inch intervals.
Morning Glory Glory Bee II, Stearns	100% Polyester	1/2″	Nice loft, wash gently and dry flat when possible.
Super Fluff Europa	100% Polyester	3/8 – 1/2″	Very dense; holds up well; machine washes and dries well.

Choosing Backing Fabric

At one time, backing a bed-size quilt required piecing fabrics to make a backing piece large enough to accommodate the massive width and length. Today, manufacturers make it easy to back these monstrosities. Backing fabrics are available by the yard in 90- and 120-inch widths in a variety of colors and prints, as well as in traditional solid white and natural. In my opinion, using these large backing fabrics is the best way to go for large-size quilts because it saves so much time.

Cotton bed sheets can also make excellent backings and are available in an array of prints, colors, and sizes. Golly, you can even give your bed a coordinated look by adding matching pillowcases and dust ruffles! Just remember to undo the hem at the top of the sheet so you won't have any strange seamlines or layers of fabric in your backing. You don't need to undo the side and bottom hems because you'll cut them away later.

Before purchasing backing fabric, determine the width and length of the backing piece needed. Allow an extra few inches along each side as a fudge factor. For example, if the finished size of your quilt is 75 inches x 90 inches (to fit a full-size bed), you need a backing piece that's *at least* 80 inches x 95 inches. You can purchase either a 3-yard cut of 90-inch-wide fabric (which gives you a 90-inch x 108-inch surface area) or a $2^1/3$-yard cut of 120-inch-wide fabric (which gives you a 120-inch x 84-inch surface area). It never hurts to purchase a little extra fabric, especially considering the fact that it's very difficult to cut these large-width fabrics perfectly straight at the store, so you may end up with a backing that isn't perfectly square.

If you want to use one of the fabrics used for the quilt top for the backing fabric, stitching the backing isn't as terrible as it sounds. Determining the amount of 44- or 45-inch-wide fabric needed just requires a bit of planning on your part. For example, using the quilt measurements in the previous example, you would need to purchase two 44- or 45-inch x $2^3/4$-yard cuts of fabric.

Why purchase two lengths of fabric rather than just one $5^1/2$-yard length, you ask? The answer is simple: to eliminate your margin of error. How upset would you be to get your fabric home, prewash, press, and then cut it, only to discover that you mismeasured, and you're now 8 inches short on one length? If you purchase your fabric in two lengths, the measuring is done for you. Plus, the folks doing the cutting at the store always allow an extra $1/2$ inch or so when cutting, which only helps the situation in the long run.

For the example quilt size in the previous paragraphs, you can stitch the two lengths together for the backing in one of two ways:

- First, you can simply stitch the two lengths of fabric together along one long edge, pressing the seam allowance open and layering this backing panel with the batting and quilt top (see Figure 2-3). This puts a seam down the center of the quilt and means that you need to be fairly accurate when centering your batting and quilt top on the backing.

- The alternative is to cut one of the lengths of fabric directly down the center, making two 22-inch x 2-$3/4$-yard strips (see Figure 2-4). Stitch one of these strips to each long side of the uncut length of fabric and press the seams open. This distributes the seam lines toward the outsides of the quilt and can make it easier to center your quilt top and batting — no one will notice if you end up slightly off-center!

You can piece the backing for other sizes of quilts in a number of ways. The method you choose depends on the actual size of backing needed. You can use any method for piecing your backing, but remember that the more seams you have, the more difficult it is to quilt through the quilt layers due to the extra thickness in the backing's seam areas.

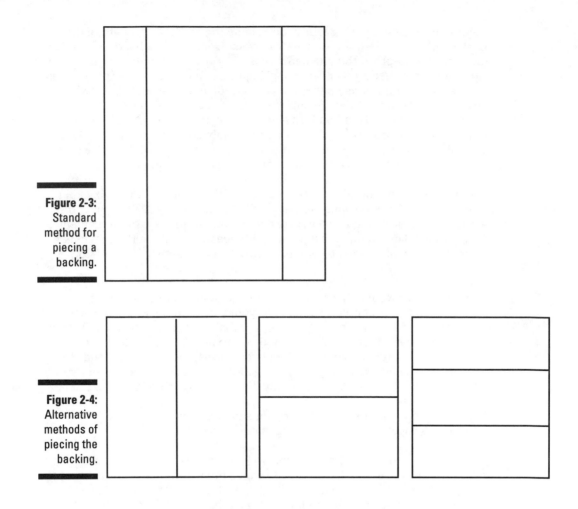

Figure 2-3:
Standard
method for
piecing a
backing.

Figure 2-4:
Alternative
methods of
piecing the
backing.

Chapter 3

A Patch in Time:
Designing Quilt Blocks

*P*atchwork is nothing more than taking individual pieces of fabric called "patches" cut out in basic, geometric shapes and stitching them together to form more complex patterns. It's a bit like putting a simple children's puzzle together, with each piece placed in its designated spot. In the case of patchwork, the puzzle pieces are made of fabric. Sounds simple enough, right? Let's get to it.

Only a few shapes are necessary for basic traditional patchwork designs: squares, triangles, rectangles, and long strips. Of course, curved shapes such as the Double Wedding Ring are also possible, but because you're probably new to quilting, I discuss only the most basic design elements in this chapter.

The breadth of creativity available with patchwork ranges from elegant simplicity to incredibly intricate Picasso-like fabric art. This creative aspect of quilting, combined with its practicality and eco-friendliness in recycling scraps of fabric into useful treasures, has made patchwork the most popular form of quilting.

Finding Inspiration in Traditional Quilt Block Designs

As you read through this or any other quilting book, you'll probably notice that all quilt blocks have names. Some names describe the blocks' motifs — Maple Leaf, Turkey Tracks, Flower Basket — but others seem way out there: Robbing Peter to Pay Paul, Johnny-Round-the-Corner, Corn and Beans, and Broken Dishes.

Where did the original creators of these blocks come up with those strange names? The answer lies in the popular culture of the day and what was going on in the quilters' lives at the time. The following listing speculates on how certain block names came to be:

✔ A passing flock of flying geese may have inspired the Flying Geese (see Figure 3-1) or Birds in the Air blocks.

✔ The Mariner's Compass may have been made by the wife of a seafaring gentleman; Water Wheel by a miller's wife.

✔ Log Cabin blocks (see Figure 3-2) are so named because they're made from narrow strips of fabric that resemble the pine logs pioneers used when building their homes.

Figure 3-1:
Flying
Geese
design.

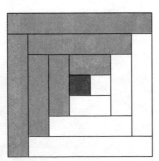

Figure 3-2:
The Log
Cabin block
design.

Some blocks were named by their makers to honor prominent individuals, as was the case with the Lincoln's Platform block. Others express the quilter's religious devotion, as in the Jacob's Ladder, Dove in the Window, Tree of Life, and Cross and Crown blocks.

A number of block names seem to just express the frustration of the era: Robbing Peter to Pay Paul (see Figure 3-3) was probably named during hard times and Drunkard's Path during prohibition. Kansas Troubles expresses the emotions experienced by farmers during the dust bowl years, and Road to California commemorates the great gold rush in the late 1800's.

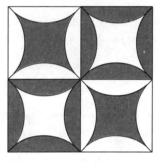

Figure 3-3:
Robbing
Peter to Pay
Paul block
design.

Still others were named purely for fun. Consider the Puss in the Corner, Wild Goose Chase, and Jack in the Box quilt blocks. Perhaps Old Maids Ramble in Figure 3-4 was named simply because Auntie Martha couldn't stop gossiping during a quilting bee.

Figure 3-4:
The Old
Maids
Ramble
block
design.

I'll stop now — perhaps someone should name a block *Cheryl's Rambling Again*. But you should know that block design names in many ways resemble the names of nighttime constellations — they don't always look like the names they are given, but rather loosely describe the object from which the design got its name. These traditional quilt blocks continue to be the foundation used by quilters today for their most beautiful and creative efforts.

A bogus letter from one anonymous quilter to another

Read the following pseudo-letter. It's a perfect example of how seamlessly quilt names reflect the real life they're so much a part of. Can you guess the quilt block names? I've underlined them so you don't miss them!

(Sunbonnet Sue is a traditional quilt design in itself. Check out a book with traditional quilt block designs to see how these blocks shape up.)

Dear Sunbonnet Sue,

It's been a rough week <u>down on the farm.</u> I just found <u>a hole in the barn door</u> —the one on the same side of the barn as the <u>weathervane.</u> Anyway, the <u>hens and chicks</u> escaped through that darn hole and ate up all the <u>corn and beans</u> I had planted in <u>grandmother's flower garden.</u> After I saw what they did to <u>my rose of Sharon,</u> I rounded the critters up and locked them in the old <u>log cabin,</u> where I found a cowering <u>puss in the corner.</u> Since puss looked guilty too, I locked him in there with the others.

I was going to head up the <u>road to Kansas</u> that afternoon, but postponed my trip. <u>Handy Andy</u> came over for a visit instead. You know, he was actually my <u>grandmother's choice</u> for a husband, because he looked better in a <u>bow tie</u> than <u>overall Bill.</u> With all the <u>Kansas troubles</u> right now, Andy still can't afford a <u>wedding ring,</u> so he gave me a <u>cut glass dish</u> and a <u>dresden plate</u> instead. How's that for a strange engagement gift! Too bad I dropped them, because I ended up with just a bunch of <u>broken dishes!</u> I almost broke grandma's <u>cake stand</u> with my elbow as I swept up the <u>bits and pieces.</u>

Don't give me any lip about this, because I remember when you started dating that Clay fellow. <u>Clay's choice</u> of an engagement gift was a <u>cherry basket.</u> Well, at least it wasn't breakable. You know, I never really did like him, 'cause he was always playin' with his <u>whirlygigs</u> or fiddlin' with the <u>churn dash.</u> I was pleased when you dumped him!

Well, I guess I have to go now—you know how us <u>old maids ramble!</u>

Love,

Edith

Choosing Your Quilt Block System: Four-Patch or Nine-Patch

You may hear seasoned quilters talking about their latest projects, often referring to the blocks as "four-patch" or "nine-patch" or some other number of patch. Although it sounds like Latin or Greek to the untrained ear, the grid-based system by which quilt blocks are designed is very easy to learn — and it actually makes sense.

This patch system is based on a simple grid filled with the various geometric shapes used in quilting. The two most common patch systems used in block design are the four-patch and the nine-patch, but others are often used for more complex designs. I stick to the two most basic treatments in this chapter.

Basic four-patch design

When a quilter refers to a *four-patch block,* she (or he — many men have taken up quilting as well) is talking about a block that's based on a grid of four squares, as shown in Figure 3-5.

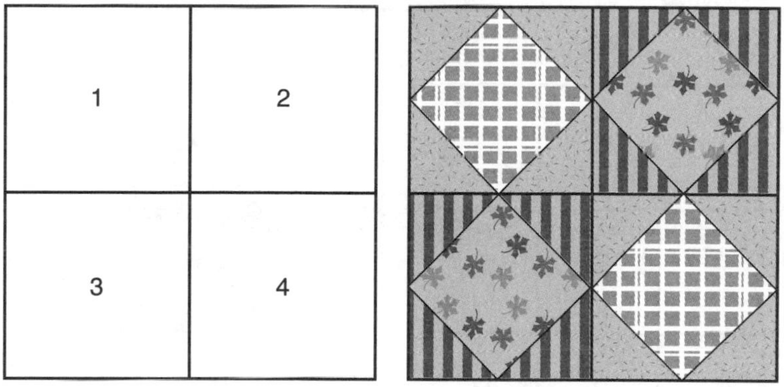

Figure 3-5:
A four-patch grid.

Describing a block as a four-patch does not necessarily mean it is made of only four pieces of fabric. It can be made of many! Rather, it describes the way the block is laid out, which is basically in four units. Each unit can be made of one or more pieces stitched together. Take a look at the figure diagrams if your brain feels like mush after reading the last few sentences.

The four-patch block can be relatively simple in nature, like the block shown back in Figure 3-5, or more complex, like the Variable Star shown in Figure 3-6.

Basic nine-patch design

A *nine-patch block* is similar to a four-patch block, but its design is based on a grid of nine squares rather than four. Each of the nine squares can also be broken down into additional units, but the block remains a nine-patch block. Notice the Pinwheel block next to the grid in Figure 3-7. This block is based on the same nine-patch grid.

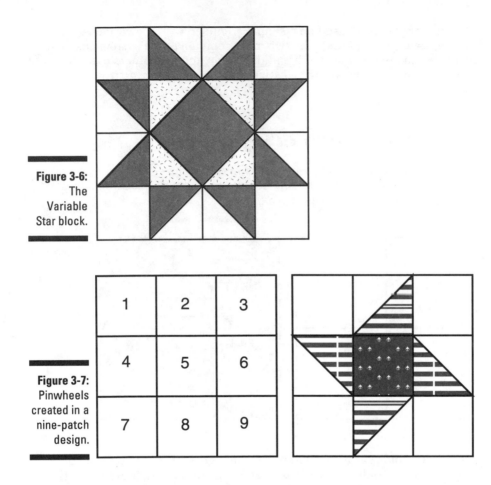

Figure 3-6:
The
Variable
Star block.

Figure 3-7:
Pinwheels
created in a
nine-patch
design.

Note that the grid need not be made of equal-sized squares. The Churn-Dash (also known as the Hole-in-the-Barn-Door) variation shown in Figure 3-8 is also based on a nine-patch grid, but the center areas are stretched to give it a different look. Although the nine units vary in size, the block stays true to its nine-patch origins.

The quilt block shown in Figure 3-9 is also a nine-patch block, even though some of the units in the nine-patch are broken down into additional units. The block is still a true nine-patch block.

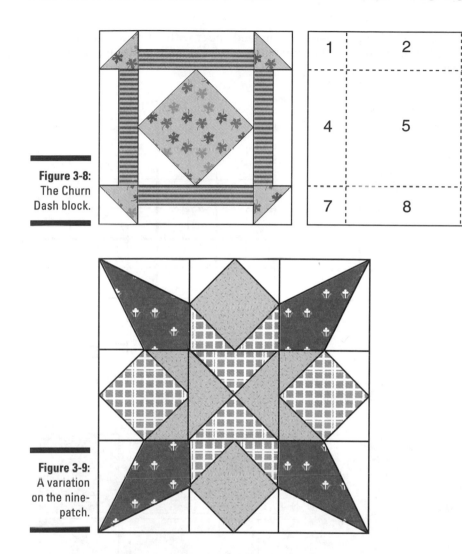

Figure 3-8:
The Churn
Dash block.

Figure 3-9:
A variation
on the nine-
patch.

Using Graph Paper to Map Out
Your Quilt Block Designs

Do you remember that only a few shapes are necessary for basic traditional patchwork designs? Now you have the chance to play with those basic shapes — the squares, triangles, rectangles, diamonds, and long strips — and create a new block of your own.

On a sheet of graph paper — I recommend paper with four, eight, or ten squares per inch — mark the nine-patch and four-patch grids shown in Figure 3-10.

Nine-Patch   Four-Patch

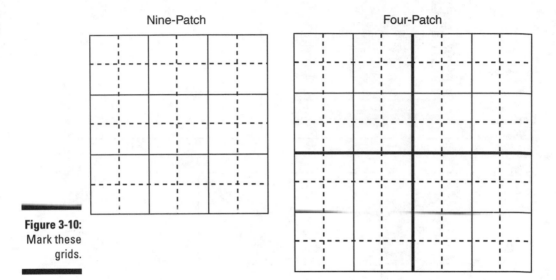

Figure 3-10:
Mark these
grids.

Fill the grids with some of the shapes shown in Figure 3-11 and discover how many quilt block designs and possibilities you can create!

Figure 3-11:
Mix and
match
these
shapes to
create the
blocks for
your grid.

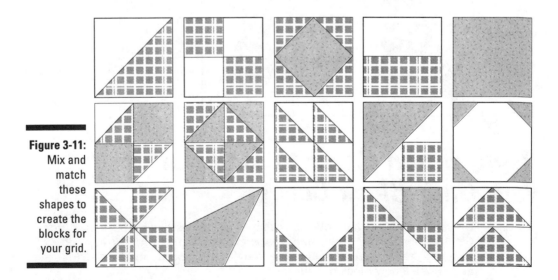

Play with as many variations of shapes as you please. Reverse the direction of the pieces, too! You can color them in with colored pencils or felt-tip markers, or sketch in some textures to differentiate between the various fabrics you would like to use. Don't limit yourself to the options shown in Figure 3-11 — make up your own designs! And when you create one you're especially fond of, name your design. After all, it's your own creation.

Creating Full-Sized Block Patterns from Your Graph Paper Doodles

After you design your quilt block in miniature on graph paper — assuming you don't go blind squinting at all those tiny squares and give up on quilting forever — you're ready to create a full-sized pattern of your block design that you will use when making templates. (See Chapter 4 for tips on creating templates and cutting out patches.)

The block's size depends on the number of blocks you will need for your project and the size of your finished project (see Chapter 5 for help choosing a layout and determining how large the finished project should be). For example:

- ✔ If you're making a single-block throw pillow, a 14- to 16-inch block is your best bet. A 12-inch block would likely require the addition of some borders (unless you want a very small pillow), and an 18-inch block might be great on the floor but could overwhelm your sofa. If you're planning a wall hanging or bed quilt, use a 10-, 12-, or 14-inch block, because anything larger would just look too strange on something as large as a bed (although it has been done!). It's really all a matter of personal preference.

- ✔ If you're using the four-patch system and your project calls for a 4-inch block, each of the patches in the block will be 2 inches square. If your project requires a 6-inch block, each patch will be 3 inches square. If your project is made up of 12-inch blocks, each patch should be 6 inches square.

- ✔ If you're using the nine-patch system and your project requires a 6-inch block, each of your patches will measure 2 inches square. If your nine-patch block is supposed to measure 9 inches square, each patch unit will measure 3 inches square. A 12-inch block requires patches that are each 4 inches square.

You can adjust the size of any block you design on graph paper simply by drawing a smaller or larger grid containing the same number of squares that appear in your graph paper design (refer to Figure 3-11).

Fun stuff for cyber-savvy quilters

Did you know that you could easily design quilt blocks, and even entire quilts, on your personal computer? It's easy if you use a computer program made especially for quilters! Programs are available that allow you to designs entire quilts or individual blocks, easily figure your yardage requirements for an entire quilt of any size, and to print accurate, ready-to-use patterns from the comfort of your home office! Fabrics of various colors and prints, as well as entire collections arranged in different themes (brights, pastels, country, and more) show you what the quilt will look like in your chosen colors before you start cutting, helping you avoid costly mistakes.

Check out Quilt-Pro for Windows and Macintosh, manufactured by Quilt-Pro Systems. This windows-based program is easy to learn, fun to use, and has a well-written user's manual. To make designing quilts even easier, this program has a wonderful tutorial with an additional version online. The folks at Quilt-Pro have also printed a companion "bible" for this program titled, the *Quilt Pro Illustrated.* This book contains sketches for all 1,000 blocks, 120 borders, and 350 fabrics in Quilt-Pro library, as well as block and border design indexes.

Quilt-Pro also makes companion programs and disks to further expand the quilt design possibilities, including Foundation Factory and Quilt-Pro Collection disks. The collection disks are a great way to update your Quilt-Pro library, and each disk contains over 100 new blocks, and new border and fabric designs. These are also available for Windows or Macintosh.

Also check out the Electric Quilt Company's Windows-based design software, called EQ4. This program is very easy to use and features tutorials and online support. This company also makes special add-on packages to further expand your design repertoire, including "Sew Precise," which contains over 1,100 block patterns! BlockBase software, also made by this company, allows you to print out templates for 3,500 traditional quilt blocks, ready for use.

You can find more information about the products made by these companies on their Web sites.

Quilt-Pro **www.quiltpro.com/foundation factory/**

Electric Quilt **www.wcnet.org/Electric QuiltCo/**

You will also find addresses and phone numbers in the Appendix.

Any of these will keep your key-tapping creative fingers busy for months!

For example, if your project requires a 12-inch block, draw a 12-inch square on a sheet of paper and divide it into the same number of sections that appear in your graph paper grid. Then simply draw your design on the 12-inch square in the same manner as it is drawn on the graph paper. Now you're ready for the next step!

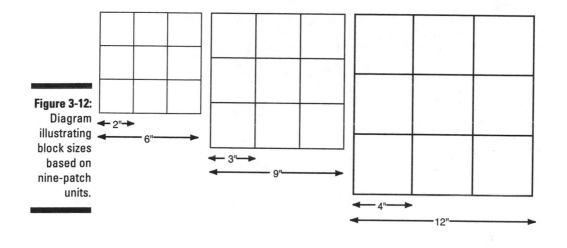

Figure 3-12:
Diagram
illustrating
block sizes
based on
nine-patch
units.

Chapter 4

Creating and Using Templates

. . . .

. . . .

Creating accurate templates is one of the most important steps in making a quilt. Your templates make the difference between a well-squared block that goes together easily and a catawampus, crooked-all-to-heck one that fights you every step of the way.

If you're wondering what the difference is between a pattern and a template, I'll share a little secret — there's not a heck of a lot of difference except that the template is cut from stiff material and the pattern is printed on paper. Both are just fine, but a template can make the work easier by having a somewhat consistent surface to trace around — rather than pinning flimsy paper to your fabrics. If you plan on making multiple blocks from your patterns or templates, flimsy paper will disintegrate faster than warm cookies in a room full of children.

In this chapter, I give you tips for everything from choosing template materials to making special templates if you plan to hand-piece your quilt. Scared that you'll goof up this template stuff? If you ever traced around your hand to make a turkey in grade school, relax, little pilgrim — you're an old pro at using templates.

Although ready-made templates are available for a variety of popular quilt block designs, making your own templates is usually cheaper, and it can even be fun. Plus, if you come up with a spectacular, intricate design that no one else has ever thought of (you clever devil!), you have to create your own templates, or your design will never be more than a pretty little sketch on paper. And if that's all you wanted, you would have bought a coloring book instead of this book, right?

Choosing Paper or Plastic

Shopping for quilting supplies can be just as overwhelming as shopping for groceries. You encounter bolt after bolt of fabric (do you choose the vanilla, the chocolate, or the strawberry, or do you settle for the Neapolitan, which will make everyone happy?), spool after spool of thread (who knew there were 73 different brands of spaghetti?), and package after package of fluffy batting (who has time to do a squeeze test on all those toilet paper brands?).

At the grocery store, the easiest decision you make probably occurs when you're asked what kind of bags you want your groceries packed in. Luckily, when it comes to choosing template material for quilts, you have that same simple choice: paper or plastic.

Scrounging up some paper

Creating paper templates from a pattern you design (or from patterns you find in this book or purchase at quilting stores) is simple and cheap. You simply trace the individual pattern pieces onto tracing paper; add seam allowances if the pattern doesn't already include them; glue the tracing paper to cardboard (use whatever type of glue you have handy), old file folders, or other heavy card-stock paper; and then cut out the templates. (The section "Transferring Patterns onto Template Materials," later in this chapter, takes you through this process step by step.)

Springing for plastic sheeting

If the kids taped together all the cardboard in the house to make a 10-foot-tall robot named Zorbot, or you don't want to eat four boxes of Serious Sugar Surge cereal before you can start your quilting project, don't despair! Many quilting supply stores carry a transparent, flexible plastic sheeting specially designed for creating quilting templates.

With this material, you trace individual patch patterns directly onto the plastic, add seam allowances, and then cut out the templates (see the following section, "Transferring Patterns onto Template Materials," for detailed instructions). No gluing is involved, so using this product saves you a few steps. Just keep in mind that this material can be a bit expensive. You won't find a secret decoder ring at the bottom of the package either. Bummer.

If you're making a larger quilt and will trace around the templates often as you create your blocks, you may want to use the plastic template material or make an additional set or two of cardboard templates. Cardboard template edges eventually become compromised due to wear from repeated tracings, making the templates inaccurate. If you want to try to preserve them for posterity (like that fruitcake you still haven't opened from three Christmases ago), you can purchase some self-sticking laminating sheets and stick them to both sides of the templates before cutting them out. Hey, you never know when you're going to need them again, right?

Going with the Grain

All woven fabrics have a *straight grain* that runs parallel to the *selvage edge* of the fabric, and a *cross grain* that, as the term implies, runs across the straight grain of the fabric at a 90 degree angle. To make your life easier, I simply call both the straight grain and cross grains of the fabric *on grain*; *bias* is simply bias, on the diagonal.

The selvage is the un-cut edge of the fabric that appears very tightly woven and often contains the name and copyright information for that particular fabric manufacturer. Always cut off the selvage edge before cutting out your pieces of fabric. This area is difficult to stitch through by hand or machine.

Before you make any templates or cut into any of your fabrics, you will need to mark the *grainline arrows* on your patterns to help you place your template along the proper grain line of the fabric you are cutting (see Figure 4-1). These grainlines will help you build your blocks in such a way that they will not stretch out of shape while stitching.

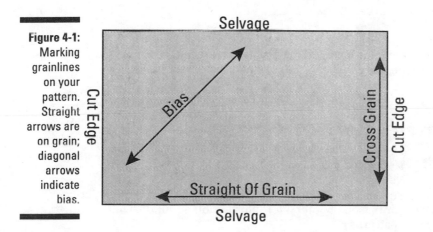

Figure 4-1: Marking grainlines on your pattern. Straight arrows are on grain; diagonal arrows indicate bias.

Be sure you have any templates for the outside edge of the block on-grain rather than on the bias. In the case of triangles, proper placement is essential. Bias edges stretch, and should not be placed along a block edge, as it can cause distortion in the finished block. You should also try to avoid having two bias edges together whenever possible, so you don't have two edges of "stretch" stretching together!

Keep in mind that there will be times when, no matter what you do, you may have two bias edges together or a piece of bias along an outside edge. There's no need to panic — just be sure you don't accidentally stretch the fabric when cutting or sewing. You may also want to stitch those pieces first so they will have the support of each other and the line of thread to help stabilize the bias edge.

Figure 4-2 shows how *not* to mark the grain lines on your patterns and templates. Notice where the bias edges of a triangle end up in the wrong version. This block is a good candidate from some major distortion!

Figure 4-2:
Oops! Inside area has bias on all four sides, and there's a bias edge on the outside of the block.

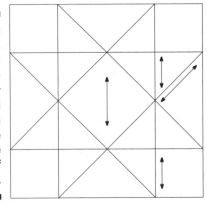

Always use care when handling bias fabric pieces. The more they're handled, the more they're stretched and distorted!

Transferring Patterns onto Template Materials

Follow these steps for making templates from patterns that you create (creative spirits, see Chapter 3 for information about designing your own quilt block patterns):

1. **Make several copies of your pattern before you cut or otherwise permanently alter the pattern**

   This way, you always have a spare on hand in case your kids decide to make paper airplanes out of your tax forms and quilt block patterns. It could happen.

   If you are using a photocopier to copy the patterns, be sure to measure the copies for accuracy! Some machines tend to stretch the patterns in one direction, throwing off the accuracy of your templates!

2. **Letter or number each pattern piece so you'll know where it belongs in the quilt block after you cut apart the pattern, as shown in the illustration that follows.**

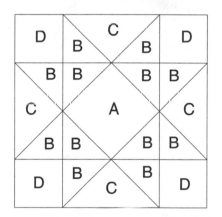

   Trust me on this one.

3. **Carefully cut out the pattern pieces.**

   Use an old pair of scissors to cut templates — NOT your fabric-cutting scissors. Fabric scissors were never meant to slice, dice, cut through tin cans, and still slice a tomato paper-thin. (I think I've been watching too much television.) You will dull your important fabric-cutting-only scissors if you cut your heavy paper or plastic templates.

   Cut only around the outside (cutting) edge, and discard any pieces that are duplicated in the quilt block pattern; you only need to make one template for each basic piece. For the block template shown in the illustration in Step 2, for example, you need one each of pattern pieces A, B, C, and D.

4. **Trace these pattern pieces onto the tracing paper or plastic sheeting, spacing the pieces at least one inch apart in all directions.**

5. **Using a ruler, carefully draw a line exactly $^1/_4$ inch outside the outline of each pattern piece, as shown.**

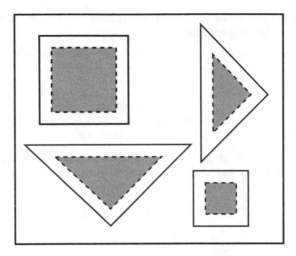

This new line is the cutting line, the line along which you will cut out the template and then later cut out the fabric patches. (The first line you drew is your stitching line.)

The space between the two lines (¹/₄ inch) provides the correct seam allowance for constructing your quilt block; make sure that the spacing between the lines is accurate and that all angles are sharp.

Use a flexible curve to trace curves on any rounded templates. You can find them at most office supply or engineering supply sores.

6. **Mark a small dot on each template wherever two seams converge.**

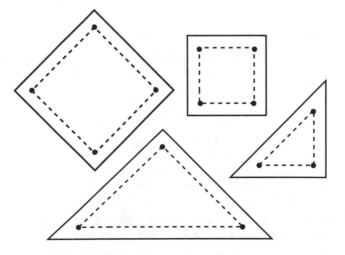

These dots act as guides when stitching — by matching up the dots on the fabric pieces, you ensure that the pieces are correctly aligned.

7. **Transfer the grainline arrows from your pattern pieces onto the templates, as shown.**

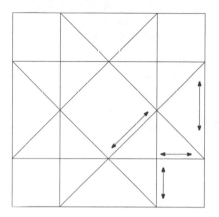

8. **If you traced your pattern pieces onto tracing paper instead of plastic sheeting, glue the tracing paper pieces to lightweight cardboard or other heavy paper.**

   Doing this adds durability and makes your templates easier to handle.

9. **Cut out the templates along their outer (cutting) lines as shown, using older scissors, not your fabric-only scissors!**

Making window templates for hand piecing

If you plan to hand piece your blocks (see Chapter 8 for more about hand piecing), you may want to make *window templates* so that you can easily mark lines on your fabric pieces indicating where you should stitch.

The great thing about a window template is that you are able to trace two lines on the wrong sides of your fabric — the outside cutting line, and the inside stitching line. You will then have a visual aid for perfect hand piecing — simply have your stitches follow the marked inside line!

Another "bonus" in using window templates is that you can center a design element from the fabric in your piece. Perhaps a bouquet of flowers or a special emblem?

Here's how to create a window template in two easy steps:

1. **Make a template from plastic or cardboard by following the previous steps.**

   I know, I know — that adds up to more than two steps already, and you're still in the first step (maybe someone should tell *The X-Files* about this). Making that basic template is simple enough, though, right?

2. **Cut out the template's center along the inside line (this is the line you drew when you traced the pattern's shape onto the plastic), as shown.**

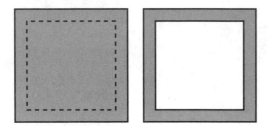

   Discard this center piece, or save it for another project if it looks big enough to make another template out of someday.

You can now use this window template to mark both the cutting lines and the stitching lines on your fabric pieces. Don't believe me? Read the section, "Putting Pencil to Fabric."

Making templates for ready-made patterns

To make templates from ready-made patterns, including those in this book, simply trace the patterns onto tracing paper or plastic template material and cut them out, as you do for your own pattern designs. On ready-made quilting patterns, cutting lines are always indicated by solid lines, and stitching lines are always indicated by dotted lines.

Make sure that you cut out template pieces along the cutting lines and *not* the stitching lines, or that king-sized bed quilt will end up looking like a place mat. (Then you'll have to decide whether you still want to make the matching bedskirt and pillow shams!)

Putting Pencil to Fabric

After you make your templates, you're ready to transfer their shapes to your pre-washed and freshly pressed fabric. Don't try to trace templates on a wrinkled piece of fabric or you will set yourself up for disaster. Wrinkles can hide behind the template, making your cut fabric pieces inaccurate. Remember, neatness counts!

Lay a template on the wrong side of the fabric (the back side of the fabric's design), paying special attention to match up the fabric's grainlines and the direction of the template's grain arrow. Trace around the template using a well-sharpened water-soluble pencil. Re-sharpen the pencil often to keep your lines accurate. If you are using a window template, be sure to trace the inside (stitching) lines, too.

 To prevent templates from slipping on fabric as you trace around them, try gluing small pieces of sandpaper to their backs. You can also make no-skid templates by applying a thin layer of rubber cement to their backs. (Just make sure that the rubber cement is dry before you use the templates, or you'll end up with a globby, boogery mess all over your fabric.) Rub off the rubber cement and apply a new layer as it becomes coated with fabric lint and loses its grip.

See Chapter 7 for step-by-step instructions for cutting out your patches.

Chapter 5

Playing with Blocks and Borders: Which Way Should They Go?

In This Chapter

▶ Using sets to arrange your blocks

▶ Choosing among straight sets, strippy sets, diagonal sets, and more

▶ Selecting borders

After you select a block design (see Chapter 3) and create the templates you need (see Chapter 4), you're almost ready to cut into your fabric yardage and start stitching. But first, you need to determine

✔ How many blocks you need and how you should arrange them

✔ The type of borders you should cut

To determine the number of blocks and types of borders, to take out your graph paper and start sketching — this is the fun part! (If you have no graph paper, get some. Believe me, you'll need lots of it.)

The number of blocks you need to stitch depends primarily on the size of the quilt you intend to make and the manner in which you plan to set the blocks (*setting the blocks* is quiltspeak for the layout of your design). In this chapter, I talk about the most common settings for quilt blocks and describe some border variations to help you plan your quilt.

Setting Up Blocks

The arrangement of blocks in a quilt is called a *set*. You can arrange quilt blocks in literally hundreds of ways, but in this book I just review the most common sets you're likely to see. Within the sets are additional components such as sashing, cornerstones, and borders, which I discuss one at a time.

The straight set and sashing

The most common and easiest set is the *straight set.* In this arrangement, the blocks are set one against the other in orderly rows that run in vertical and horizontal lines. Take a look at Figures 5-1 and 5-2 for examples of a straight set. Figure 5-1 shows nine blocks stitched together in three rows having three blocks each; the blocks are placed *block-to-block,* meaning that one block is placed square with the other. The **Blue Star Placemat** in the projects section (Part IV) uses this set.

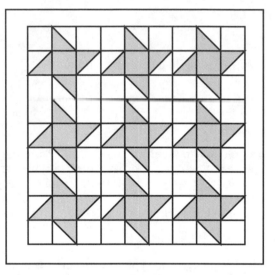

Figure 5-1:
Diagram of a straight set arranged block-to-block.

Figure 5-2 shows the same blocks as in Figure 5-1, but this time the blocks are separated or framed by thin strips of fabric called *sashing* or *lattice.* Adding sashing to the blocks gives the quilt a completely different look, don't you think? The sashing or lattice strips can be plain, or you can insert squares in the lattice, as you see in Figure 5-2. These are called *sashing squares.* You can find sashing used in a straight set in **Pieced Blossoms, Scrappy Bloomers, Snow Crystals,** and several other projects in Part IV.

The diagonal set

The second most common set is the *diagonal set.* In this arrangement, you place the blocks diagonally, on their points, at a 45-degree angle from the sides of the quilt. Blocks set on their points are also said to be *on point.*

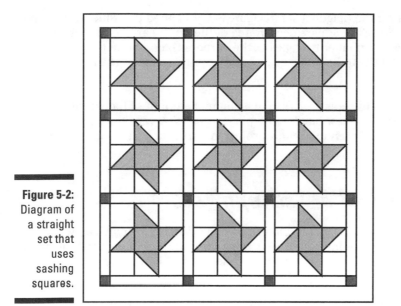

Figure 5-2:
Diagram of
a straight
set that
uses
sashing
squares.

In Figure 5-3, you see nine blocks set alternately with four plain squares.

Figure 5-3:
A diagonal
set gives
you a great
look with
just a few
blocks.

Notice that for the diagonal set in Figure 5-3, you need two differently sized triangles to form the square center area of the quilt: Large triangles are used at the sides and smaller triangles at the corners to complete the square center area of the quilt. You can also add sashing strips to the blocks if you'd like.

The diagonal set makes great use of a minimal amount of blocks, as you can alternate just a few blocks with plain squares. A very traditional look! The **Pastel Nine-Patch mini-quilt** project in Part IV uses this simple but versatile set.

The vertical or "strippy" set

Another popular set for quilt blocks is the *vertical* or *"strippy" set,* which is one of my favorites. Instead of forming orderly rows of blocks, you place the blocks in vertical strips separated by other strips (hence the name, strippy!).

In Figure 5-4, I show a straight strippy set with two rows that have the blocks set diagonally on their points, and the middle strip set normally, just to show you that you can set them either way. The **Pieced Hearts** project in Part IV of this book is a great project for strippy aficionados.

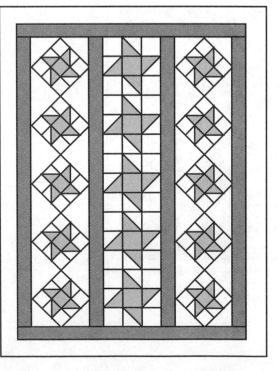

Figure 5-4:
Diagram of a straight strippy set with two rows of diagonally set blocks.

Figure 5-5 shows an offset strippy in which I place the blocks diagonally on their points. This really plays up the offset look and gives the pattern movement. Notice that the center strip is offset from the outer strips by the addition of pieced triangles to the top and bottom of the strip.

Figure 5-5:
Diagram of
an offset
strippy
straight set
arranged
block-to-
block.

The medallion set

Some quilters prefer to set their blocks in the *medallion set*. In this set, a single block or group of blocks acts as a central focal point. This focal point is then surrounded by different types of sashing, other types of blocks, and borders (see Figure 5-6).

The **Traditional Basket** wallhanging in Part IV uses this type of set. You can create so many different styles of medallion quilts that I can't go into much detail. Just let your imagination fly!

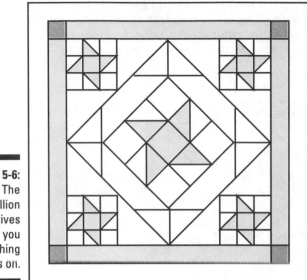

Figure 5-6:
The
medallion
set gives
you
something
to focus on.

Making a Run for the Border!

A *border* is a strip (or strips) of fabric that frame the edges of the quilt. Your entire quilt top is usually bordered, but you can also have borders surrounding your quilt blocks or as part of the quilt block design.

A quilt's borders can be wide or narrow, pieced or appliqued, or a combination of techniques. Always try to choose a border that complements rather than clashes with your blocks.

For example, if you have stitched together some busy-looking blocks in bright colors, consider adding a simple border. Its simplicity will complement the complexity of your blocks. If you choose a border as complicated as your block design, that complex border could detract from your design by making it impossible to tell where the block ends and the border begins. In contrast, if your blocks are simple and traditional, multiple bands of borders may be just what you need to set them off. The idea is to make sure that all the elements of your design combine to make it eye-catching.

Selecting a border type

Although you can have dozens of border options to think about when planning your quilt, you most likely will use one of two basic types.

The easiest and most common border style is the *plain border,* shown in Figure 5-7. You can stitch the plain border with squared corners or with mitered corners, depending on your expertise. A *mitered corner* is stitched at a 45-degree angle to the sides of the quilt.

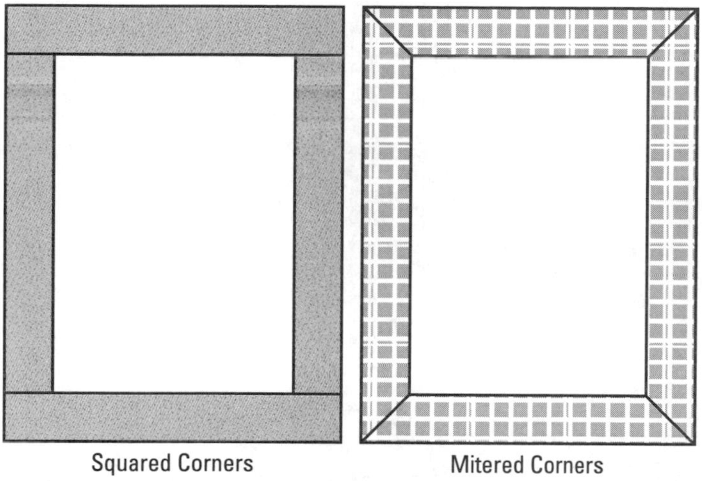

Figure 5-7:
A plain border can have squared or mitered corners.

Squared Corners   Mitered Corners

The squared-corner border is the simpler of the two to stitch. You can use a single wide length of fabric, or you can use several different plain borders together in one quilt.

Borders with cornerstones are simple borders with the addition of a square in the corner of each border (see Figure 5-8). The cornerstones can be a complementing or contrasting fabric, or you can use pieced or appliqued blocks that complement the center area of your quilt.

If you have been admiring quilts for a while, you're probably familiar with other options for borders, such as the popular checkerboard border in Figure 5-9, but most are simply variations on the plain and cornerstone borders.

Calculating border size

Calculating border size is really pretty simple. Just total all the finished measurements and add your seam allowances.

For example, suppose that the quilt in Figure 5-10 is made of 10-inch square blocks with one-inch wide sashing strips, and you want a finished border that is 10 inches wide.

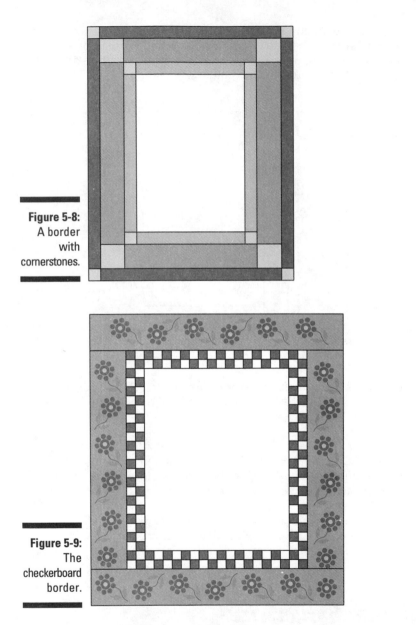

Figure 5-8:
A border
with
cornerstones.

Figure 5-9:
The
checkerboard
border.

To find the size you need to cut for the borders:

1. **Find the size of the side borders by adding up the blocks (three 10-inch-square blocks = 30 inches) plus the sashing (four 1-inch-wide strips = 4 inches): 30 inches + 4 inches = 34 inches**

   The finished size of your side border will be 10 wide x 34 inches long, but this is not the cutting measurement — yet. You need to add your $1/4$-inch seam allowances *to each side* of this measurement, because this

10-inch block   Border   Sashing

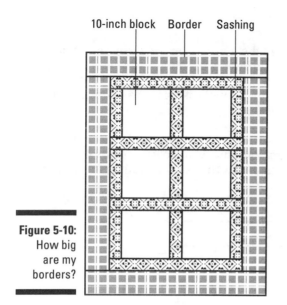

Figure 5-10:
How big
are my
borders?

figure is the *finished* measurement. You certainly have not yet stitched the borders in place, so the borders are not finished, right? The seam allowances are the areas of fabric along the edges that will be taken up by the stitching. This area needs to be added to the finished measurements, or the border strips will be too narrow and too short after you stitch them to the quilt top.

2. **Add ¹/₄-inch seam allowances to all four sides of the finished measurement.**

   This results in 10¹/₂ inches x 34¹/₂ inches as the cutting size of the side borders. Now to cut two borders using this measurement — one border for each side.

3. **Find the measurement for the upper and lower borders by adding the blocks (two blocks at 10 inches = 20 inches) plus the sashing (three strips that are 1 inch wide = 3 inches) and the finished width of the side borders that you fiddled with in the previous steps (two borders that are 10 inches wide = 20 inches).**

   Now you have a *finished* measurement of 10 inches wide by 20+3+20= 43 inches long.

4. **Add the ¹/₄-inch seam allowances to all four sides of the 10-inch x 43-inch length.**

   The final measurement for the upper and lower borders is 10¹/₂ inches x 43¹/₂ inches. You need to cut two of them this size — one for the top edge and one for the bottom.

Did you have any trouble?

Okay, I know; when you assembled the quilt center area, your stitching probably wasn't exactly perfect, and your seam allowances were not quite $1/4$ inch. You may even discover that the left side of your quilt center is longer than the right side of your quilt. That's okay; we can tweak it into shape by creatively cutting the borders!

Here's a nice simple method for cutting your borders while squaring up the quilt top at the same time, making those uneven measurements jive once again! To keep things simple, assume that the border width in Figure 5-11 is 10 inches.

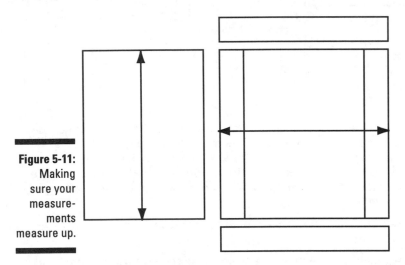

Figure 5-11:
Making
sure your
measure-
ments
measure up.

1. **Measure the length of the quilt top down the center.**

2. **Round off the measurement to the nearest inch (assume this quilt center is 33 inches long).**

   Since the border is going to be 10 inches wide, you now have a measurement of 10 inches x 33 inches.

3. **Add $1/4$-inch seam allowances to all four sides.**

   This makes the length to cut $10^1/2$ inches x $33^1/2$ inches.

4. **Measure the quilt from side to side and include the borders.**

   Assuming that the width of the quilt is 22 inches, and your side borders are 10 inches wide, your unfinished measurement will be 10 inches + 10 inches + 22 inches.

5. **Add the $1/4$-inch seam allowances to all four sides.**

   You've now got a cutting measurement of $10^1/2$ inches x $42^1/2$ inches.

Stitching the borders to your quilt

Before you stitch the border to your quilt, you need to prepare the border strips so that everything will (hopefully) come out okay. You don't want to end up with too little or too much border fabric in proportion to your quilt top (kind of like ending up with too much cake at the end of your frosting).

First, fold each of the four border strips in half to find the centers of the strips and press the center of each border to form a crease, or place a pin at the halfway point to mark it. Find the centers of all four sides of the quilt top as well in the same manner (fold and press or mark with a pin). After you mark the centers, you're ready to stitch.

As shown in Figure 5-12, align the center of the border with the center of the quilt top, having the right sides together. Pin through the layers at the center marking to hold them together while stitching. Add a pin to each end to hold the ends together, too.

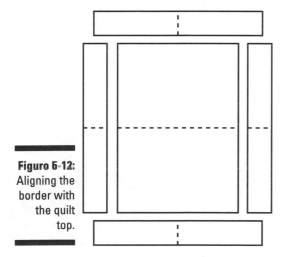

Figure 5-12:
Aligning the border with the quilt top.

Stitch the border to the quilt along its length, easing in any excess fabric using the technique described next:

✔ Be sure to ease the excess fabric in place when you stitch.

To do this, place the side that has the excess (whether it be the border or the quilt top) next to the feed dogs of your machine. These feed dogs will help ease the extra length for you. Now, start stitching, holding back the top (shorter) layer slightly and allowing those feed dogs to do their job of feeding that lower layer of fabric as shown in Figure 5-13.

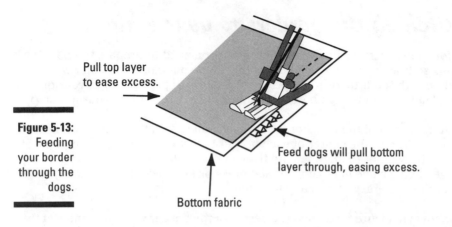

Figure 5-13:
Feeding
your border
through the
dogs.

Pull top layer
to ease excess.

Feed dogs will pull bottom
layer through, easing excess.

Bottom fabric

> ✔ Stitch the borders to the quilt, placing the side that needs easing toward the feed dogs and pulling back on the top layer to ease.

After stitching the borders to the quilt top, press the borders outward and the seam allowances toward the border fabric.

Part II
Sharpening Your Sewing Skills

The 5th Wave   By Rich Tennant

"I see that you're still collecting scraps for your quilting projects."

In this part . . .

Okay. It's obvious, I know. But you can't make a quilt without a little needlework. You don't have to be a champion stitcher to create a quilt, but it helps if you know the basics and then some. This part helps you through the careful work of choosing the right tools and then cutting, pressing, and piecing together your quilt top, with a spot of appliqué thrown in for added elegance and flair.

Chapter 6

Threads and Needles
and Gadgets, Oh My!

*W*hile you're selecting your fabrics, you may want to purchase the threads and needles and other supplies you need to complete your quilting. Unfortunately, as with most things, no one choice is right for every situation.

Want to buy a simple spool of quilting thread? There's no such thing. You'll find yourself facing an endless array of little spools of every thickness and color imaginable. You may choose a spool of thread just because it matches your fabric, and you bring it home. Did you make the right choice? There's a good chance you didn't.

A Thread for Each Reason

Just as there are different sizes of nuts and bolts for almost every purpose, so is the story with thread. You can choose all-purpose or buttonhole-twist or rayon or cotton or silk. What about woolly nylon? Do you need monofilament, extra-fine, or metallic? Are you hand quilting or machine quilting? Do you want basting thread or darning thread. Cotton, mercerized cotton, and nylon thread all come in a wide range of colors. Which thread is the best thread for your project?

For help with thread selection at-a-glance, see Table 6-1. I explain the uses of the different threads in the sections that follow.

Table 6-1	Picking Threads
For	*Use*
Piecing, hand/machine and all assembly	All-purpose thread, mercerized cotton thread
Appliqué, hand	All-purpose thread
	Silk thread
	Cotton thread
	Single-strand of embroidery floss (in a pinch when you have nothing else on hand)
Appliqué, machine	Buttonhole twist for blanket/buttonhole stitch Nylon monofilament for invisible appliqué
	Rayon machine embroidery threads for satin-stitch or other decorative-stitch appliqué
	All-purpose for satin stitch appliqué
	Metallic threads for special appliqué effects
Quilting, hand	Extra-strong hand-quilting thread (polyester core)
	Cotton quilting thread
Quilting, machine	Nylon monofilament for invisible stitches
	All-purpose for general machine quilting
	Buttonhole twist for prominent-looking stitches
	Metallic thread for glittery effects in quilting

Assembly threads

For assembly, such as when you are stitching together the pieces of fabric in a quilt block, or assembling the quilt blocks into a quilt top, choose an *all-purpose thread* to coordinate with your fabrics. All-purpose thread is the most common thread and is available in nearly every color known to the human eye. You can use it for both hand and machine stitching. All-purpose thread is strong and durable because it's made from mercerized (treated) cotton with a polyester core (called poly-core).

Some quilting "purists" prefer to use nothing but 100 percent cotton in their quilts, and this is fine too —100 percent cotton thread is also available in a reasonably nice range of colors, but be sure to select one that has been *mercerized* (treated with a caustic soda), which adds strength and durability to the thread — you want your project to eventually become an heirloom, right?

Machine-quilting threads

For machine quilting, you have a few thread options: all-purpose, monofilament, buttonhole twist, and metallic. For standard, every-day machine quilting, you can use all-purpose thread. Some manufacturers also market thread that is identified as specifically for machine quilting, but in some instances the thread is really all-purpose thread that has been re-packaged as machine quilting thread. It's not an attempt at deception, but rather the manufacturer's way of helping you select the right thread.

If you prefer to have your stitching be "invisible," you can choose one of the nylon monofilaments that are available in clear and smoke colors. The clear is great for bright fabrics mixed with white or off-white, while the smoke is best for darker fabrics. It's durable and hides all manner of mistakes.

For a fun and different effect, try using buttonhole twist or a metallic thread for machine quilting. Buttonhole twist is a heavier version of all-purpose thread and has a nice, thick dramatic effect. Try using buttonhole twist in a contrasting color for extra pizazz! Metallic thread looks beautiful in a holiday project, but do try different brands whenever possible — some of them tend to break easily when stitching.

Using metallic threads in machine quilting will dull your needle quickly. Be sure to insert a fresh needle in your machine after using a metallic thread.

Appliqué threads

For machine appliqué, all-purpose thread is once again an option, but you can also throw in rayon machine-embroidery threads, metallics, and buttonhole twist:

✔ Rayon thread is very fine and has a beautiful luster. Its sole purpose in life is as a decorative thread only — do not use it for assembly, it's just not strong enough. Use rayon thread for satin-stitch embroidery.

✔ For a special glittering effect, try stitching your appliqués with metallic thread.

✔ The buttonhole twist is a very thick thread, used mainly for topstitching. However, in this book, I recommend it for appliqué because buttonhole-stitch appliqué gives a look that nearly duplicates hand embroidery!

Nylon monofilament is the thread of choice for invisible machine appliqué.

For hand appliqué, all-purpose thread or silk threads are good choices.

Hand-quilting threads

Hand-quilting thread is available in a couple of different forms. The first is a polyester-core, cotton-wrapped thread with a polished finish; the other is 100 percent cotton with a polished finish. Both are slightly heavier than all-purpose thread.

The polished finish on the quilting threads provides abrasion resistance, making it easier to stitch, and helps keep the thread from tangling. If you run into knotting and tangling problems during hand quilting, however, run your thread through a beeswax cake before threading your needle. The beeswax acts as a lubricant and helps prevent any handling problems. You'll find it in the same departments as needles and quilting supplies in most fabric stores.

As for the other threads you may find in the store, ignore them for now. They're another story, some other time, another project. They're just not suitable for quilting.

Sewing Basket Essentials: Scissors and Needles and Other Stuff

A few basic supplies should be in every sewing basket:

- ✔ Scissors for cutting fabric
- ✔ Scissors for cutting paper and miscellaneous materials (so that you don't dull the scissors used for cutting fabric)
- ✔ Hand sewing needles
- ✔ Seam ripper
- ✔ Measuring tape or stick
- ✔ Marking pencils and tailor's chalk
- ✔ Needle threader
- ✔ Thimble

✔ Straight pins (the nice long ones with the plastic balls on the ends, sometimes labeled as "quilter's'pins") and pincushion to keep them contained

✔ Large safety pins

✔ Glue stick

Other basics to have on hand include a sewing machine with extra machine needles in size 11(80), an iron (be sure to keep the steam reservoir empty unless instructed otherwise), and an ironing board along with a pressing cloth.

The following sections explain the importance of some of these tools.

Scissors

You need *at least* two pairs of scissors. One should be reserved for fabric cutting **only.** Nothing dulls an expensive pair of fabric scissors faster than using them for cutting paper or cardboard. Tag this pair of scissors with a skull and crossbones if necessary. Hide them if you have to. Lock them away. Whatever you do with them, be sure to remember where you stashed them and tell other family members about your scissors rules. Let the would-be scissors-snaggers know that if you catch them using your fabric scissors for anything other than fabric, they'll face some severe consequences (I'll leave the punishment up to your imagination).

If your scissors have become dull, you can have them sharpened through most fabric and craft stores. The stores normally contract with a local sharpening service that will pick up and deliver freshly sharpened scissors to the store within a few days. If you use the cheapies (something you may want to consider if you DO have scissors-snaggers in your household), toss them or relegate them to the kitchen junk drawer (I admit it, I have one) when they become dull — they are not worth the expense to sharpen.

In addition, be sure to include a pair of all-purpose scissors for cutting templates or clipping patterns.

You may also want to throw in some fabric snippers for trimming threads, or small scissors for cutting appliqués. Although they are not truly necessary, they are nice to have (and we quilters do love our gadgets). These also should be reserved for cutting fabric and thread only. Figure 6-1 shows how these scissors look.

Figure 6-1:
Assorted
scissors
and thread
snips.

Needles for sewing by hand

Purchase needles for general sewing and for quilting. A "household assortment" of needles is handy because it usually contains a variety of needle lengths and widths.

When selecting needles remember, the *smaller* the number, the *larger* the needle.

Household needles are called *sharps,* which are fine (very narrow) needles with small round eyes. They call them "sharps" because they are — they penetrate the fabric (even multiple layers) easily. Sharps are suitable for hand piecing and appliqué.

Sharps in size 8 or 9 work well for quilting, but choose a needle that you're comfortable with. Some folks prefer a small needle, others like 'em big! If your hands are large, you certainly don't want a teensy-weensy needle to work with — it'll feel more like a splinter than a sewing tool. If your hands are small, choose a smaller needle, rather than one that feels like a metal toothpick with a thread hanging out one end.

If you have trouble threading these general-purpose needles, you can buy a package of easy-threading needles with slotted eyes.

For hand quilting, select needles called *betweens.* These are also fine needles, but they're generally shorter than sharps and are made especially for quilting or other detailed handwork. Size 8 is a good size for the beginner, but many long-time quilters prefer size 12, which is a really tiny needle — its diminutive, narrow size allows the quilter complete control and enables the quilter to take quite a few very small stitches onto the needle before passing it completely through the quilt. A longer needle actually gives you less control while quilting because your fingers are further from the fabric.

Seam ripper

Unless you're one of those lucky people who never, ever makes a mistake, you definitely need a seam ripper, shown in Figure 6-2. (As my own grandmother used to say, "As ye sew, so shall ye rip!" Mistakes are a common aspect of quilting. Get used to it, bucko.)

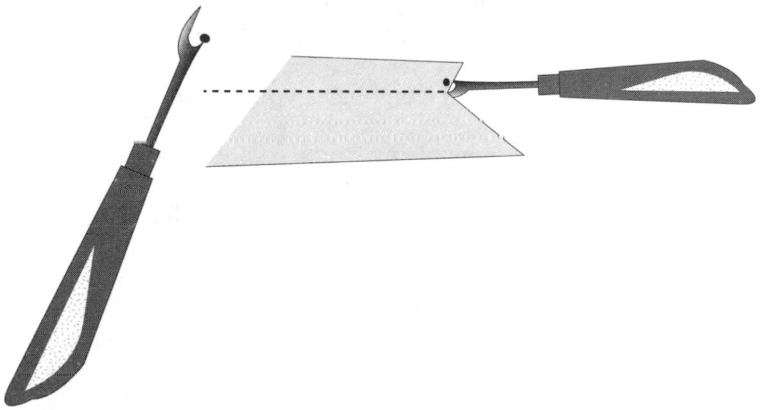

Figure 6-2:
Seam
ripper.

Practice using the seam ripper on a few scraps of fabric sewn together, making sure that you cut only the thread without ripping into the fabric. Keep your seam ripper handy when sewing and be sure to replace it now and then — seam rippers dull with use. Seam rippers are cheap, so don't fret about replacing them. You may want to keep several on hand because they tend to get lost easily. I provide tips on the fine art of seam ripping in Chapter 8.

Measuring tape and marking implements

Measuring tapes are handy for a number of things: checking seam allowances, creating patterns, measuring fabric, and so on. This tool is another goodie to hide deep in your sewing basket to avoid having it permanently borrowed by "Not Me," that mysterious scapegoat living in most households. Figure 6-3 shows a retractable measuring tape.

Figure 6-3: A retractable measuring tape is handy for quick and precise measure-ments.

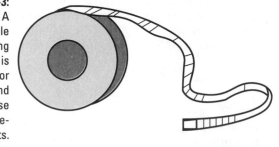

A standard #2 pencil is handy (the kind of pencil you needed in grade school to fill out those standardized tests), but don't use it for marking fabrics. For that job, you need an assortment of water-soluble marking tools. Look for pencils and pens specifically designed for marking on fabrics. These are guaranteed to wash out and won't harm your the material.

Personally, I don't use pens of any kind — not even those meant for use with fabrics. I use only fabric-marking pencils or tailor's chalk. They wash out beautifully and never soak through to the other side.

WARNING! Never, never, never ever, ever, ever use a standard pen or marker. They may become permanent, especially after pressing. The dark lines also show through on the other side of the fabrics, making them unsightly in your finished quilt.

TIP I like to use EZ brand wash-out chalk pencils. They're available in blue, white, and yellow. I also like the Berol Marking Pencils available in silver, white, blue, yellow, rose, and #4 graphite. They all wash out easily.

WARNING! Beware of anything that says "fade-away" or "vanishing fabric marker." These marks fade rapidly, and you may have to re-mark your fabric when you least expect it (like in about 48 hours — less, if you leave the fabric in direct sunlight).

Needle threader

A needle threader (see Figure 6-4) is handy to have in your sewing basket, whether you have trouble seeing or are simply trying to thread a needle in low light. The nicest type has a magnifier on one end.

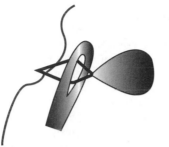

Figure 6-4:
A needle
threader
eases the
task of
joining
needle and
thread.

Thimble

Eventually (maybe even at first!), you're going to prick your finger with a needle. And you probably don't want blood on your quilt top (though I tell you how to get blood spots out in Chapter 12). A thimble will help protect your fingers from needle sticks. Several different types of thimbles are available, including varieties made of metal, plastic, and leather (see Figure 6-5). Others are adjustable or fit around long fingernails.

Figure 6-5:
Let your
thimble get
the point so
you can
quilt in
comfort.

Get a thimble that fits your finger snugly, without being tight. Because thimbles are inexpensive, try a few different styles. You may find that you like certain thimbles better for different applications.

Most right handed quilters wear their thimbles on the middle finger of their right hands, using it to help push the needle through the fabric without piercing the skin of their "pushing" finger. It's also helpful to wear a thimble on the "receiving" finger — the one positioned under the work to help guide the needle (this is either the middle or index finger on most folks). You're a lefty? Reverse these tips!

Pins and pincushions

Straight pins are helpful for holding pieces of fabric together and holding appliqués in place. A pincushion prevents the pins from rolling off your work surface and onto the floor — and later into someone's foot!

I prefer the magnetic pincushions. They're an easy target to hit (you only have to get the pins close enough for the magnets to attract) when you're pulling pins with one hand and guiding fabric through the machine with the other. They also work great when you accidentally knock the whole sha-bang off your work table and they scatter all over the floor. Hold the empty or near-empty pincushion a few inches above the floor in the area surrounding the spill and watch them fly back to the pincushion!

Be wary of pin spills on carpet, however. If the pins are lodged in the fibers, the magnet may not pull them out, and you will most certainly end up with one sticking right through your house slippers. (I know what you wear while sewing — don't play coy with me!)

Safety pins are handy for holding the layers of a quilt together for machine quilting, among other things. Choose the large-sized nickel-plated brass finish pins so you won't have problems with rust stains. You can also purchase special basting safety pins from quilting supply stores (see Figure 6-6). These pins are slightly curved, making them easier to open and close through the layers of a quilt.

Figure 6-6:
A curved safety pin helps you baste through the layers.

Glue stick

A glue stick may not sound like a typical sewing basket staple, but it can help hold small appliqués in place in areas where pins are just too large or cumbersome. You can purchase either a standard glue stick from an office supply store or glue specifically designed for fabrics at a fabric store. Both work and wash out well.

More Basics and Nice-to-Haves

Some supplies won't fit into a sewing basket, but they're essential to successful quilting nonetheless. Other supplies are just plain nice to have — you could do without them, but why should you? In no particular order, here's a list of the large essentials and the portable nice-to-haves:

- Sewing machine and extra machine needles
- Iron and ironing board
- Pressing cloth (handy when pressing specialty fabrics like metallics or lame)
- Rotary cutting supplies: rotary cutter with extra blade, plastic see-through ruler for quilters, cutting mat
- Assorted plastic quilting templates, such as squares and triangles
- Quilting frame and hoops
- Graph paper and tracing paper
- Colored pencils for layout design ideas
- Masking tape
- Spray bottle of ouchie-fixer (you're bound to go "ouch!" at least once) and a supply of bandages

The following sections tell you why you need these tools and which are just nice to have around.

Rotary cutting supplies

With a rotary cutter, you can accurately cut through multiple layers of fabric, drastically decreasing the time spent cutting out strips and patches. Most can be used by right or left handers; I recommend that you purchase a large-sized cutter. They are more comfortable to handle than the smaller ones.

To protect your cutting surface, purchase an 18-inch x 24-inch or larger rotary cutting mat. Choose a cutting mat that's marked with 1-inch grid markings and bias lines.

A 6-inch x 24-inch clear plastic ruler and other sizes of clear plastic rulers and templates can also help you cut your fabric pieces quickly and accurately. Figure 6-7 presents a variety of rotary cutting supplies.

I explain more about rotary cutting in Chapter 7.

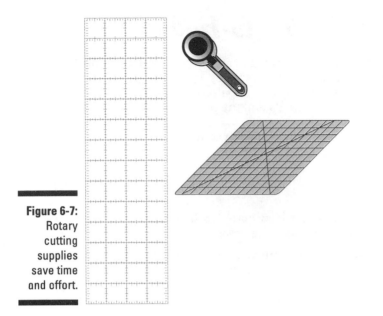

Figure 6-7:
Rotary
cutting
supplies
save time
and effort.

Quilting frames and hoops

The beginning quilter may want to stick to smaller projects that can be easily quilted in hoops. Large projects can also be quilted in hoops, but they can be heavy and cumbersome — after all, the weight of the project sits in your lap when using a hoop! A hoop consists of two circles of plastic or wood that are nestled together to securely hold the layers of the quilt taut for hand quilting (see Figure 6-8). A screw eye on the outer circle allows you to tighten and loosen the tension of the hoops as necessary. Hoops of varying sizes are available in any quilting or fabric store.

A 20-inch-diameter hoop is a good all-purpose hoop. You may want a larger hoop — up to 30 inches or so — for a large-scale project such as a bed quilt. Remember, the smaller the hoop, the more you will have to unfasten it to move around on your quilt.

Once you are quilting regularly and working on larger or more advanced projects, you may choose to invest (they can be quite expensive) in a floor-standing quilt frame (see Figure 6-9). Check with your local quilting or fabric store for quilting frames. They are also advertised in the backs of quilting magazines. For your convenience, I provide the names and phone numbers of quilting stand manufacturers in the Appendix.

Most quilting frames are free-standing and take up quite a bit of space. Hoops, on the other hand, are easier to transport and are available in large sizes, some with optional floor-stands. I talk more about quilting with hoops in Chapter 12.

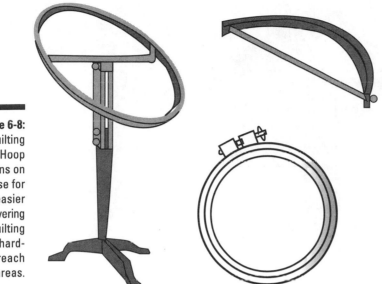

Figure 6-8: A quilting hoop. Hoop spins on base for easier maneuvering and quilting those hard-to-reach areas.

Graph paper, tracing paper, and colored pencils

Use these tools for sketching ideas and working out designs. Colored pencils and graph paper allow you to experiment with different color combinations and ways of setting the blocks in your quilt. Tracing paper is handy for tracing patterns from books and magazines.

Masking tape

Masking tape is an indispensable tool for basting quilts together. I keep tape on hand in 1/2-inch, 1-inch, and 2-inch widths for my quilting projects. It sticks without stickiness.

Ouchie fixer and bandages

You know what these are for. Expect to use at least one a day (more in the early days of your quilting career).

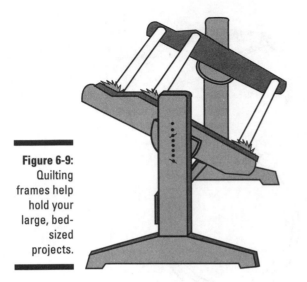

Figure 6-9:
Quilting
frames help
hold your
large, bed-
sized
projects.

Chapter 7

Cuts and Creases: Pressing Matters

*Y*ou may be wondering, "why bother with a section on cutting?" Everyone knows how to cut using a pair of scissors, right?

Although everyone certainly knows how to use a pair of scissors, few may realize the importance of cutting accurately, especially when it comes to quilting! Accurate cutting is just as important as accurate piecing if you want your project to turn out well.

Also important to the cutting process is laying out the pieces efficiently to avoid waste — fabric can be expensive, and you want to be certain you have enough to complete your project.

Finally, proper pressing, just like accurate cutting and stitching, can mean the difference between a well-made block and a crooked, misshapen one. Having smooth seams makes the stitching process much easier and gives your quilt its crisp neatness.

In this chapter, I review basic tips to make your cutting and pressing go smoothly.

General Cutting Tips

Most quilting instructions tell you to cut the largest pieces — usually the borders and sashings — first. This is a good rule to follow even when the directions do not specify the cutting order. Cutting the borders and sashings first makes more efficient use of a large length of fabric, and cutting those long strips first will save you from having to piece them together or buy more fabric later. You then cut the smaller pieces from the remaining fabric.

Before cutting into your fabric, take a close look at the block you want to make and figure out which way the grain of the fabric should go on each piece (refer to Chapter 4 for information about grainlines). Lay your templates on the fabric, placing as many similar pieces together as possible. For instance, place triangles together with their longest sides facing, and neatly line up squares (see Figure 7-1). Rearrange your templates as many times as necessary to make them all fit.

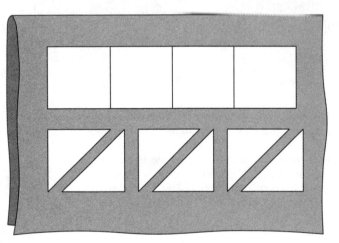

Figure 7-1:
Neatly line up triangles and squares.

Trace lightly around your templates with a washable pencil or tailor's chalk.

Remember that the inner (broken) line on the templates is the stitching line and the outer (solid) line is the cutting line.

Cut out the shapes neatly using a sharp pair of fabric scissors. When using scissors, I recommend cutting through just one layer of fabric at a time — or use a rotary cutter for better precision. When cutting through multiple layers of fabric, a rotary cutter works best.

Keep your shears sharp to the very tip of the blades. Nice sharp tips make it easier to trim appliqués and those hard-to-reach places!

If you've kept your fabric-cutting scissors hidden away from those who dishonor their sacredness by cutting paper, cardboard, or other taboo items with them, your cutting line should be sharp and clean. If you have a wavy thing going or discover little nicks in the edges of your fabric, *your scissors are not sharp enough!* Have them sharpened or toss them and purchase a fresh pair! Keeping scissors sharpened is easier than risking the ruin of your fabric by cutting inaccurate or sloppy-looking pieces.

My scissors are good-quality, heavy-duty sewing shears, which I have professionally sharpened once a year. They are certainly expensive, but they're worth every penny because of the amount of cutting I do. I keep a pair of "cheapies" on hand for take-along projects. If you buy inexpensive scissors, however, just toss them when they become dull. Sharpening cheap scissors is just not worth the expense.

To keep your templates from slipping as you trace, glue a piece of fine-grain sandpaper to their backsides, or brush a thin layer of rubber cement onto their backsides and allow them to dry.

Rotary Cutting Basics

Using a rotary cutter with a see-through ruler and rotary cutting mat (see Chapter 6 for information about rotary cutting supplies) is by far the quickest and most accurate method of cutting fabric. I urge you to get acquainted with this tool — you'll love it!

You may find this method of cutting referred to by other quilters as *template-free cutting*. Instead of tracing around your templates with a pencil and cutting the pieces out one-by-one, you cut multiple pieces at once based on a specific size.

To prepare your washed and pressed fabric for rotary cutting, re-fold the fabric the way it was when it came home with you from the store — fold the fabric along the center, right sides together, keeping the tidy selvage edges (not the ragged cut edges) together. Press along the crease. Then place the fabric on the cutting mat and square up one end of the fabric by placing the ruler along one of the lines on the mat, as shown in Figure 7-2.

Slice off the uneven edge of the fabric with the rotary cutter, placing the blade against the ruler and cutting *away* from you in *one continuous motion*. You don't need to cut a large strip to square-up your fabric — cut just enough to make the edge even.

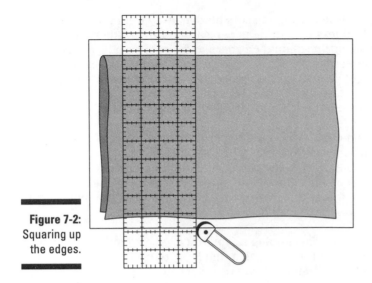

Figure 7-2:
Squaring up
the edges.

Cutting strips, squares, and rectangles

To cut strips of fabric, align the marking on the ruler the width of the strip you wish to cut. For example, if you want 2¹/₂-inch strips, find the 2¹/₂-inch mark on the ruler and place this along the squared-up edge (see Figure 7-3).

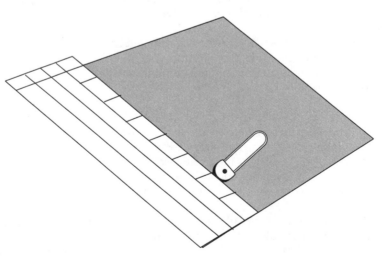

Figure 7-3:
Lining up
your fabric
for cutting.

Slice off the strip with the rotary cutter. The number of strips you cut in one swipe will depend on the number of layers you are cutting through. For instance, if you are cutting a strip of fabric with the fabric folded in the same manner as in Step 1 in the preceding section, you will have a strip of fabric $2^1/_2$ inches x 44 inches. You can then cut this into smaller strips as needed.

Use this same method for cutting all strips, no matter their width.

You can cut squares the same way you cut strips. The only difference is that you then cut your strip into individual squares, as shown in Figure 7-4. Because of the double thickness of fabric, you will have two squares for each cut.

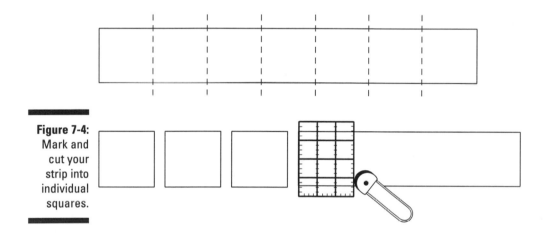

Figure 7-4:
Mark and cut your strip into individual squares.

Cut rectangles the same way you cut squares (see Figure 7-5).

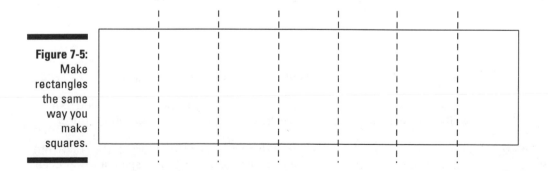

Figure 7-5:
Make rectangles the same way you make squares.

Cut as many rectangles as you need. Just remember that you are cutting through a double thickness of fabric; therefore, you'll have two rectangles for each cut. For example, if you have cut a $3^1/_2$-inch x 44-inch strip of fabric in the manner previously described, you can slice off $6^1/_2$-inch units to make $3^1/_2$-inch x $6^1/_2$-inch rectangles. It's that simple, and your hands aren't even sore from handling scissors!

Cutting triangles

For simple template-free triangles with 45-degree angles, cut squares first and then cut each square in half diagonally, as shown in Figure 7-6.

Figure 7-6: Start with a square to make a triangle.

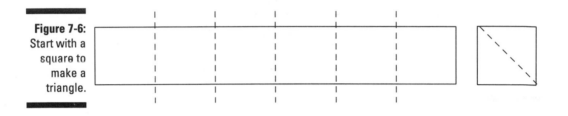

To cut other types of triangles, such as the 60-degree triangle shown in Figure 7-7, you can pre-mark your strip and cut along the lines.

Figure 7-7: Mark your strip for 60-degree triangles.

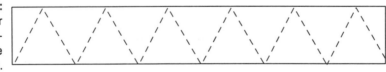

A wonderful alternative to premarking your strip, however, is to purchase a special ruler for cutting a specific type of triangle (see Figure 7-8).

These rulers are also see-through and are heavy-duty plastic, so you can easily use them in conjunction with your regular ruler and rotary cutter.

When cutting triangles, whether with scissors or the rotary cutter, take into account that the longest side of the triangle also needs a seam allowance! If the finished size of the triangle is to be 2 inches, do not cut a $2^1/_2$-inch square in half to make triangles; you will not have a seam allowance for the

Figure 7-8:
Specially
sized
triangle-
rulers
help you.

long edge! Instead, measure your template (which includes seam allowances) from the corner to the tip along the bottom edge. You will find that the square from which you will cut your two triangles needs to be $2^7/_8$ inches wide to accommodate the seam allowances on all three sides. Figure 7-9 shows how to indicate seam allowances.

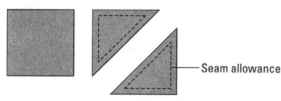

Figure 7-9:
Don't forget
to mark
your seam
allowances.

—— Seam allowance

Confused about seam allowances on triangles? Use your template as a cutting guide in conjunction with your see-through ruler! Simplify your life by laying your template against the fabric, aligning the side edges (see Figure 7-10). Place the ruler directly over the template, aligning the edges of the ruler with the edges of the template. Cut your strip the exact width of the template. Then use the template as a cutting guide for the triangles in the same manner.

So many different rotary cutting tips and techniques can be used that it is impossible to cover them all in this chapter. Many wonderful books have been written specifically for rotary cutting methods if you want more detail. Check out the booklist in the Appendix for a list of my favorites.

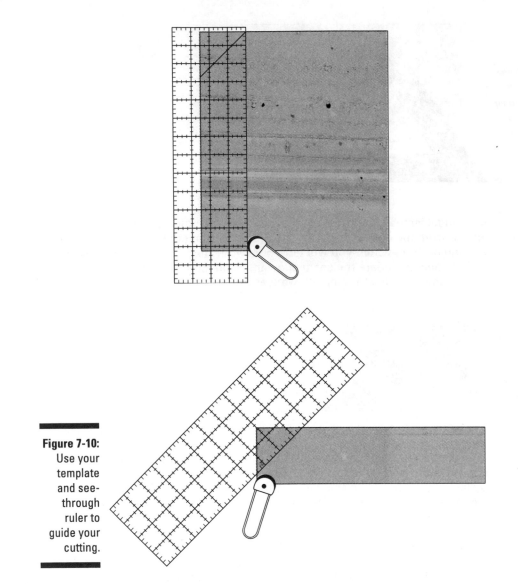

Figure 7-10:
Use your
template
and see-
through
ruler to
guide your
cutting.

Organizing Your Cut Pieces

You need to have a way to keep those cut pieces neat and organized. Not
only will doing this help keep your work area clean and keep the pieces from
getting mixed up, you also will be able to notice at a glance what you have
already cut and what still needs to be done.

To keep all those little pieces neat and organized, stack them by color, type,
and so on. Then store them using one of the following methods:

✔ Place individual stacks of cut pieces in little clear plastic sandwich bags to keep them tidy.

✔ Thread a needle and insert it into a stack, pulling the needle through the entire stack of pieces at once, as shown in Figure 7-11. Leave a 3-inch tail of thread and then insert the needle through the stack again, going in the opposite direction. Cut off the thread, leaving another 3-inch tail. To use the pieces, simply pull one off the top of the stack. The thread will hold the remainder in place!

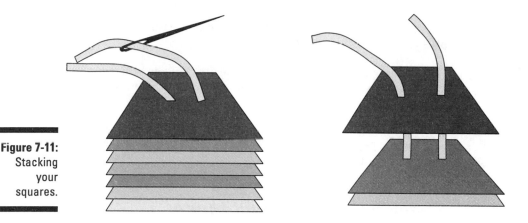

Figure 7-11: Stacking your squares.

Store your bags or threaded piles in a pretty basket or box, ready for use. If you are working on more than one project at the same time, store the pieces in separate baskets or boxes.

Proper Pressing

Proper pressing techniques are not difficult to perform or to remember.

First, be sure that you're *pressing,* rather than ironing — a critical distinction. Do not slide your iron across the fabric, as you do when ironing. Instead, lift the iron to a new location and then lower it downward as shown in Figure 7-12 (this is what makes it pressing, rather than ironing!). You don't need to press down on the iron — the weight of the iron will do the job.

Figure 7-12:
Lift, rather
than slide,
your iron
when
pressing
fabrics.

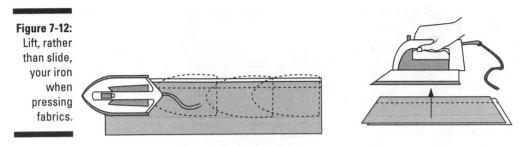

Sliding the iron across the fabric tends to distort bias edges and can really stretch your pieces out of place.

Keep your iron within easy reach while stitching so you can press as you stitch. I always keep my ironing board within just a few steps of my sewing and cutting area.

Don't purchase an iron with an automatic shut-off if you plan on doing a lot of quilting. The iron will shut off at the most inopportune times, so you will be re-setting it constantly.

Pressing seam allowances

Be sure to press the seam allowances together in one direction, rather than pressing them open. When you press a seam open, only the stitching thread keeps those patches together. Pressing the seam allowances to one side provides an added layer of fabric across the seam, making the seam stronger and more durable.

To press your seam allowances:

Set your iron for cotton with no steam, and then

1. **Press the closed seam first to set the stitching. Then unfold the pieces and press them open.**

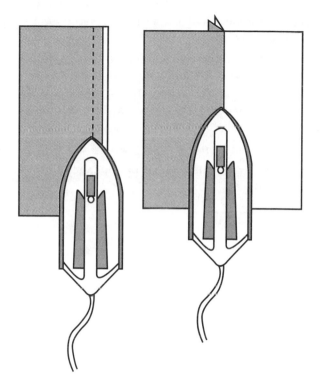

2. Press the seam allowances toward the darker fabric to avoid dark shadows that show through the lighter fabrics in the finished quilt.

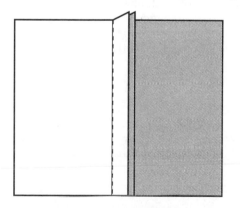

3. **Whenever large numbers of seams meet, press them in opposite directions to avoid bulk.**

   This may mean that sometimes you have to go against Step 2 and press towards a lighter fabric. Stuff happens!

   When you need to press toward the lighter fabric, hand trim a small bit of the seam allowance from the darker fabric to avoid any shadow showing through the lighter fabric.

4. **Always press a seam before stitching across it with another seam.**

5. **Press intersecting seam allowances in opposite directions to avoid bulk in the seam.**

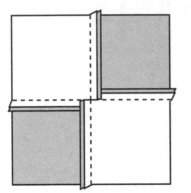

When pressing long strips such as borders, change the direction of the tip of the iron each time you lift and lower it, as shown in Figure 7-13, to ensure that your strip won't favor one side and stretch out of whack. If you forget to press, accidentally sliding the iron along the strip, the seam may curve, resulting in a less-than-straight strip of fabric.

Figure 7-13:
Lift, turn, and lower your iron to ensure that you're correctly pressing long strips.

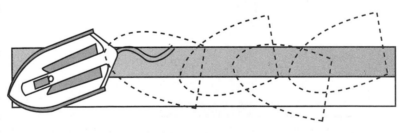

If you're having a bit of trouble getting a seam to lie flat, try a bit of water. Use the water only where needed rather than spraying an entire block. Keep some water in a shallow bowl and apply it with a finger just where you need it.

Chapter 8
Positively Perfect Piecing

● ●

In This Chapter

▶ Machine and hand piecing techniques

▶ Timesaving sewing tips

▶ Cheryl has a penchant for "P" words

● ●

*P*erfect piecing does not require profuse preparation, but some preliminary planning (placing pieces together in pairs) will better prepare you for producing perfect patchwork. It is permissible to pause and ponder this paragraph for a moment, as I am presuming you are profusely perplexed by my peculiarly preposterous postulating. It could be worse — I probably could have penned this particular paragraph as a prose poem.

What my previous prose means is that accurate piecing requires preparation. Not only will this preparation ensure success, but the job will proceed more smoothly and quickly.

In this chapter, I show you all the piecing tricks and techniques you need to know so that you can make accurately pieced blocks. I also tell you how to sew more efficiently in units using chain piecing and how to repair the inevitable mistake. Well-formed points and perfectly square blocks are within reach if you follow just a few basic rules, so don't be shy — dive on in!

Perfect Machine Piecing for the Impatient

Your grandmother might have spent her free time painstakingly piecing her quilt squares by hand, but today, you have the good fortune to be able to piece by machine. As a self-described "machine queen," I prefer to do everything I can with the aid of my sewing machine. Elias Howe, the wonderful wizard who patented the very first sewing machine in 1846, is truly my hero.

Although the rules are basically the same for both hand and machine piecing, machine piecing dramatically reduces the time it takes to complete a quilt top. (If you like to stitch on the go or simply don't want to use a machine, see "Hand Piecing for the Purist" later in this chapter.)

The following sections tell you how to set up your machine and start piecing. Chances are, if you're attempting to make a quilt (even if it's your first), you already know something about the basic workings of a sewing machine. If you don't use a sewing machine, just skip on over to the area for hand piecing.

Setting up your machine

Piecing by machine is a breeze. It's fast, accurate, and easy. But before sewing a single stitch, you need to make sure that your machine is set up properly by following these steps:

1. **Thread both the upper part of the machine and the bobbin with a neutral-colored all-purpose thread (one that will coordinate with all of the fabrics you are stitching together).**

2. **Set the stitch length to its default setting (usually 12 to14 stitches per inch, depending on the machine).**

3. **Insert your machine's patchwork presser foot (discussed in the following section) so you will be assured of an accurate ¹/₄-inch seam allowance.**

Then prepare your previously cut patches for stitching (see Chapter 7).

Using the presser foot

Whether you sew by hand or by machine, your *seam allowance* (the area of fabric taken up by the seam) is always exactly ¹/₄ inch wide — no more, no less. Your seam allowance is probably the most important factor to keep in mind when piecing, whether your block is simple or elaborate.

Some machines come with a special patchwork presser foot that measures exactly ¹/₄ inch from the needle hole to the outside edge of the foot. To stitch an accurate seam allowance, simply keep the edge of your fabric aligned with the edge of the foot (see Figure 8-1).

If this type of foot didn't come with your machine, you may be able to purchase one made specifically for your brand of machine from a sewing machine dealer. Some machines can be fitted with a "generic" foot, also available at sewing machine dealers.

Figure 8-1:
The presser
foot aligned
with the
raw edge of
the fabric.
The needle
is ¹/₄ inch
from the
edge of the
fabric.

Be sure to bring in one of your machine's existing feet when looking for one of these helpful goodies, as machines can vary by manufacturer. It's better to be prepared than to be sorry later! Bringing home a foot for a straight-shank machine (straight up and down), only to find that your machine has an angled shank (angles to the rear), would be a bummer!

Before you use the foot, be sure to check its accuracy. To do this, place a lightweight piece of paper in your machine and lower the presser foot. Then make a few stitches. Before removing the paper from the machine, mark a pencil line along the edge of the presser foot. Remove the paper from the machine and measure the distance from the needle holes to the pencil line. If this measurement is exactly ¹/₄ inch, you're in great shape!

If the measurement isn't accurate, use the tape trick described in the next section, "Using the great tape trick," to help keep your seam allowances accurate.

Using the great tape trick

If you prefer not to bother with a patchwork foot, or if you discover that your patchwork foot isn't accurate, you can make your own stitching guide with a piece of masking tape.

Measure ¹/₄ inch from your needle and place a piece of tape on the throat plate (that slab of metal with the hole in it that the needle goes up and down, and up and down, and up and down through) so that the right edge of the tape is at the ¹/₄ mark. This tape is your seam guide. You may need to replace it often if you do a lot of stitching.

Checking the tension

Make sure your machine is stitching properly before you attempt to machine piece anything. A machine that has its tension improperly set can result in pieces that pucker when stitching or in seams that separate slightly after stitching.

Checking the tension is especially important if you are using an older machine that has not been professionally serviced in a while, or if it's a hand-me-down, borrowed, or a garage sale find. Poor tension is not much of a problem with newer machines, as they are usually equipped with safeguards to keep the tension properly set.

To make sure your tension is properly set, you need to run a little test. Stitch through a double layer of fabric on your machine using a light-colored all-purpose thread in the machine and a dark colored all-purpose thread wound on the bobbin. Then take a close look at it. Does the dark bobbin thread show on the top of the fabric, having been pulled to the top surface? Does the light machine thread show on the bottom of the fabric?

If either situation is the case, you need to adjust the tension on the machine (refer to the owner's manual, too — each machine is different; this information is intended as a "pointer" for you). In my experience, when these things occur, something's been tightened too much — rarely has anything been loosened:

- ✔ **If the dark bobbin thread is pulled to the top surface:** Loosen the upper tension on the machine just slightly. Sew another test piece and look at it again. Keep doing this until the stitch is even on both sides.

- ✔ **If the top thread is being pulled to the bottom:** Your bobbin is probably adjusted too tightly. Loosen the adjusting screw slightly — $1/4$ turn at a time is fine. Stitch another test piece until the tension is right.

Another method for testing your bobbin tension is to hold a threaded bobbin case in the palm of your hand. Hold the thread from the bobbin between your thumb and first finger. While holding on to the thread, let go of the bobbin. Did it drop? If so, tighten the tension screw very slightly. It didn't go anywhere? Lightly shake the thread. If it still didn't budge, loosen the screw very slightly. A perfectly tuned bobbin case will yield when lightly shaken. There's sort of a fine line between too tight and too loose, but doing this will at least give you a clue.

Keeping your needle sharp

Be sure to change your sewing machine needle often. Believe it or not, I have run into people who have said, "What, change my needle? Why should I? It still sews, and I've had it in my machine for 10 years." YIKES!

Changing needles regularly is something I just can't drill into you enough! It's absolutely essential!

That needle is important to the tension, to properly formed stitches, and to the fabric itself. A needle that has become dull and rounded leaves larger holes than necessary in your fabric and can mess up your tension by allowing thread to travel through the holes. A needle that has a burr on it will catch the fabric's fibers, causing it to pucker. A burr may also cause your machine thread to break or get fuzzy while stitching.

I usually insert a new needle in my machine on a biweekly basis — after 40 to 50 hours of sewing. You'll see other quilters changing their needles less or more frequently, depending on their machines, the types of fabric they are sewing, or their own personal preferences. Always keep a fresh pack of needles on hand.

Chain piecing to save time and thread

When stitching many units together, whether for a pillow or an entire quilt, group your pieces together in pairs ahead of time, as shown in Figure 8-2, so that you can *chain piece* them together (stitch them in groups). Chain piecing not only saves time by grouping tasks and eliminating a few tedious steps, it also saves thread by not having a tail of thread at the beginning and end of every single unit you stitch.

Figure 8-2:
Group the
pieces in
pairs and
place them
next to your
machine.

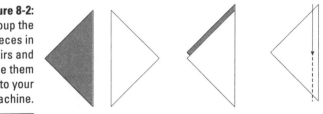

Here's how chain piecing works. Suppose that your project requires you to sew 12 blue triangles to 12 white triangles. To chain piece them:

1. **Place one of each color triangle together, with right sides facing.**

2. **Stack the 12 groups together to the right of your machine, facing the direction in which you need to sew them.**

   For example, if you are stitching them together across their longest side, place the stack next to the machine so that the longest side (the side you will be stitching) is on the right. This way, when you reach for the next pair of triangles, you simply feed the pair through the machine the way you picked it up. You don't need to fiddle with it, turning the triangles every which way before you figure out what sides to stitch!

3. Stitch the first unit as you normally would; however, instead of lifting the presser foot and removing the unit once you stitch it, simply start the next unit right behind it.

4. Stitch all the units in a chain, without cutting the thread, as shown in the following illustration.

5. When you finish stitching the units together, press them flat and cut them apart. Then press the units open, making sure you press the seam allowances towards the darker fabric.

Proceed to the next steps as usual!

Hand Piecing for the Purist

Some quilters prefer to hand piece their blocks. They enjoy sticking with tradition, and like the feel of the fabric flowing through their hands as they stitch. I call them "quilting purists" for lack of a better term.

As ye sew, so shall ye rip!

We're human. We make mistakes — sometimes lots of them! That's why it's important to learn how to use a seam ripper properly.

Notice that I said "seam ripper" and not "fabric ripper." The whole point of using one of these handy little tools is to undo the seam on a botched stitching job — not to rip through the fabric and ruin an entire patch.

To use a seam ripper correctly, insert the tool's sharp point under the first stitch, cutting the stitch. Cut the thread in the same way every five or six stitches, or until you can easily separate the two pieces of fabric. If the fabric pieces are difficult to separate, cut the thread at closer intervals, but don't forcefully separate the pieces — you risk ripping them or distorting their shapes.

Always keep your seam ripper on hand when piecing blocks, and make sure that it's in good shape. If your seam ripper becomes dull or rusted, throw it out and invest in a new one.

Always store your seam ripper with the cover on. This not only keeps it sharp and keeps moisture out, it also keep you from getting stabbed while rummaging through your sewing supplies!

Although hand piecing is certainly a traditional and time-honored approach to patchwork quilting, it has an added benefit: It's portable. By stashing just a needle, thread, fabric pieces, and small scissors in your purse or briefcase, you can work on a project virtually anywhere.

If you commute, try piecing instead of staring out the train window. If you travel, tuck your supplies in your carry-on bag and use your flight time for stitching. Quilting certainly beats reading the emergency evacuation guidelines over and over again or playing tic-tac-toe on the back of an airsick bag for the hundredth time! You also can carry your supplies when taking the kids to baseball practice or ballet lessons. You may even find yourself making a few new friends who share your interest in quilting, or who would like to learn but have been too afraid to try it. Become a quilting advocate!

You'll find little difference between hand piecing and machine piecing, with the hand-piecing exception of template preparation (see Chapter 4) and the beginning and ending of your stitching.

You still use a ¼-inch seam allowance, just as you would if you were machine piecing your project. However, because you don't have the machine's presser foot as a stitching guide, you need to mark seam allowances directly onto the wrong sides of your fabric pieces to keep your seam allowances accurate.

To accurately mark your seam allowances, make a window template for each piece, as shown in Figure 8-3.

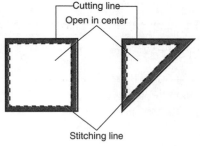

Figure 8-3:
Window
templates
with center
openings
for marking
seam lines.

A window template is simply a pattern template with a hole or window in the center for marking your seam line.

To use the template, lay it on the wrong side of the fabric you want to cut and trace around the template's outer edge with a washable pencil (refer to Chapter 6). This first line is your cutting line. Next, trace around the inside edge of the template. This second line is your stitching line.

To hand stitch the fabric pieces together, place them right sides together. For ease of handling, you may want to place a pin at each end of the stitching line and another at the mid-point to hold the layers together and prevent them from shifting as you stitch.

Cut a length of thread no longer than your arm and thread a hand-sewing needle with a single length of thread, as shown in Figure 8-4. Knot the longer end. This knot is your *waste knot* and will be cut off later.

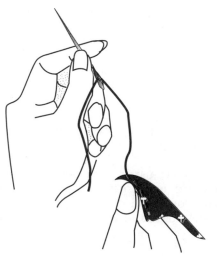

Figure 8-4:
Thread a
hand-
sewing
needle with
a single
length of
thread,
knotting the
longer end
of the
thread.

To begin stitching, start your thread just inside the piece and backstitch to the beginning. Then reverse your stitching direction and stitch across the entire length of the stitching line, making small, even stitches. Try to space these stitches as consistently as possible — shoot for eight to ten stitches per inch. When you reach the opposite end of the stitching line, reverse the direction of your stitching again and backstitch three or four stitches, as shown in Figure 8-5. Cut off the thread, and carefully cut off the waste knot from your starting point.

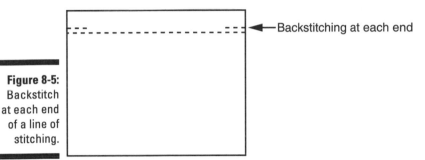

Backstitching at each end

Figure 8-5:
Backstitch at each end of a line of stitching.

After you become comfortable with hand stitching, you can eliminate the waste knot. You simply backstitch a few times at the beginning and then backstitch again at the end.

Piecing Blocks with Set-in Seams

At times during the piecing process, chain piecing is not appropriate, such as piecing blocks that have set-in seams. *Set-in seams* are components that need to be inserted into the block at an awkward angle, rather than stitched as a tidy unit. Figure 8-6 illustrates a set-in component. Notice that stitching the unit in place requires two seams (one on each side), rather than one. (The **Pieced Tulips Breakfast Set** in Part IV includes a set-in element in a block.)

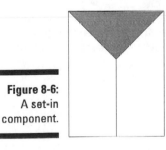

Figure 8-6:
A set-in component.

When working with templates for set-in components (see Figure 8-7), you see a *dot* at the corners where seam allowances converge. These dots are very important as they indicate where you are to begin and end your stitching. Be sure to transfer these dots to the cut pieces of fabric before stitching the pieces to the other components.

Figure 8-7: A set of templates for set-in components. Notice the "dots."

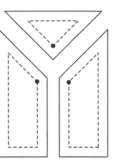

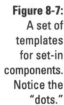

Do not go past the dots when stitching — you need to STOP AT THE DOT, rather than stitching to the end of the unit.

After you stitch along one side and end your stitching at the dot, rotate the pieces in the other direction and sew the final seam. The stitching order would be like the diagram shown in Figure 8-8.

Figure 8-8: The order of stitching on a set-in seam.

Remember! The stitching lines must not cross each other. And if you don't stop at the dot, you will end up with a pucker forming at the convergence of the seams. Sewing set-in pieces is not rocket science — just stop at the dots.

Chapter 9

Do You Know the Way to Appliqué?

ppliqué, a very elegant and versatile technique for creating quilt blocks, has been found on ancient textiles from nearly every culture. Historically, appliqué had been used mostly by the upper classes because it requires twice the amount of fabric as patchwork, and hence, twice the cost. An appliquéd quilt, being made up of additional layers of fabric, was more expensive to produce than a patchwork quilt, which consists of a single layer of fabric that has been pieced together, along with its filler and backing materials.

The term *appliqué* is French (oui!) and means "to apply," which is basically what you do — you apply bits of fabric to the top of other fabric. Unlike patchwork, where the pieces are cut and stitched together, appliqué is made by layering pieces one upon the other on a base or background fabric. The layers are stitched in place by hand or machine. Appliqué pieces can be any shape, enabling you to use curved designs impossible with traditional patchwork.

Appliqué: Stylistic Versatility

Appliqué is very versatile, enabling the quiltmaker to consider an infinite number of design possibilities! Styles of appliqué can range from traditional and folksy to contemporary or even *avant garde*, depending on the likes and skills of the quilter. Appliqué techniques can also be combined with patch-work to create blocks, and can also be used to add interest to other designs.

One of the most well-known forms of hand appliqué is the *Baltimore Album style,* which reached its highest point of popularity in 19th century Baltimore, Maryland. This style of appliqué, worked in traditional shades of red and green on white, has been enjoying a revival in recent years. Fair warning — this style is not really suitable for the beginning quilter due to the use of dozens of tiny appliqué pieces. Sure, it looks absolutely gorgeous, but some appliqué experience is a necessity! Practice on appliqué projects that have larger or fewer pieces, and build your skills before attempting this type of project on a large scale.

Because of appliqué's versatility, you can work using a number of different methods that vary in their degree of preparation and difficulty. I stick with the most basic stuff in this book — such as using freezer paper to help you turn under seam allowances — to give you a good foundation for developing your appliqué skills. You can substitute any of the appliqué methods for those that are listed in the individual projects if you like. I also cover fusible appliqué to make your quilting life even easier.

When you feel ready to move on to more difficult projects, a number of books specifically devoted to appliqué are available to guide you through the more advanced techniques. You may even decide to take a class and discover new methods of appliqué in a hands-on setting. I suggest a number of useful guides in the Appendix.

Appliqué Basics for Hand and Machine

A few rules apply to both hand and machine appliqué:

- ✔ First and foremost, select materials that are suitable for your project.

  Because appliqué consists of as many built-up layers of fabric as you like applied to a base, you don't want any heavy-weight fabrics. Stick to the fabrics that are most suitable for other quiltmaking techniques, as outlined in Chapter 2. You can add a bit of specialty fabrics if you like, such as gold or silver lamé, but make sure they, too, are lightweight, and that they can be laundered in the same manner as the other fabrics in your project.

- ✔ Second, before stitching any shapes to your background fabric, pre-mark the background fabric so that you'll have an easier time placing your appliqués later.

  To mark your background fabric, place the background fabric over the pattern and trace lightly using a water-soluble pencil or tailor's chalk through the fabric. These tracing lines will eventually disappear when you wash the project later.

➤ Finally, before cutting any fabrics, decide on the method you wish to use for appliqué.

Do you wish to do traditional hand appliqué with turned-under seam allowances? If so, you need to add seam allowances to appliqué patterns that do not already include them before cutting out any pieces.

If you choose fusible-web machine appliqués, your pieces will not require seam allowances at all.

In this chapter, I show you a few techniques using both types of appliqué — appliqués that require seam allowances and appliqués that do not. This list of techniques is by no means complete; there are as many different ways of doing appliqué as there are quilters.

Doing Seams: Appliqués with Seam Allowances

In this type of appliqué, whether stitching the pieces to your background fabric by hand or machine, you prepare the edges of the appliqué by turning under its seam allowances before stitching the appliqué to the background fabric. The seam allowances are $1/4$ inch, just like every other seam allowance you find in quilting (You may notice that some seam allowances in other quilting books are a mere $1/8$ inch. Don't worry about that right now. Build your skills before you stitch appliqués with narrower seam allowances).

The advantage to this type of appliqué is that the seam allowances are turned under and are hidden away beneath the appliqué itself. This gives your quilt a very polished, traditional look, and the appliqués seem to float on the background fabric because the stitches used to stitch them in place are hidden as well. It requires more time to produce than fusible webbing appliqué, but the results can be breathtaking!

To make an appliqué with a turned-under seam allowance, trace your appliqué template on the fabric. If the template includes seam allowances, cut out the shape along your marked line. If it does not have a seam allowance, cut out the shape $1/4$ inch from your marked line.

You will know if your template includes seam allowances by looking at it — does it have one solid line around the outside, or does it have a solid outside line and a dashed inside line? If it has a dashed inside line, the seam allowance has been included in the template, as shown in Figure 9-1. If it does not, you will need to add it.

Figure 9-1:
The left
template
includes
seam
allowance,
the one on
the right
does not.

Methods for turning under the seam allowance

After cutting out the appliqué shapes, you need to turn under the seam allowance, using one of the following methods: turn-and-baste appliqué, freezer-paper appliqué, or glue-stick appliqué.

Remember !!!! When turning under the seam allowances around curves or inverted points, you need to clip the seam allowance to make it lie flat. When turning under the seam allowance at a corner, turn up the point first and then turn up the seam allowances on either side of the point. Figure 9-2 illustrates how this is done.

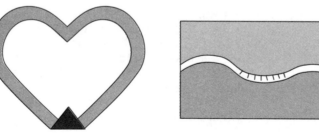

Figure 9-2:
Working
your way
around
curves,
corners,
and points.

Turn-and-baste appliqué

Turn-and-baste appliqué is very time-consuming, but gives good results. After tracing and cutting your appliqué shape with seam allowances, turn the seam allowance to the wrong side of the appliqué. Be sure to clip into the appliqué's seam allowance around any curves or inverted points.

Secure the seam-allowance folds by basting them in place by hand. To do this, thread a needle (any kind) with a length of thread, and stitch around the appliqué shape $1/8$ inch from the folded edges in running stitch. You will remove the basting thread after stitching your appliqués to the background fabric, so don't worry about the color of your basting thread.

After you baste the seam allowance around all the edges, as in Figure 9-3, the shape is ready to be appliquéd.

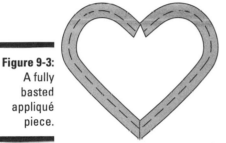

Figure 9-3:
A fully basted appliqué piece.

Freezer-paper appliqué (or English paper appliqué)

Freezer-paper appliqué is my favorite technique when using appliqués that have seam allowances, and it is the method you will be using for several of the projects in this book. In my humble opinion, this is the best method to use when preparing your pieces for machine appliqué because you're gathering the seam allowance of your appliqué around an inside shape, giving you smooth, accurate results with very little fuss.

You can purchase freezer paper at any grocery store; it's usually located on the same aisle as the aluminum foil and plastic wrap. Be sure to purchase freezer paper that has wax on one side and plain paper on the other. The wax on the freezer paper is what makes this technique work.

To use freezer-paper appliqué:

1. **Cut out your appliqué with seam allowances included, as you would for turn-and-baste appliqué.**

2. **Trace your appliqué pattern *without* seam allowances on the wax-free side of the freezer paper and cut out.**

3. **Center the freezer paper shape on the wrong side of the appliqué shape, placing the waxy coating towards the fabric. With an iron set on "cotton," press the freezer paper to the appliqué fabric.**

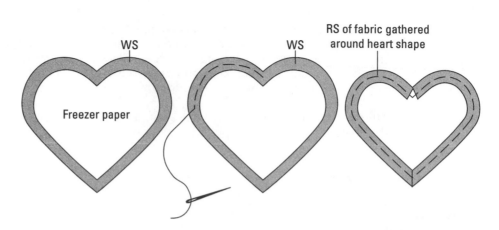

You only need to press long enough to melt the wax (don't worry, it won't harm the fabric in any way).

4. **Clip your curves and points as you would for turn-and-baste appliqué.**

5. **With a hand sewing needle and thread to match the appliqué fabric, sew a running stitch around the seam allowance, pulling the thread slightly to gather the seam allowance around the shape. Knot your thread at the end so the gathering stitches won't slip.**

6. **Press the appliqué with the freezer paper still inside.**

The shape is now ready to be appliquéd.

Glue-stick appliqué

Glue-stick appliqué is similar to the freezer-paper method, but instead of freezer paper you use plain white paper (copier paper or computer paper works great). You secure the seam allowances by using a glue stick. You can purchase glue sticks made for use on fabrics in quilting and sewing supply stores, but it really isn't necessary. The glue sticks from the office supply store work just as well.

My favorite glue-stick brand is the UHU stick. It always gives me great results and washes out of my fabrics thoroughly. If the end of your glue stick feels a bit dry, cut off about $^1/_4$ inch of the glue stick with a knife and start fresh.

Prepare your fabric and your paper as you would for the freezer paper method (without worrying about any waxy coating):

1. **Place a small amount of glue on the center of the back side of the paper shape and press the paper shape to the wrong side of the appliqué fabric. This will hold it in place on the fabric as your turn under the seam allowance.**

2. **Working in increments (so your glue doesn't dry before you fold under the seam allowance), apply a line of glue around the edge of the**

paper shape, immediately pressing the seam allowance onto the glue. Hold the fabric in place for a moment until it stays of its own accord.

3. **Continue adding glue around the edges of the paper until all of the seam allowances are glued down.**

The shape is now ready to be appliquéd.

Hand stitching the appliqués

After you prepare your appliqué pieces, you're ready to stitch them to the background fabric!

Arrange your prepared appliqué pieces on the background fabric. Pin, baste, or glue them in place to keep them from falling off. Work from front to back — appliqué any pieces that will be lying under another one first, followed by the overlapping piece (see Figure 9-4). You can remove the overlapping piece temporarily if it helps you appliqué the piece underneath — just be sure to replace it later.

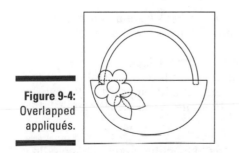

Figure 9-4:
Overlapped
appliqués.

Thread a needle (either a sharp or a between) with thread to match the color of the first appliqué. Using the ladder or tacking stitches (so your stitches will be nearly invisible), stitch around the edges of the appliqué.

If you are using the freezer-paper or glue-stick method of appliqué described previously in this chapter, appliqué around the shape to within ³/₄ inch of your starting point. Using tweezers or your fingers, remove the freezer paper from the opening. The freezer paper will peel off the fabric very easily; the glued paper may need a spritz of water to soften the glue before removal. After removing the paper, finish your appliqué stitching.

If you are using the turn-and-baste method, remove the basting stitches after stitching around the appliqué.

If you have many appliqués piled on top of one another, you want to reduce some of this bulk before attempting to quilt it later! To do this, trim away the fabric ¹/₄ inch from the stitching of the appliqués on the wrong side of the background fabric and cut away the excess bulk (see Figure 9-5).

Figure 9-5:
Eliminating
bulk.

Use this with both hand and machine appliqué techniques to reduce bulk.

Machine stitching the appliqués

To machine appliqué the pieces in place on the background fabric, pin, baste, or glue the pieces to the background fabric as for hand appliqué.

Place a piece of tear-away stabilizer, cut to fit the background fabric, on the wrong side of the background fabric and pin it in place. This stabilizer is essential to proper machine appliqué because it adds support to the fabric, preventing it from being shoved through the hole in the throat plate while stitching.

Be sure to use the stabilizer for all methods of machine appliqué, including those using seamless appliqués. For more about stabilizer, see the sidebar, "Stabilizer: How stable is it if you can tear it away?" later in this chapter.

Stitch around the edges of the appliqués using any of the methods described in the sections that follow.

Stabilizer: How stable is it if you can tear it away?

A stabilizer is a nonwoven product, made from polyester, which is used to support the project as you stitch. You can purchase it at any fabric store.

The stabilizer holds the project above the feed dogs, preventing the material from being crammed through the machine's throat plate hole while sewing. Different types of stabilizers are available for different uses. All of the references in this book are for *tear-away stabilizer*.

Don't confuse tear-away stabilizers with those that need to be washed out or cut away after you finish the appliqué. Look for those brands that are called Tear-Away or Stitch and Tear.

Invisible machine appliqué (or blind-stitch appliqué)

Blind-stitch or *invisible machine appliqué* mimics the look of hand appliqué, but takes a fraction of the time to complete.

To do invisible machine appliqué, thread the top of the machine with nylon monofilament. You will find this thread at any sewing, quilting, or fabric store. Use clear monofilament for stitching over light to medium fabrics; use the "smoke" color for stitching over darker fabrics. These two threads will be virtually invisible to the eye.

Don't substitute fishing line, even though it's similar and you think it could suffice! Fishing line is much heavier than the monofilament made for sewing and could damage your machine. Besides, what would you use as line if you decided to plop yourself next to the ol' fishin' hole after sewing?

Load your bobbin with a neutral color of thread, preferably one that matches your backing fabric. Set your machine to the *blind stitch* (refer to your sewing machine owner's manual). The blind stitch looks like Figure 9-6 and consists of a length of straight stitch followed by an inward zigzag.

Figure 9-6:
The blind stitch.

Change your machine's foot to one with an "open toe" (again, refer to your manual). An open toe foot allows you to see where you're going much better than a standard foot, because it is open at the front.

Carefully stitch around each of the appliqué shapes, with the straight stitch just outside the appliqué (into the background fabric) and the zigzag stitch into the appliqué, as shown in Figure 9-7.

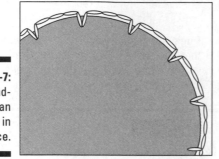

Figure 9-7: Blind-stitching an appliqué in place.

Straight-stitch appliqué (or topstitching appliqué)

The *straight-stitch* method is exactly as it sounds — you stitch around the appliqué, using the machine's most basic stitch. The only trick is that you must try to stitch as close to the edge as you can comfortably get (see Figure 9-8).

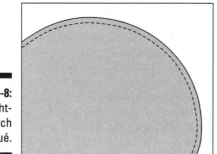

Figure 9-8: Straight-stitch appliqué.

How far you get from the edge depends on your skill level and your bravery quotient. For some folks, this is $1/8$ inch from the edge. Experienced sewers often topstitch so close to the edge that it's difficult to see if the stitches are on the appliqué at all!

You may want to save this technique for use at a later time, when you have acquired a bit more experience.

Zigzag appliqué

Zigzag appliqué is the lazy quilter's version of satin stitch, which I discuss under "Look, Ma, No Seam Allowances." Needless to say, I'm fond of the zigzag appliqué stitch. I like being lazy at times.

In zigzag appliqué, you can load your machine with whatever thread you choose (all-purpose, monofilament, or buttonhole twist) in any color you want (matching or clashing).

Stitch around the edges of the appliqué in a loose zigzag, as shown in Figure 9-9.

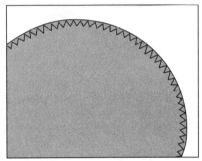

Figure 9-9:
The zigzag
technique.

This technique is very similar to satin stitch appliqué, except for the fact that satin stitch is dense (tighter, closer together) and covers the raw edges of appliqué completely — which is why it's used for appliqués that do not have seam allowances. The looser zigzag method of appliqué is just plain fun!

Look, Ma, No Seam Allowances! Fusible Machine Appliqué

Appliqué without seam allowances basically falls under the domain of fusible machine appliqué. Why? Because using sewing machine techniques and fusible webbing is the easiest way to keep the edges from fraying on appliqués that do not have turned-under seam allowances. This is important if you expect your quilt to be used, loved, and laundered.

Buying fusible transfer webbing

For fusible machine appliqué, you need to purchase *fusible transfer webbing*. The instructions in this book call for fusible webbing that has a paper backing on one side. This webbing is made by several different manufacturers and even comes in different weights — standard, lightweight, and heavy-duty.

For the purpose of machine appliqué for quilting, stick to the standard weight of fusible webbing. This is an all-purpose weight and is ideal for any fabrics you may be using. The lightweight variety is meant for sheer, light-weight fabrics and has considerable flexibility. The heavy-duty weight is a bit stiff and is best suited to heavier fabrics, such as denim or canvas.

Some of the typical brand names you find this stuff listed under include WonderUnder, Stitch Witchery, HeatnBond, and Trans-Web. Any brand will suffice. When in doubt, ask the store personnel for advice — that's what they're there for.

Webbing products are normally found in the section of the store containing interfacing. Sometimes, the fusible webbing is kept under the counter, and you have to ask for it (which is rare). Fusible webbing is sold from the bolt by the yard or pre-packaged in varying sizes. I prefer to buy it by the yard.

Fusible webbing does *not need* to be prewashed (in fact, you would ruin it if you did). When storing fusible webbing, don't fold it! This can sometimes cause the webbing material to separate from the paper, rendering it almost useless. Instead, roll it with the insert it came with (you don't want to lose it because it contains important instructions) and secure it with a rubber band.

Preparing for machine appliqué

You need to prepare your pattern template differently for machine appliqué. Read these instructions carefully, or you'll find yourself with everything facing the wrong direction.

To better illustrate the importance of these directions, I am going to use the letter "Q" as an appliqué shape:

1. **Trace the appliqué pattern directly from its source onto tracing paper. Mark the side facing you as you trace RS (right side). Turn the paper over and mark the other side WS (wrong side).**

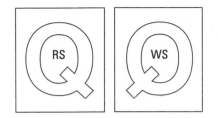

I know seeing writing on the opposite side of the paper backward is annoying, but you'll get used to it.

2. **Place your traced pattern RS down on your work surface (or WS up depending on which way you look at the world).**

   To keep the pattern from scooting around as you trace, tape it down along with two corners.

3. **Place your fusible webbing over the pattern, with the paper side up (facing you).**

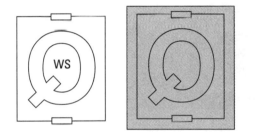

   The webbing is nearly transparent, so you can easily see the patterns through it.

4. **Trace the pattern onto the fusible webbing using any pencil.**

   You may be wondering why you trace the appliqué in the opposite direction; I'll get to that in a moment.

5. **Cut out the shape "roughly."**

   You don't need to cut the shapes perfectly along the lines at this point; that would just be a waste of time. You cut out the shapes neatly after fusing them to the fabrics.

6. **Using a hot iron, fuse the appliqué to the wrong side of the appliqué fabric, having the webbing (rough) side toward the fabric and the paper facing upward, toward you.**

   For iron settings, refer to the manufacturer's insert that accompanies your brand of webbing.

7. **Now you can cut the shapes out neatly!**

   As you may have noticed, the "Q" has been facing the wrong direction this whole time. It's supposed to. The next steps will show you why.

8. **Remove the paper backing from the appliqué by peeling it away, exposing the adhesive which has been fused to the wrong side of the fabric.**

9. **Place the appliqué goopy side down on the background fabric.**

   Tada! . . . It's now facing the right direction!

10. **Fuse the appliqué to the background fabric.**

Your appliqué is now ready to be finished by one of the machine-appliqué techniques described n the following sections.

Using machine-appliqué techniques

I'll continue using the same appliqué in this section because "Q" is for Quilt (what else?). And it's such a neat shape!

To prepare your project for machine appliqué, cut a piece of tear-away stabilizer the same size as the background fabric. Pin the stabilizer to the wrong side of the background fabric at the corners. For information about this stabilizer, see the sidebar on stabilizer earlier in this chapter.

Satin stitch appliqué

Everybody loves satin stitch! It looks gorgeous, can be stitched in different widths depending on preference, and completely encloses the raw edges of the appliqué under a barrier of thread, making the appliqué very durable. This stitch is a composed of zigzag stitches spaced very close together — so close that you are unable to see the fabric through the thread.

Load the top of the machine with a dark color thread and wind a lighter color in the bobbin, because you are going to test your stitch quality in a moment. Look through your machine's presser feet and find one with an open toe. This differs from a closed-toe foot in that the front area of the foot is cut away (see Figure 9-10). Using an open-toe foot allows you to see where you're going much easier than using a closed-toe foot.

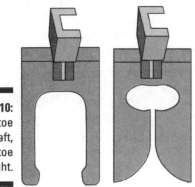

Figure 9-10:
Open-toe
foot on left,
closed-toe
on right.

Satin stitching requires your machine to be in good working condition. To set your machine for satin stitching, refer to the owner's manual. Beginners should start with a width of $1/8$ to $1/4$ inch. Anything narrower can be a bit difficult to handle and will require more experience. The width of the satin stitch can be controlled by the knob for *stitch width*. The density of the satin stitch (how closely spaced it is) is controlled by the knob for *stitch length*.

Test sew a line of satin stitching on a scrap of fabric with another scrap of fabric fused to the center of it, and look at the stitch:

✔ Is the stitching nice and even or are there skipped stitches? Does the stitching need to be denser, or should it be less dense?

If you can still see the edges of the fused fabric through the line of satin stitching, the stitching should be denser, and you need to shorten the length of the stitch. If the satin stitching is bunching up on itself in front of the presser foot, increase the length of the stitch. Increasing or decreasing stitch length does not alter the width of the satin stitch. The width of the stitch is controlled by a different knob, remember?

✔ Now look closely at the ridge of satin stitching. Can you see any of the light-colored bobbin thread on the surface?

If you do, you need to loosen the upper tension on your machine very slightly. Test sew again and check the quality. If you continue to see the bobbin thread, keep adjusting the tension in small increments until none of the bobbin thread is seen on the surface. If this does not work, you may need to increase the tension of the bobbin thread (see Chapter 8 for additional instructions on proper tension settings). If nothing works, have your machine serviced professionally.

Once your stitch is perfect, it's time to sew the appliqués in place:

1. **Replace the upper and bobbin threads to whichever thread you will be using for appliqué.**

2. **Place your project under the presser foot and begin to lower the needle.**

Before lowering the needle to the point that it enters the fabric, note whether the needle is positioned to the left or to the right. If the needle is to the left, lower the needle so that it goes through the fabric in the appliqué. If the needle is to the right, it needs to go into the background fabric.

If your satin stitch is in proper form, use a neutral thread in the bobbin. This way, you won't have to change the color of the bobbin thread each time you change the upper thread to match the appliqués!

3. **Stitch around the edges of all of the appliqués, having the left swing (zig) of the needle in the appliqué and the right swing (zag) into the background fabric.**

Many beginning quilters complain that their satin stitches are bumpy and uneven. By following a few simple steps, you can avoid these complaints. You need to use a bit of caution when you approach a corner or curve or when stitching along a point. When approaching these areas, slow down and follow these instructions:

To stitch inside corners: Stitch beyond the corner as far as the stitch is wide, and leave the needle in the fabric where indicated by the dot on Figure 9-11 (in the left-hand position). Raise the presser foot, leaving the needle in the fabric, and turn the fabric so that you are ready to stitch along the next side. Lower the presser foot and continue stitching. You will have crossed over the stitching where you left off on the previous side.

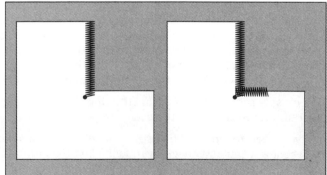

Figure 9-11:
Turning an inside corner.

To stitch outside corners: Stitch to the end of the appliqué and leave the needle in the fabric at the right-hand position, indicated by the dot in Figure 9-12 (at the point of the corner). Raise the presser foot and turn the fabric so you are ready to stitch the next side. Lower the presser foot and continue stitching. This will give you a nicely finished corner.

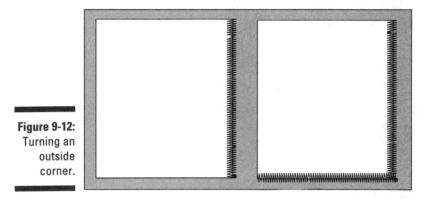

Figure 9-12:
Turning an outside corner.

To stitch around curves smoothly: Pivot the fabric as you sew. If you are stitching along an inside curve (see Figure 9-13), leave the needle in the appliqué (left-hand swing of the needle), raise the presser foot, and turn the fabric just slightly. Lower the presser foot and continue stitching. Repeat this until you have stitched along the entire curve. The number of times you need to pivot depends on the curve: A slight curve needs fewer pivots than a tight one.

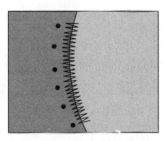

Figure 9-13:
Stitching an inside curve.

Stitching along an outside curve is identical to that of an inside curve, except the needle is stopped in the background fabric (right-hand swing of the needle). Raise the presser foot and pivot the fabric as many times as needed to stitch around the curve smoothly (see Figure 9-14).

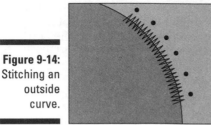

Figure 9-14:
Stitching an outside curve.

To stitch along a sharp point: Gradually decrease the width of the satin stitch as the point narrows, as shown in Figure 9-15.

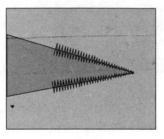

Figure 9-15:
Narrow the width of the satin stitch as you approach a sharp point.

After you turn the point, increase the width again and begin stitching along the opposite side of the point.

Now that you are either thoroughly confused or have a vague notion of what to do, read the previous steps ten more times (just kidding, you're ready!) and then just jump in and stitch all the appliqués in place. The stuff I just covered will be instinctive once you begin stitching. When you finish stitching the appliqués, remove the pins holding the stabilizer and tear the stabilizer from the backside of the project. It will tear away easily.

Use a tweezers to pull off any small bits that are too tiny for your fingers to grasp.

Machine blanket stitch (or buttonhole stitch)

The machine blanket stitch closely mocks hand blanket stitch, but is stitched so much quicker! It gives your appliqué projects a primitive look that today's quilters love.

Blanket stitch can be done it any color, but the most commonly used color is black. Therefore, I am only going to refer to black in these instructions. If you choose to use a different color, simply substitute it for the black. (A real no-brainer tip, eh?)

After fusing your appliqués in place and backing them with stabilizer, set your machine to the blanket stitch as shown in Figure 9-16 (refer to the owner's manual). You want to use your open-toe foot with this method of appliqué, too.

Figure 9-16:
The machine blanket stitch.

Wind your bobbin with black all-purpose thread and insert it in the bobbin case. As for the top thread, you have two options: All-purpose thread and buttonhole twist (topstitching) thread. Some quilters prefer to have a heavier thread on the edges of their appliqués, which is why they use the buttonhole twist. Others prefer to use all-purpose, which is a bit lighter in appearance. (For a complete run-down of threads, see Chapter 6.)

Test sew a piece of fabric in the blanket stitch to make sure you are making a good, solid stitch. If it looks ragged or has skipped stitches, refer to your owner's manual and Chapter 8 for tips on adjusting tension.

When your stitch looks perfect (just like the picture in the manual), stitch around the edges of the appliqués. The straight-stitch edge of the blanket stitch should be *in the ditch* at the edge of the appliqué (as close to the appliqué as possible); the long "legs" of the stitch need to be in the appliqué itself, as shown in Figure 9-17.

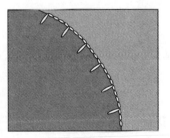

Figure 9-17:
The finished blanket stitch.

Turning corners and stitching around points can be a matter of trial and error with this method of appliqué. Keep in mind that this is supposed to be a "primitive-looking" type of appliqué, and perfection is not necessary. If you're worried about it, use Figure 9-18 as a guide.

When you have finished stitching the appliqués in place, remove the pins and tear away the stabilizer.

TIP

Blanket stitch on-the-go

After fusing the appliqués in place, you can proceed to stitch them in place with hand blanket stitch if you prefer! Stabilizer is not necessary (it'll just get in your way). Use black pearl cotton or two strands of embroidery floss in a large-eyed needle to appliqué the pieces in place. The following diagram shows the hand-embroidered blanket stitch.

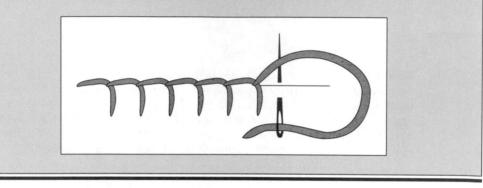

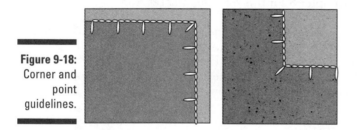

Figure 9-18:
Corner and point guidelines.

Appliqué Using Decorative Machine Stitches

Does your machine have tons of neat stitches that you've never used? Great! Use them for appliqué!

Some of the denser, tighter stitches, such as those shown in Figure 9-19, can be used on fused appliqués. Simply substitute them for the satin stitch or blanket stitch in the "Look, Ma, No Seam Allowances" section.

The **Scrappy Pines Lap Quilt** in Part IV is a great project on which to use decorative stitches.

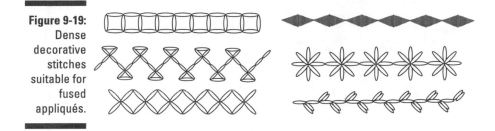

Figure 9-19:
Dense
decorative
stitches
suitable for
fused
appliqués.

You can also use the looser, open decorative stitches shown in Figure 9-20; however, these stitches are best suited to appliqués with turned-under seam allowances as discussed in "Doing Seams: Appliqués with Seam Allowances," earlier in this chapter. If you use these looser stitches on appliqués that don't have seam allowances, you could wind up with frayed fabric edges poking through your beautiful stitching!

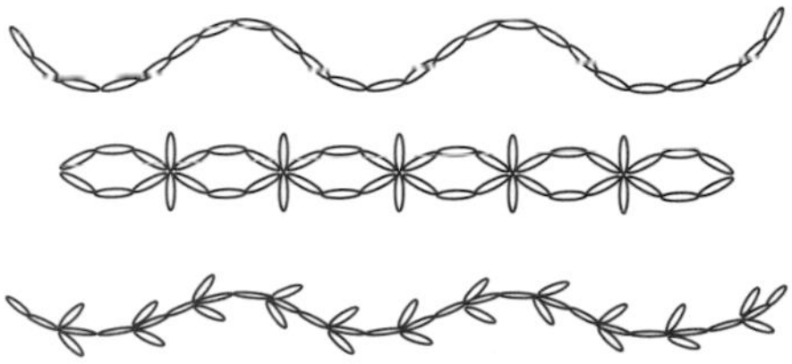

Figure 9-20:
Loose, open
decorative
stitches.

Experiment with your machine's stitch repertoire on scraps of fabric and be creative!

Part III

Ahead at the Finish: Quilting the Pieces in Place

In this part . . .

This part helps you put top layer, batting, and backing together so that it stays put and looks fantastic. You can choose your quilting approach, baste the sandwich in place, and bind the edges for a piece you'll be proud of. Now's the time to see the quilt you've been picturing in your head take actual shape. Happy quilting!

Chapter 10

The Plan of Attack: Deciding How to Quilt Your Quilt

. . . .

In This Chapter

▶ Stitching for hand or machine quilting
▶ Stitching to enhance your design
▶ Stitching that fills large areas

. . . .

*A*fter you have your plan and cut and stitch your pieces, you're ready to quilt your quilt. What, you say! What have I been doing up to now? I thought I was quilting. Well, you're right in a way. You've been piecing and/ or appliquéing a quilt, but it's not a quilt until you assemble the three sandwich layers into one fluffy project, and that's where the real quilting begins.

As with piecing your quilt, you have the choice of hand stitching or machine stitching. But before you decide to hand or machine quilt your project, you need to think about what your project will be used for. Is it going to get much use and regular washing, such as a baby's bib? Is it for looks rather than function, such as a wallhanging or a holiday vest? You will also need to decide if you want to finish this project in a hurry, or if you prefer to take your sweet time.

Here are two important points to consider when deciding to machine or hand quilt:

✔ Machine quilting is quick — real quick. However, it can sometimes have a less-than-heirloom look, and your skill level at this point does not allow you to create intricate quilting designs by machine. Intricate machine quilting designs require a bit of experience (which I'm certain will come later!).

✔ Hand quilting is slow — real slow. But for the beginning quilter, decorative quilting patterns are best worked by hand (it's much easier) rather than machine. You have complete control over your quilting when doing it by hand.

I think you may have guessed that I'm a "machine queen" by now. I prefer to hand quilt only when I'm working on something I consider "heirloom quality." Your choice of technique, however, is totally up to you.

Although both hand and machine quilting are suitable for any use, the spacing of the quilting may not be, and you also need to consider the manufacturer's recommended quilting intervals when making your decision (refer to the batting section in Chapter 2). All of these factors combined will help you determine how to quilt your quilt.

If you have the opportunity to look closely at antique quilts, you will notice that the quilting is very closely spaced. This spacing keeps those cotton fibers from migrating into corners and creating lumpy pockets in great-granny's quilts. Granted, granny didn't have the batting selection available today, so she rolled out large wads of cotton wadding or wool wadding instead of batting for her quilts.

Even though today's battings are treated with special finishes that help keep the fibers together, not going beyond the intervals discussed in Chapter 2 as the widest recommended intervals for placing your quilting stitches is very important to the finished project.

Fiber migration is common in most battings — even the ones that state otherwise on the wrapper. Any fiber batting can migrate if not quilted and laundered properly. The quilting stitches that you set are the ones that keep the three layers of your quilt functioning together as one unit. The denser the quilting (the closer your stitches are to one another), the better the quilted item will perform as a wallhanging, bedcovering, placemat, or whatever you intend.

For instance, if you make a quilted vest that you know you will love to wear and you expect to wash it often, space your quilting intervals closer together. The more an item is washed, the more you risk having the fibers migrate into pockets. Those closer intervals help hold that batting in place, reducing the chances of fiber migration.

Today, you can quilt at wider intervals than granny could without ending up with a lumpy mess, but you still must keep the recommended intervals in mind when deciding how to quilt your project. Be sure to read the package carefully before selecting a batting (refer to Chapter 2 if you need more information about batting).

Outline Quilting to Enhance Shapes

You have a wide range of choices (and you can even invent your own!) when it comes to choosing quilting-stitch patterns. I cover the most useful in the sections that follow.

By far the most popular method of quilting is to enhance the shapes of the patchwork or appliqué with some type of outline quilting. Outline quilting can be either in-the-ditch or ¹/₄ inch from the seamlines:

- ✔ *In-the-ditch quilting* is stitching very near — almost on top of — the seams in a patchwork block (see Figure 10-1). Its name comes from the fact that the seam areas form a sort of "ditch" that is very easy to follow. In-the-ditch quilting is a good choice for machine quilting, but can be difficult to hand stitch.

  When hand quilting, do your in-the-ditch stitching on the side of the seam that has the least amount of bulk for ease of handling.

- ✔ *Quarter-inch quilting* is also referred to as *echo quilting*. The quilting lines "echo" the shape of the piece as you stitch ¹/₄ inch from the seam line on each piece (see Figure 10-2). I talk more about echo quilting in the "Free-style fillers" section later in this chapter.

  Using quarter-inch quilting, you avoid stitching through those thick, multiple layers in the seam allowances! Quarter-inch quilting is best suited for hand quilting, when you are learning to quilt. It can be machine quilted as well but it requires a bit of experience to do it properly (it is a free-motion stitch — the feed dogs are disengaged, requiring you to hand guide the quilt).

Figure 10-1:
In-the-ditch
quilting is
difficult to
do by hand.

When outline quilting with appliqué, you can space the stitches very close to the shape of the appliqué — much like in-the-ditch quilting. You can then use the filler stitches described in the next section to fill in the outside areas of the block, or continue to echo the shape of the appliqué until you fill the entire area.

You can use quilting as a way to enhance your appliqué blocks as well, as shown in Figure 10-3.

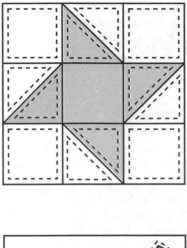

Figure 10-2: Decorative quilting patterns for blocks and borders.

Figure 10-3: A matching set of traditional feather-quilting patterns for blocks and borders.

Notice that the block in Figure 10-3 is outline quilted with additional quilting to the inside of the flower and along the centers of the leaves to better define the design. Beautiful!

Filler Patterns for Quilting Large Areas

The following types of geometric quilting designs are suitable for both hand and machine quilting and are easy to stitch. These stitch designs are used to fill large areas on a quilt and are usually referred to as *filler patterns*. You can use these patterns on the entire quilt or just for areas of the quilt in which you need to fill a large amount of background. The choice is yours.

Cross-hatch quilting

Cross-hatch, also known as *grid quilting,* is one of the most common and traditional-looking filler options, as you can see in Figure 10-4. Cross-hatch quilting is quick and texturally interesting. Plus, if you use the following masking-tape technique, you don't need to pre-mark this pattern on your quilt top before stitching (although you certainly can mark the quilt top before basting if you wish). I discuss marking patterns for quilting in Chapter 11, just before basting.

Figure 10-4: Cross-hatch quilting.

To quilt this pattern without marking the top, decide first how far apart you wish to have the lines. Will they be spaced ¹/₂ inch apart or 1 inch apart?

After making your decision, run to the hardware store or art supply store and find a roll of masking tape the width you need (if you don't already have some on hand). I'm not kidding! This works beautifully and is so accurate, it's scary! I have rolls of tape on hand in widths as narrow as ¹/₈ inch and ¹/₄ inch, as well as tape that is ¹/₂ inch, 1 inch, 1¹/₂ inches, and even 2 inches wide. You need only purchase one roll in the width of choice because the tape will last quite a while. After you find your tape, lay out a strip of tape 12 inches or so in length on your basted quilt at a 45-degree angle to the sides of the quilt (see Figure 10-5). Hand or machine quilt along the sides of the tape — the tape does the spacing for you!

You do not need to end your stitching just because you get to the end of the tape — lift the tape and move it along to the next spot and continue stitching. The tape can be peeled off and moved as many times as needed, but when it starts to lose its stickiness, discard the tape strip and get another.

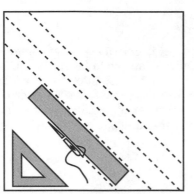

Figure 10-5:
Let your
tape do the
spacing.

Diamond quilting

A variation on the cross-hatch quilting is *diamond quilting*, shown in Figure 10-6.

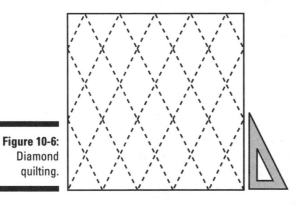

Figure 10-6:
Diamond
quilting.

Diamond quilting can also be worked with the masking tape method described in the previous section, but instead of placing the tape at a 45-degree angle, place it at a 30-degree angle to the sides of the quilt.

You can do other fun variations with the tape method. Use the illustrations in Figure 10-7 for inspiration!

Clamshell quilting

Clamshell quilting is an easy-to-stitch filler that requires pre-marking before you baste together the layers of your quilt.

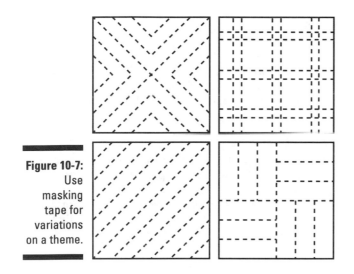

Figure 10-7:
Use masking tape for variations on a theme.

Make a template from a circle of cardboard and a compass. Although the circle can be any size, 3 to 4 inches in diameter suits most quilt battings. Mark a line through the center of the circle across the diameter. Mark another line vertically through the radius only. These lines act as guides when tracing around the template onto your fabric. Trace the upper section of the template on the fabric as shown in Figure 10-8.

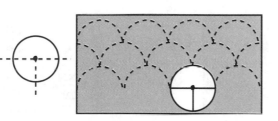

Figure 10-8:
Creating a quilted clamshell using circle tops.

A variation on this theme is called *orange peel quilting*. Use the same template as for clamshell quilting, but instead of tracing around only the top half of the circle, trace around the entire circle, using the circle's markings as a guide (see Figure 10-9).

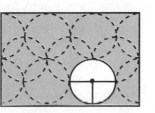

Figure 10-9:
Orange peel quilting uses the whole circle.

Free-style fillers

Free-style fillers are a bit more complicated than the geometric fillers discussed previously, but they're well worth the extra effort. Instead of following a specific grid or pattern, you cut loose and do whatever feels good! Although the fillers take a bit of time to master, you'll be beautifully rewarded!

Echo quilting, which I mentioned previously, is one type of free-style filler that you often see. It consists of multiple lines of quilting stitches that run parallel to the edges of any shape, "echoing" the shape. Space the lines approximately ¼ inch apart. Because this type of quilting is rarely pre-marked, you need a bit of practice to get your lines evenly spaced. You can pre-mark the lines if you wish, but it takes quite a bit of time and really isn't necessary. If the lines not perfectly spaced at ¼ inch, you really won't notice because the overall effect is quite casual and relaxed.

Figure 10-10 shows two variations on echo quilting: one echoes an appliqué; the other echoes patchwork shapes.

Figure 10-10:
Echoing figure shapes with your quilting stitches.

Another popular form of free-motion filler is *stipple quilting.* Stipple quilting takes some time to master by hand, but it's a breeze to do on the machine. Figure 10-11 shows an example of stipple quilting.

Keep in mind that stipple quilting will act to flatten an area. Stipple quilting is most commonly used in appliqué blocks because this flattening effect enables the appliqués to stand out nicely, giving them a puffy look.

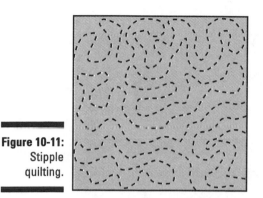

Figure 10-11:
Stipple
quilting.

Decorative Quilting Patterns and Stencils

Other quilting options include decorative quilting patterns and stencils. These can be found in books specializing in quilting designs, and can be found in quilting and fabric shops as pre-cut stencils. You will find decorative quilting patterns and stencils available in many types of designs — florals, geometrics, meandering vines, feathers, and more, in both traditional and contemporary styles.

There are two types of decorative quilting patterns and stencils: those used in the blocks (see Figure 10-12) and those intended for borders (see Figure 10-13). You often find them in matched sets so you can create a coordinated look.

Figure 10-12:
Decorative
patterns
and stencils
intended for
borders.

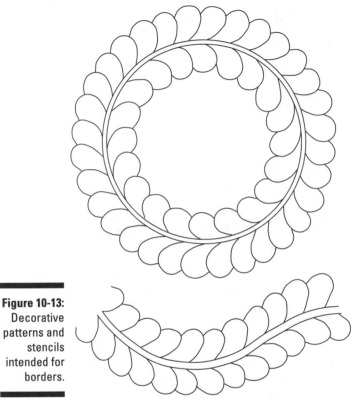

Figure 10-13:
Decorative
patterns and
stencils
intended for
borders.

Note: Quilting stencils are not the same stencils sold for painting decorative borders on your walls — they are specially cut templates intended for quilting. Quilting stencils have narrow slits cut into them. You trace the design onto your quilt top by running your marking pencil through the slits to mark the lines, as shown in Figure 10-14.

To mark your quilt top with a decorative quilting design from a book, you need to trace the design onto a piece of paper and transfer the design using one of the methods described in Chapter 11 on preparing your quilt for quilting.

Once you understand the most common types of quilting approaches, the time has come for you to baste your quilt and start quilting!

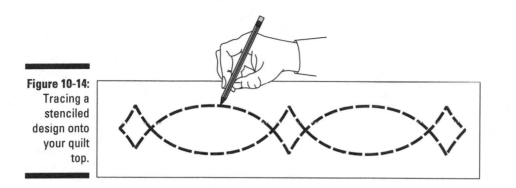

Figure 10-14:
Tracing a
stenciled
design onto
your quilt
top.

Chapter 11

Assembling the Quilt Sandwich

*G*ood going, quilter! Once you complete your quilt top, you're ready to layer it with the batting and backing fabrics to assemble your sandwich and prepare it for quilting. You're almost home with a finished quilt!

Remember that before you can assemble the sandwich, you'll have to make the following decisions:

✔ How do you want to quilt your quilt?

Remember that quilting here refers to the actual stitching pattern you will use to sew the three layers together so that the batting doesn't shift or bunch. You want a sturdy and decorative stitch pattern for your quilt top and back.

You may have already chosen a nice design such as a floral border or a geometric block design for your quilting stitches. If not, you may want to refer to Chapter 10 for inspiration. Additionally, many quilting books specialize in these designs; you can easily find them at any fabric store, craft shop, or bookseller.

✔ Are you quilting by hand or by machine?

See Chapter 10 for issues to consider when making this decision, including the size of the project (small or large).

You also must plan whether to mark your quilting design on the fabric or simply stitch along seamlines. In this chapter, I explain how to mark your quilting design on the fabric. Then you can finish by assembling the layers and basting them together.

Marking Your Quilting Stitch Designs

You have many ways to transfer your quilting designs to your quilt top. For the sake of simplicity, however, I just discuss the most common techniques. Remember to use only a water-soluble marking pencil or chalk (see Chapter 6 section) when marking the design.

If you are planning on stitching (this is the REAL *quilting!*) a decorative motif or border into your quilt (such as the leaf design in the **Traditional Basket** project in Part IV), always mark the design before you assemble the quilt sandwich.

If you plan on quilting in a grid pattern, along seamlines, or around the shapes in your quilt top, you don't need to premark your quilting lines, as you will simply be following the grid, seam, or shape. (See Chapter 12 for a more detailed discussion.)

Following are ways to guide your quilting stitches:

- ✔ **Trace the design.** If your fabric is light in color and the design has nice dark lines, you may be able to transfer the design directly from its source by laying the fabric on top and tracing it. You need to do this before you layer your quilt sandwich, so you will need to mark the design on the entire quilt top.

- ✔ **Use a window or light box**. Tape the design to a window or light box and place the quilt top over the design. Tape the quilt top in place, too, if you feel you don't have enough arms to hold it up while you trace. Trace as usual. I use a window quite often, even though I do have a light box in my sewing room. It's convenient — especially on smaller projects — and I get the chance to be nosy and see what the neighbors are up to at the same time. By the way, before you tape it, make sure there's no icky stuff on the windowsill that could soil the fabric.

- ✔ **Use dressmakers' carbon paper**. Be sure to make a test sample first on a scrap of fabric to be absolutely certain this stuff will wash out! This type of carbon paper comes in many colors to a package. Use as light a color as possible on your fabric — just dark enough (or light enough if you have used darker fabrics) to see it. To transfer the design, pin the dressmakers' carbon face-down over your quilt. Center the design to be quilted over the carbon, and transfer it to the quilt top by tracing over the design with a regular pencil, peeking to make sure it is transferring properly.

Don't use heat transfer paper! It will become permanent as soon as you iron the design on the fabric!

✔ **Make a template.** If you are using a simple design, such as a heart, cut the design for quilting from lightweight cardboard or heavy paper (an old file folder works great). Place the cut-out on your quilt top and hold it in place with one hand while tracing around it with the other. Trace designs from purchased quilting templates in the same manner.

I recommend marking your entire quilt top before layering the quilt sandwich.

Basting Top, Back, and Batt Layers Together

When you finish marking your quilting designs, you are ready to layer the quilt top with the batting and backing.

To assemble the quilt layers, follow these steps:

1. **Place your backing fabric right side down on a flat work surface. (The wrong side of the fabric should be facing you.)**

   You can use a table (be sure to protect the surface of a wooden table before you start pinning!) or a floor (more on the floor thing in a moment; see the section "Taming the Bed-Size Beast").

2. **Center the quilt batting over the wrong side of the fabric.**

3. **Carefully center the quilt top over the batting.**

4. **Hand baste the layers together.**

To baste the layers together, first thread a large, general-purpose sewing needle with a length of thread no longer than your arm. Put a knot in the far end.

Starting at the center of the quilt, insert the needle at an angle through all three layers so that you can bring the needle back up through the fabric about 1 inch away from where you started. Continue basting in this manner. You'll be making some huge running stitches — two to five per inch — through all three layers of the quilt top.

When you run out of thread, just clip it, leaving a $\frac{1}{2}$-inch tail. (You can use these tails to pull out the basting stitches later.)

Be sure to start each new length of basting thread at the center: Basting outwards from the center keeps the layers nice and flat and helps avoid bunching in the batting and puckering in the backing fabric or quilt top.

Cut off the knots after ending each length of thread so you don't stitch over them later. Don't worry about the basting threads working their way out — they won't.

Your fully basted quilt should resemble Figure 11-1.

For small- to medium-size projects, you can pin baste the layers together using nickel-plated safety pins (they won't rust if they get a bit moist). Be sure to pin from the center outward, as for hand basting, and through all three layers of the sandwich. Space the pins 3 to 4 inches apart for best results — if placed closer together, they just get in the way.

Remember that the more pins you put in the quilt, the heavier the thing becomes — which is why I only recommend pin basting for small- to medium-size projects.

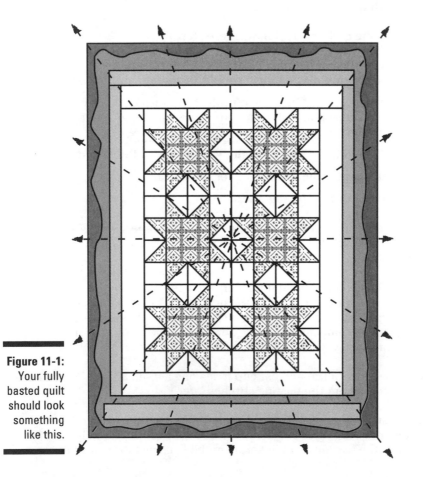

Figure 11-1:
Your fully basted quilt should look something like this.

When machine quilting, be sure to remove each pin before stitching over it. (You may leave pins in place when hand quilting.) Never jump over pins with your machine — you could break the needle and put your eye out.

When you finish basting, the sandwich is ready for you to quilt by hand or machine. In Chapter 12, I present tips to help you successfully through the final quilting process.

Taming the Bed-Size Beast

Although hand or pin basting small- to medium-size quilts is simple enough to do on a table or other work surface, basting quilts of bed-size (mammoth) proportions can be a challenge.

The solution? Tape the beast to the floor — yet another use for the ever-helpful masking tape you should have included with your supplies (see Chapter 6 if you forgot this crucial item; then hie thee to the hardware or art supply store to stock up). You have a golden opportunity to put it to use. Knee pads aren't a bad idea either — if you've got some lying around from your roller-blading phase, use them!

Make sure you have a clean floor by sweeping or vacuuming before laying out the quilt (the batting is a magnet for every fuzz bunny, bit of dirt, speck of lint or any mystery gunk on the floor).

1. **Tape the backing to the floor first, with the right side of the backing fabric facing the floor and the wrong side facing you.**

2. **Tape the corners to the floor, stretching the fabric slightly to smooth any wrinkles or creases. Then tape the sides in place.**

3. **Repeat with the batting and quilt top. Lay the batting over the backing and tape it in the same manner. Then, center the quilt top over the batting and tape it to the floor, too.**

Don't be shy with the tape! Be generous — use as much as it takes to make everything lay nice and smooth and secure. You don't want the sandwich coming loose when you start basting. After taping, your sandwich should look something like Figure 11-2. Hey, it's weird, but it works.

Then baste the quilt as described in the earlier section "Basting Top, Back, and Batt Layers Together."

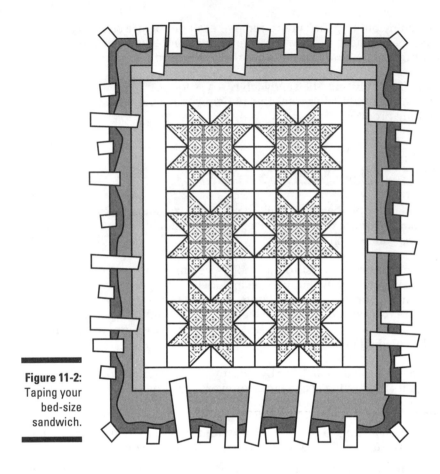

Figure 11-2:
Taping your
bed-size
sandwich.

Chapter 12

Ready, Set . . . Quilt! Hand and Machine Quilting Tips

My goodness! If you're reading this chapter, I assume that you've pieced and/or appliquéd your quilt top, selected your batting, and have already basted the whole shebang together. You've selected your quilting patterns, if any (if you're stumped, see Chapter 10) and marked them on your quilt top. Now you're poised and rip-roarin' ready for the quilting!

I find the actual quilting process — sewing the sandwich together with neat, lovely, and oftentimes patterned stitches — the most rewarding. Not only do I get a rush to see everything taking shape, but the project now actually looks like a real honest-to-gosh quilt. And it's almost finished!

Whether you're hand quilting, machine quilting, or tying your project, the following sections guide you along.

Using the Hoop for Hand Quilting

So, you've chosen to do it the old-fashioned way, quilting by hand. Good for you — the ghosts of quilters past are very proud! And the meticulous hand quilters of the present honor you as well!

Here's a very simple process for hand quilting your project once you have basted everything together and have decided how you want to quilt your quilt.

For hand quilting, I recommend that you place your project in a hoop (see Chapter 6 for more about hoops). You can certainly quilt smaller projects such as pillow covers without a hoop, but if you're a beginner, you're likely to find using a hoop more comfortable until you have a bit more experience with quilting.

You can also place your project in a quilting frame, following the manufacturer's directions for your individual frame. However, because of the expense, most beginners don't have frames, so I won't go into detail about frames.

Center a block or some other element face up over the inner portion of the hoop and place the outer portion of the hoop over the inner part, securing the quilt between the two circles or ovals. Hand tighten the wing nut snugly to keep the fabric taut.

Threading the needle 'n' hiding the knot

Next, cut a length of quilting thread (it's heavier than all-purpose, remember?) about as long as your arm — from the shoulder to the tips of your fingers — and thread a quilting needle (a size 7 or 8 *between* needle works nicely). Make a small knot in the long end of the thread.

No self-respecting quilter would ever want knots showing on the quilt's back side! So the first thing you need to do as you start to quilt is to hide the knot. Not only is hiding the knots a tidier way to quilt, but the actual quilting stitches are made stronger because the knots won't be subject to abrasion from use.

To hide the knot, simply insert the needle into the quilt top 1 to 2 inches from where you plan to begin stitching. Where you start doesn't matter; just pick a spot that looks promising — corner or the tip of a design element would be a good spot.

After inserting the needle in the quilt top, dig the needle slightly into the batting, pull the needle back up through the quilt top at the point where you intend to start — you won't have pierced the backing yet — and then pull the thread through. When you get to the end of the thread where the knot is located, give the thread a little tug, so that you pull the knot through the quilt top and lodge it in the batting, as shown in Figure 12-1. Doing this hides the starting knot in the quilt batting.

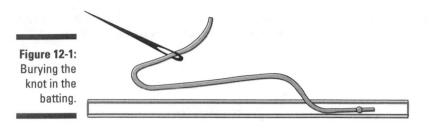

Figure 12-1:
Burying the
knot in the
batting.

Hand stitching your quilt

Turn the hoop in your lap so that the direction of the quilting runs from
the upper right (2:00) to the lower left of the hoop (7:00) as shown in
Figure 12-2. Quilting in this direction enables you to quilt toward
yourself.

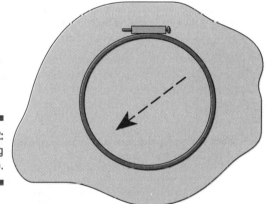

Figure 12-2:
Positioning
the hoop.

Place your handy-dandy thimble on the middle finger of your right hand.
(Be careful not to accidentally flash anyone the "bird" while donning the
thimble. Beginning quilters should never try to start a riot at the quilting
guild.)

If you are left-handed, reverse the direction of everything mentioned in this
section. You're probably used to doing this anyway, so I probably didn't
need to mention it; lefties are all highly intelligent. (This message was
brought to you today by my left-handed husband and teenage daughter, who
love to remind me that Albert Einstein was "lefty," and I am a mere "righty.")

Follow these instructions to hand stitch your quilt:

1. **Place your free hand (the left one, unless you're a lefty) under the
   hoop directly under the stitching area.**

2. **Insert the needle straight down into the quilt about ¹/₁₆ inch from the point where the thread came up through the quilt top.**

You should feel the point of the needle as it pierces the quilt backing. Ouch! Sorry, but feeling the needle-prick is the only way to know that the needle is through all the layers. If you'd rather not get this point, try placing a soft leather thimble on the "receiving" finger under the quilt.

Some quilters like to use a spoon under their quilt, holding it in the receiving hand. The curved bowl of the spoon also assists them in bringing the needle back through the surface. Try it! But do keep the bandages and ouchie spray handy, too, while you're at it. After all, this *is* a learning experience.

3. **Bring the needle back up through the quilt top by rocking the needle upwards after you feel it pierce the backing.**

Load two or three stitches onto the needle following Steps 2 and 3 before you pull the needle all the way through the quilt. As you become accustomed to hand quilting, you will find that you can load more stitches on the needle at one time, speeding up the process considerably.

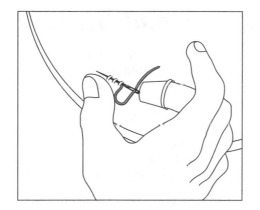

4. **After you pull the needle through, insert it again about ¹/₁₆ inch from where you came out of the fabric, near the last stitch, and repeat this process along your marked lines.**

5. **When you only have about 8 inches of thread left in your needle, *backstitch* by inserting your needle into the starting point of your last stitch and up through the ending point of the last stitch, creating two stitches in the same spot.**

6. **Insert the needle into the quilt top, travel through the batting for an inch, and come up to the surface again (it's a bit like swimming underwater). Cut the thread tail close to the quilt top.**

Thread the needle with a fresh length of thread and keep going until the quilt is quilted!

TIP

Getting the blood out

Whenever needles and fingers come together, occasionally blood happens, and your pristine fabric is dotted with drops. Deal with these as soon as they occur.

Here are the two best options:

Option #1 (my favorite): What I always tell people to do (some people HATE this) is to lick the spot — yes, lick it. The saliva in our mouths contains certain elements that help break down proteins, which is why it works. It's fast and easy, and you barely miss a stitch.

Option #2: Use a cotton swab dipped in warm water (not hot or cold, as that will set the stain) and gently blot. You can even put a little bit of mild soap on the swab if it helps. Don't saturate the area — just blot until the swab absorbs the stain.

Then run for your thimble and get on with it.

Machine Quilting Tips and Tricks

If you have chosen to machine quilt your project, you need to prepare your machine for the chore at hand. Each machine quilting technique requires a different type of presser foot and machine setting, so read through the following information carefully.

If you have pin basted your quilt together, you must remove the safety pins as you approach them! Do not, under any circumstances, attempt to stitch over a safety pin. Not only does stitching over them make them difficult to remove, but it's dangerous! You could easily break your needle, sending a fragment of the needle into your eye.

Preparing large-size projects

If you are quilting a large project, such as a bed quilt, be sure you have a large surface to the rear and to the left of your machine to help you support the weight of the quilt. These large-size projects are very heavy and can easily pull your machine right off the table and onto the floor!

Prepare any quilt larger than 36 inches x 36 inches for quilting by rolling it as follows.

Lay the basted quilt on the floor and roll the two sides towards the center, leaving a 12-inch swath of quilt unrolled, as shown in Figure 12-3. This is where you will begin machine quilting. Secure the rolls with safety pins or bicycle clips.

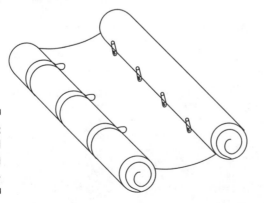

Figure 12-3:
Rolling and
securing
the quilt.

You can find bicycle clips at the sporting goods store and at some quilting stores. As you see in Figure 12-4, *bicycle clips* are flexible metal rings with a small opening. They hold your pants leg against your body while cycling so that your pants don't get caught in the bicycle chain.

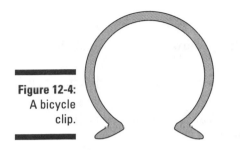

Figure 12-4:
A bicycle
clip.

Bicycle clips function the same way on a quilt. Just think of the rolled edges of the quilt as the "leg" and put the clip over this rolled leg, holding it securely in place.

Using straight-line quilting for the beginner

Straight-line quilting is the easiest form of machine quilting. The results are always good, and it's quick, too!

Begin by inserting an *even-feed presser foot* in your machine, as shown in Figure 12-5. These presser feet are also known as *walking feet*. If your machine did not come with an even-feed foot, make a trip to the sewing center to get one. Bring your machine's manual with you so the clerk can help you find the right foot for your model.

Figure 12-5:
An even-
feed foot on
the left,
compared
to regular
foot on
the right.

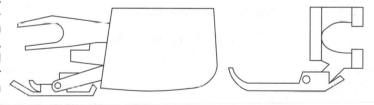

An even-feed foot makes machine quilting smoother and pucker-free because it feeds the layers of the quilt through the machine evenly. Without it, the feed dogs (those teeth under the needle) will only feed the bottom layer of fabric through the machine, leaving the batting and top layers open to puckering because they're not being fed through the machine at the same rate.

To start machine stitching:

1. **Thread the top of the machine with a coordinating shade of all-purpose thread.**

   If you would like the stitching to be invisible, use clear nylon monofilament as your top thread.

2. **Load the bobbin with all-purpose thread in a color to match or coordinate with your backing fabric.**

3. **Set the stitch length on the machine at 6 to 10 stitches per inch.**

4. **Place the unrolled center area of the quilt in the machine and take one stitch.**

5. **With the needle up, stop and raise the presser foot. Pull the top thread tail so that the bobbin thread tail comes up through the hole in the stitch you made in Step 4.**

   You now have both tails on top of the quilt.

6. **Lower the presser foot and begin stitching by taking two stitches and then stopping.**

7. **Put your machine in reverse and take two stitches backward to secure the thread.**

   You are now ready to stitch your quilt.

8. **Continue stitching normally (without reversing) along your marked lines, in-the-ditch, or however you have decided to quilt your project.**

9. **When you get to a corner that needs to be turned, lower the needle into the fabric and raise the presser foot. Pivot the quilt in the other direction and lower the presser foot again. Continue stitching.**

10. **When you reach a spot where you need to stop stitching, take two stitches backward to secure the thread, just as in Step 7.**

Remember, you need to secure the thread at the beginning and end every time, or you run the risk of the stitching coming undone at these starting and stopping points, resulting in an unsightly $1/4$ inch or so that is unstitched.

After you finish quilting the area you unrolled, remove the project from the machine and unroll the sides to expose an unquilted area. Continue stitching until you have quilted the entire quilt.

Choosing free-motion machine quilting for advanced projects

Free-motion machine quilting requires some practice to master, so I just give you a brief introduction in this section. Plenty of books are available devoted entirely to this subject.

Free-motion quilting is beautiful for fancy quilting patterns, with decorative possibilities limited only by your imagination. You can use it to create graceful curved designs and floral patterns, as well as the basis for stipple quilting by machine. (See Chapter 10 for more on stipple quilting.)

To do free-motion quilting, you need a special presser foot called a *darning* or *free-motion* foot. This type of foot has a rounded toe that travels just above the surface of the fabric, as shown in Figure 12-6.

Figure 12-6:
A darning foot for free-motion quilting.

Because you feed the quilt through the machine manually, free-motion quilting requires you to disengage your machine's feed dogs:

- ✔ On some machines, you disengage the feed dogs by turning a knob, which lowers them out of position.
- ✔ On other machines (especially older models), you don't lower the feed dogs to disengage them. Instead, you cover them with a metal or plastic plate. You will find this plate in your machine's bag of tricks.

Refer to your machine's manual to see how yours works.

With free-motion quilting, you do not need to adjust the length of the straight-stitch on your machine at all. The speed at which you are sewing combined with the speed at which you move the quilt around under the needle determines the stitch length. This is why practice is so important before attempting a large project in free-motion quilting.

After inserting the darning foot and disengaging the feed dogs, thread your machine and bobbin as you would for straight-line quilting. Place the quilt under the presser foot with one hand positioned on each side of the quilt, 2 inches or so from the presser foot. Use your hands to guide the quilt in the necessary direction under the darning foot.

If your fingers feel dry, or if you are having trouble moving the quilt under the machine because your fingers are sliding on the fabric, cover the first and index finger of each hand (four fingers in all) with a rubber fingertip from the office supply store.

Slowly begin stitching, taking two or three stitches in the same spot to secure the thread at the beginning. As you stitch, move the quilt, guiding it with your two hands, so that the needle follows your marked quilting lines or designs. Keeping the machine at a steady speed, move the fabric slowly and smoothly so you don't end up with gaps or overly long stitches. Slow and steady is the key here!

Free-motion machine quilting takes some time to master. I recommend starting on small projects, such as pillows, placemats, or wallhangings, before progressing to larger projects. Stipple quilting is a great first-time use for free-motion quilting because you are not required to follow a set pattern. Instead, you learn to maneuver the project under the darning foot and get some much-needed experience.

Tying Fluffy, High-Loft Quilts

If you have decided to make a big, fluffy quilt using a high-loft batting, you will want to tie the quilt, rather than quilt it! Tying is a quick, simple process in which the three layers of the quilt are held together with "ties" of fabric. The principle is the same as using a tie-tack to secure a man's necktie, keeping the two tails from flapping in the breeze.

Tying is also the best way to finish a quilt made with fluffy, high-loft batting (the loft and bulk make it difficult to stitch through by hand or machine). Tying works best with polyester battings that do not need to be quilted at tightly spaced intervals, as is the case with some of the cotton or blended batts.

What if you are pressed for time and just want to get the darn thing done? Tying is faster than hand or machine quilting.

Or was your first attempt at making a quilt just too ugly to bother quilting it by hand or machine? (You should have seen my first quilt!) Would it make a better car blanket or dog bed than wallhanging? Well then, tying it may be the best option — you might as well get some use out of it. No sense wasting all that hard work.

To tie a quilt:

1. **Thread a sharp-pointed, large-eyed needle with a 12-inch length of heavy thread. Don't knot the end.**

   For tying quilts you need heavy thread, such as pearl cotton, embroidery floss, narrow ribbon, or even worsted-weight yarn. Don't use all-purpose thread — it's just not strong enough to hold the tied layers together in this manner.

2. **Insert the needle straight down into the quilt through all layers and bring it back up in the opposite direction $1/8$ inch from where it went down.**

3. **Pull the thread tail so that you have about 4 inches of thread on one side of the quilt and the rest on the other. Tie the thread in a double knot.**

4. **Cut the two tails, leaving them about 1 inch long.**

5. **Repeat Steps 2 through 4 at consistent intervals — every 5 to 6 inches.**

Trim all of the tails to the desired length after tying — but no shorter than $1/2$ inch. Your efforts should resemble Figure 12-7.

Figure 12-7:
Tying a
quilt.

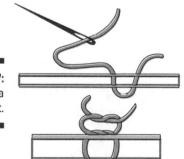

When you finish quilting your project, add a binding or other finishing touch and you're all done! On to Chapter 13 for tips on binding and finishing!

Chapter 13

Finishing Touches: Bindings and More

. . . .

In This Chapter

▶ Using bias and straight-edge binding
▶ Finishing your projects pillow-style

. . . .

*W*hen you finish stitching and quilting your masterpiece, you need to do something about those raw edges that still have batting hanging out from beneath them. Your quilt sure won't look too great left as it is!

To determine how much binding you will need, total the measurements for all four sides and add 12 inches. The additional 12 inches allows for mitering the corners of the quilt (which we will discuss later in this section) and for the overlap where the binding starts and stops (with a little extra built in, just in case). Table 13-1 provides a quick reference for the amount of binding needed for typical bed-size quilts.

Table 13-1	Binding Needs for Bed-Size Quilt
Type of Bed	*Amount of Binding*
Crib	5-6 yards
Twin	9 yards
Double/Full	10 yards
Queen	11 yards
King	12 yards

You can choose from many ways of finishing the edges of your quilt. You can use *bias binding* and *straight-edge binding*. You can fold the excess backing fabric to the front for a *self-binding*. Or you can finish it *pillow-style*.

The following sections describe the advantages of each technique.

Bias Binding

The most common method of binding is to apply bias binding around the edges of your quilt. *Traditional bias binding* and *double-fold binding* use strips of fabric cut on the bias to enclose the raw edges of the quilt. You can choose from two techniques for cutting bias strips. One way is to make a tube of fabric, mark it, stitch it, and cut the binding in one continuous strip. This is called a *continuous binding strip*.

To make a continuous binding strip:

1. **Cut a square of fabric the size needed and cut this square in half diagonally to make two large triangles.**

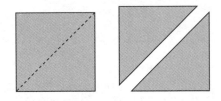

2. **Stitch the triangles together along the straight edges to make the shape that follows. Press the seam allowance open.**

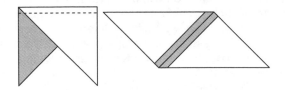

3. **Decide how wide you want to cut the strips (refer to the individual binding techniques discussed in this chapter for help determining this measurement) and mark the wrong side (WS) of the fabric using a ruler, spacing the lines the distance you need them.**

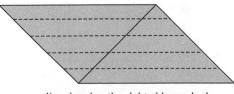

I'm showing the right side marked

4. **Stitch the short ends of the fabric together (right sides facing), offsetting the lines by one strip mark to form a funny-looking tube.**

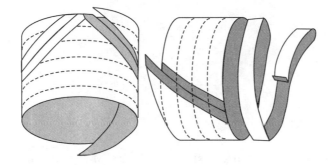

Carefully press the seam allowance open.

5. **Cut the binding in one continuous strip using scissors, starting at the offset area, cutting along the marked lines.**

Pretty simple, huh?

The second method of cutting bias strips is the one I use. I prefer this method because it's a good way to use up an odd-size piece of fabric. Because we're cutting bias strips instead of a perfect square, it doesn't matter if our choice of fabric for the binding has been cut into previously.

To cut bias strips using this second technique, simply mark the fabric in lines on a 45-degree angle to the grainline with a ruler (the ruler described in the tools chapter with the 45-degree markings comes in handy here), spaced the width needed (see the individual techniques for help determining the width to mark). Cut the strips apart using a rotary cutter (see Figure 13-1). You can also use scissors if you prefer.

Figure 13-1:
Mark the strips at a 45-degree angle and cut them apart.

Join the strips facing as shown in Figure 13-2, having the right sides together. You will notice a little "tail" on each side of the strips where they are sewn together. You need to offset the strips slightly to accommodate the $1/4$ inch seam allowance, so you end up with these little tails.

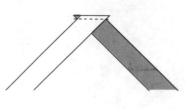

Figure 13-2:
Join the
strips with
the right
sides
together.

If you don't offset the strips as shown in Figure 13-2, you won't have a straight smooth line at the long edges near the joints!

Press the seam allowances open after you have sewn the strips together and trim off the little tails with scissors. Continue joining strips until you have enough length to bind your quilt.

Traditional bias binding

Traditional bias binding, as you would expect, is the old-fashioned way to bind a quilt. The binding is made from a wide strip of bias-cut fabric that has been folded down the center lengthwise (see Figure 13-3).

Figure 13-3:
Fold the
bias-cut
fabric down
the center
lengthwise.

Traditional bias binding is the most durable binding method because, when you are finished stitching, you actually have two layers of fabric covering the raw edges of the quilt.

I recommend using the traditional bias binding method for bed-size quilts or anything that will undergo a lot of laundering.

To make a traditional bias binding:

1. **Cut strips of fabric that are eight times wider than the desired width of the finished binding.**

For example, if you prefer a binding that is $^1/_2$ inch wide when finished, cut 4-inch-wide strips of bias-cut fabric ($^1/_2$ inch x 8):

- A 44-inch x 44-inch square of fabric produces about 13 yards of 4-inch-wide binding.

- A 36-inch x 36-inch square produces 9 yards of 4-inch-wide-binding.

- A 20-inch x 20-inch square produces only about 2.5 yards of 4-inch-wide binding.

2. **Fold under $^1/_2$ inch at the beginning of the strip (WS facing). Then, fold the strip in half along its entire length (WS facing).**

3. **Press the strip carefully — do not stretch the bias.**

4. **Place the pressed strip on the front of the quilt, having the double raw edge even with the raw edges of the quilt top.**

Show quilt as right side

5. **Along one long side of the quilt, begin machine stitching the binding in place $^1/_4$ inch from the double raw edge of the binding, starting about 4 inches from the folded end of the bias strip.**

When you begin to approach a corner, slow down a bit so that you have better control and stitch to within $^1/_4$ inch of the corner of the quilt top. (See the dot in the following illustration? That's where you stop stitching.)

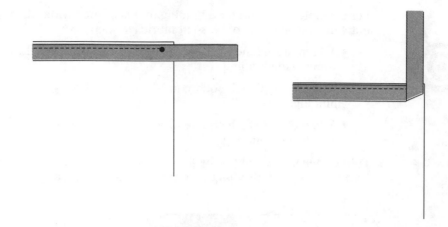

6. **Turn the corner as follows (this is known as "mitering" the corner):**

   Fold the bias strip upwards at the corner and then fold it down, having the newly made fold even with the edge you just stitched. Start stitching the strip to the *next* side at the corner.

7. **Continue stitching the binding to the edges as described in Steps 5 and 6.**

8. **To end your binding back at the beginning (what goes around comes around), trim the ending tail of the binding so that it overlaps the beginning end of the binding by about 2 inches (you left 4 inches of it unstitched, remember?). Insert the ending tail of the binding into the folded (beginning) end and continue stitching through all of the layers.**

9. **Trim away any excess backing fabric and batting with scissors.**

10. **Turn the binding to the back side of the quilt and hand stitch it in place directly over the line of machine stitching, using the blind stitch, on all four sides.**

To work the blind stitch, insert the needle through the binding and then take a small stitch into the quilt backing. Bring the needle up again about $1/8$ inch from the first stitch in the binding. In this manner, you have "traveled" $1/8$ inch and have hidden the traveling portion of the thread in the quilt backing, as shown in Figure 13-4.

Figure 13-4: Blind stitch the binding in place by hand on the back side of the quilt. 13-4b shows detail of the blind stitch.

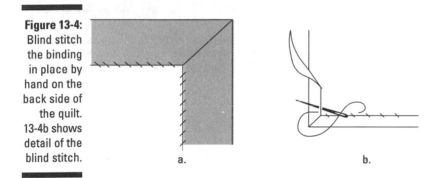

a.   b.

Double-fold binding

The *double-fold binding* method uses a single strip of fabric on the edges of the quilt. Although not quite as durable as the traditional binding, this method is just fine for most projects, such as wallhangings and table runners.

Double-fold binding is great for anything that has rounded corners, as the natural stretch of the bias along with the single layer at the edge will help you round those corners smoothly.

Double-fold binding is more economical than traditional bias binding because it uses less fabric. To determine the width to cut the bias strips, decide how wide you want the finished binding to be and cut the strips four times wider than the finished measurement. For example, if you want a $1/2$-inch-wide finished binding, cut the strips 2 inches wide ($1/2$ inch x 4). Cut as many strips as needed to measure the circumference of the project — a 25-inch x 25-inch project will require 100 inches, plus an extra 10 inches for turning the corners and overlapping the ends:

- A 45-inch x 45-inch square produces 26 yards of 2-inch-wide strips.

- A 36-inch x36-inch square produces 18 yards of 2-inch-wide strips.

- A 20-inch x 20-inch square produces 5.5 yards of 2-inch-wide strips.

Pressed for time? If so, double-fold bias tape is available pre-packaged in any fabric store. Look for the ones marked "Extra-Wide Double-Fold Bias Tape." Because it's sold in packages containing 2 to 3 yards of bias tape, you'll need several packages.

After cutting:

1. **Fold the strip in half directly down the center of the entire length of bias, having the wrong sides together.**

2. **Open the strip, having the creased side down toward your work surface.**

3. **Fold the sides of the strip towards each other, meeting at the center.**

4. **Press each side of the strip.**

5. **Fold again along the center crease and press it again in case you lost the crease when pressing the sides.**

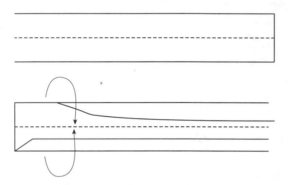

6. **Open the binding strip again and turn under $1/4$ inch at the starting end of the strip.**

7. **Place one raw edge of the binding strips along the raw edge of the quilt top and machine stitch in the ditch of the crease.**

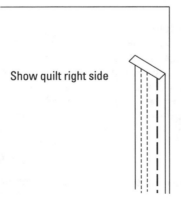

Show quilt right side

8. **Miter the corners as shown in previous section on traditional binding.**

   When you have stitched around all four sides of the quilt, trim away the excess batting and backing fabric.

9. **Fold the binding to the back side of the quilt.**

   The center crease should lie along the very edge of the quilt.

10. **Hand stitch the binding in place using the blind stitch along the remaining crease, stitching directly over the other stitching line.**

Self-Binding

Self-binding is a quick and easy way to bind small projects. Also known as fold-over binding, a *self-binding* is made from the excess backing fabric, which is trimmed to size and folded to the front side of the quilt to enclose the raw edges.

The reason I recommend this for smaller projects only, is because it is a straight-edge binding, and does not have the flexibility of a bias binding. In fact, it tends to ripple the edges of the project slightly if used on the longer sides of a project. It is fine to use on placemats and wallhangings, but I would not recommend it for use on anything larger than a baby quilt.

If you want to make your project self-binding, be sure to

~ Cut your backing fabric at least 3 inches larger than your project around all four sides. For example, if you have a 30-inch x 30-inch project, cut your backing 36 inches x 36 inches.

~ Center your quilt top on the backing fabric carefully before quilting it.

Remember that whatever you use as your backing will be seen on the front, so choose the backing accordingly.

Follow these steps to make your project self-binding:

1. **After quilting, trim away the excess batting from the edges of the quilt.**

   Be very careful not to cut through the backing fabric.

2. **Trim the backing fabric so that the excess measures two times the desired width of the binding.**

   For example, if you want a $1/2$-inch binding, trim the backing fabric down to 1 inch ($1/2$ inch $\times$ 2).

3. **Fold the backing fabric toward the front a scant $1/2$ inch and press, keeping the iron away from the batting; then fold the backing fabric over again $1/2$ inch.**

Do not press this time or you may flatten the batting at the edges of your quilt.

4. **Stitch the backing fabric that's being used as binding in place on the quilt front by machine or by hand using the blind stitch.**

Pillow-Style Finishing

This method of finishing does not use a binding at all. In *pillow-style finishing*, the raw edges of the quilt are enclosed in the quilt itself, and the quilting is actually done *after* you bind the project.

Cut your border strips $1/4$ to $1/2$ inch wider than usual when using pillow-style binding so that you don't end up with a project smaller than you intended. The seam allowance will take up the excess.

To finish a project pillow-style, follow these steps:

1. **Cut the backing and batting pieces slightly larger than the quilt top.**

2. **Center the quilt top over the batting and trim the batting to fit the quilt top perfectly.**

3. **Place a pin in the center through the layers to keep them from shifting during the next steps.**

4. **Turn the whole thing over so that the batting is facing you and the quilt top faces your work surface.**

5. **Place the backing fabric right side up on your work surface. Center the quilt top unit over the backing fabric. (You will be placing the backing and quilt top right sides together, with the batting facing you).**

6. **Pin the layers together very well.**

   Use lots of pins to tame the batting.

7. **Place the piece in the sewing machine and stitch $\frac{1}{4}$ inch to $\frac{1}{2}$ inch (depending on your preference and comfort level) around all four sides, leaving a 6-inch opening along one side for turning.**

8. **Clip the corners close to, but not through, the stitching and turn right side out through the opening.**

9. **Hand stitch the opening closed, using the blind stitch.**

10. **Pin or baste through all layers to prepare it for quilting. Then, quilt it however you want to.**

I recommend pillow-style finishing only for very small projects, such as placemats and hot pads. Anything larger can be too bulky to handle comfortably and is a pain in the neck to try and push through the sewing machine.

Part IV
Completing the Circle: Projects to Try

"She started quilting oven mitts and toaster cozies. Then, one day she saw 'Snowball' shivering next to her drinking bowl and, well, her tail's still wagging in there, so I don't see the harm."

In this part . . .

So, you've scanned through the pages of this book, picking up lots of tips and ideas here and there. As soon as your brain unfreezes from the information input, I hope you'll be eager to start your own project.

On the following pages, you'll find lots of neat, simple projects to get your creative juices flowing. To make choosing a project simple and worry-free, I have ranked them using a "thimble" system.

✔ **One thimble:** The project practically works itself — anyone can do it.

✔ **Two thimbles:** The project is easy to make but a bit more involved than a one-thimble project, but you can whip it up with little effort.

✔ **Three thimbles:** The project is a bit more challenging (you may have to put the gray-matter to good use) or a good skill-builder (but it's still fairly easy!). Save these for when you become more comfortable with quilt-talk and the quilting experience.

Now, choose your project and start slicing and dicing that fabric you've been itching to cut into!

Hand-Quilted Starburst Pillow and Trapunto Mini-Pillow

Appliqued
Bluebirds
Breakfast Set

*Pink Tulips
Breakfast Set*

Blue Star Placemat and Hot Pad Set

Pastel Nine-Patch Wallhanging

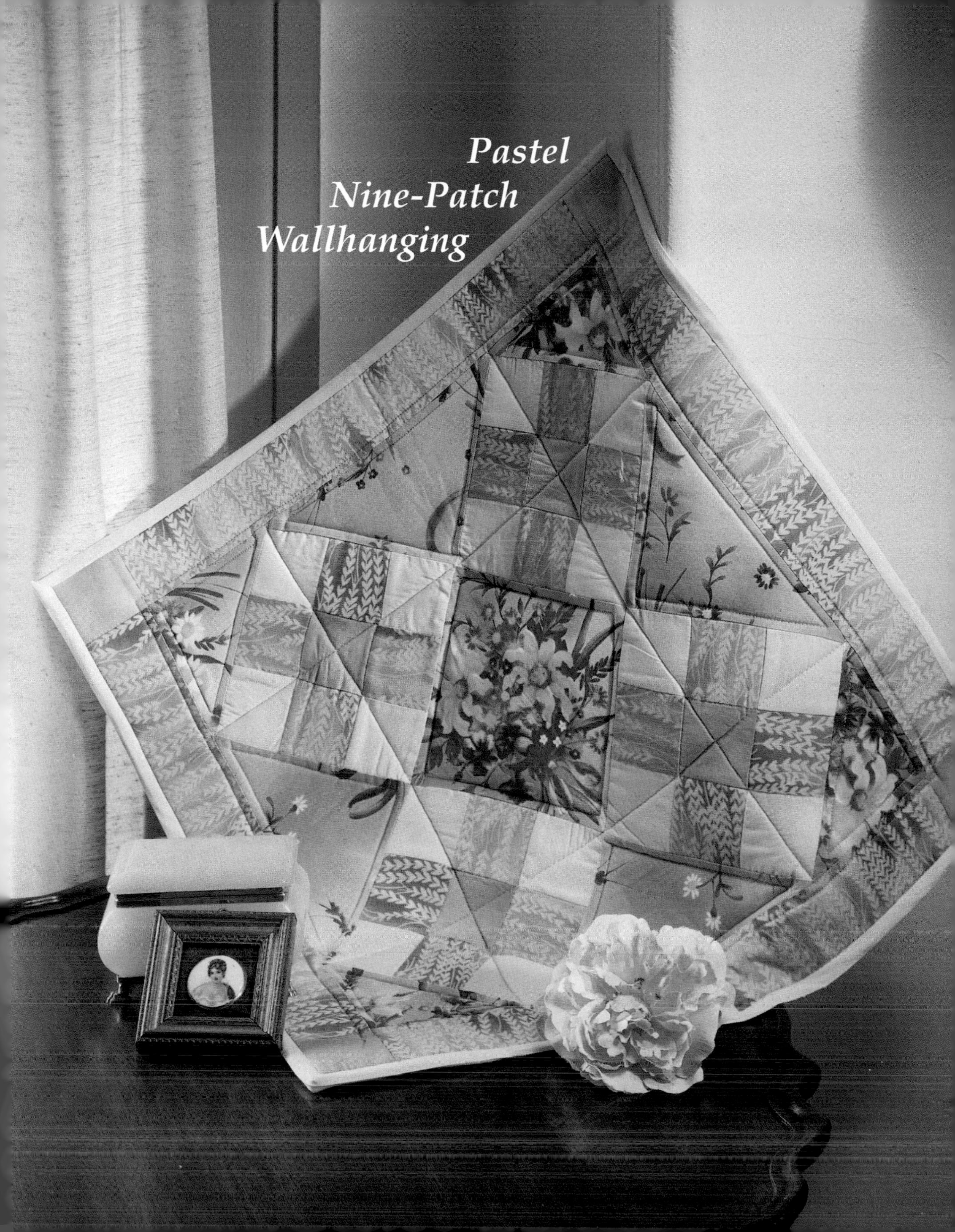

Pieced Flower Pots Wallhanging

Pieced Hearts Wallhanging

May Baskets Wallhanging

Traditional Basket Wallhanging

*Pieced Blossoms
Lap Quilt*

Winter Holly Lap Quilt

Scrappy
Pines
Lap Quilt

Scrappy Bloomers Lap Quilt

Rosy Wreath Lap Quilt

Snow
Crystals
Pieced and
Appliqued
Lap Quilt

Caribbean Dream Quilt

Project 1

Hand-Quilted Starburst Pillow

. . . .

Finished size of pillow: 14 inches square

. . . .

*A*re you ready to try hand quilting? Great! Here's a quick, fun project to get you started. The small size makes it more than manageable for the beginner. This makes a great take-along project: just whip it out of your bag whenever you find a few precious moments of spare time.

Feel free to change the colors of the fabrics to suit your own taste or décor.

Stashing Your Materials

The following list describes the fabrics and notions you need to create this pillow:

- $10^1/_2$-inch x $10^1/_2$-inch square of off-white solid fabric for center
- $^1/_3$ yard of print fabric for the outer borders
- 15-inch x 15-inch piece of off-white solid fabric for lining
- 15-inch x 15-inch piece of traditional-weight cotton or polyester batting
- 15-inch x 15-inch piece of coordinating print fabric for the pillow backing
- 2 yards of purchased piping to coordinate with the border fabric
- Off-white all-purpose thread for assembly
- Hand quilting thread (I used navy blue) and a "between" needle
- Stuffing or a 14-inch pillow form

A word about pillow forms

Some folks purchase a pillow form that's an inch or two larger than the cover in an effort to have a nice, plump pillow and avoid those sad, "saggy/soggy" corners that can result from a pillow form that's not quite ample enough.

If you do this for your own pillow projects, you may be purchasing the *wrong insert*. The ones made today are very standardized, but they DO come in different weights; some are meant for soft-squishy pillows, others are firmer for a well-stuffed look.

Another problem may be that your seam allowances are not accurate for the project you're making.

Pillow inserts come in standardized sizes — 12-inch, 14-inch, 16-inch, 20-inch, and 24-inch. Stuffing a 24-inch insert into a 20-inch pillow covering invites disasters such as split seams and other problems.

Because this is a quilted project, you automatically add thickness and support to the top of the pillow, so the corners shouldn't cave-in if you're using the right materials. I would NEVER recommend that anyone buy an oversized pillow form. Something stuffed that firmly is not a pillow but a mini-mattress! YIKES!!

Preparing the Pillow Top for Quilting

In the following steps, I explain how to transfer the quilting design onto the pillow top and prepare the top for quilting:

1. **Fold the 10¹/₂-inch off-white square into quarters and press it. Unfold the square and lay it flat.**

    The resulting creases help you arrange your quilting pattern in the center of the square.

2. **Using the creases as a guide, transfer the quilting pattern at the end of this project to the center of the square by tracing or using dressmaker's carbon and a sharp pencil.**

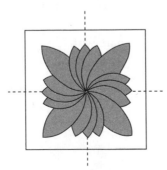

3. From the border fabric, cut two $2^1/_2$-inch x $10^1/_2$-inch strips of print fabric for upper/lower borders, and cut two $2^1/_2$-inch x $14^1/_2$-inch strips of print fabric for side borders.

4. Using the all-purpose thread and a $^1/_4$-inch seam allowance, stitch the upper and lower borders to the square. Press the seam allowances toward the borders.

5. Repeat Steps 3 and 4 to add the side borders.

6. Layer the pillow top with the batting and the lining fabric and baste the layers together to prepare them for quilting.

Quilting the Pillow Top

In the following steps, I tell you how to quilt the starburst pattern onto the pillow top. Refer to Chapter 10 if you need more information about the quilting process:

1. **Thread a quilting needle (a "between") with a length of quilting thread no longer than your arm.**

2. **Starting wherever you feel like on the quilting pattern, bury the knot in the batting and begin quilting, using the hand-quilting stitch.**

   Take small, evenly spaced stitches.

3. **On each border, hand quilt $^1/_4$ inch away from either side of the seamline around all four sides.**

Assembling the Pillow

After you quilt the pillow top, you're ready to finish the project. The following steps explain how to assemble the pillow so you that can show off your quilting skills:

1. **Machine stitch very close to the raw edges of the pillow top.**

   Your stitches should be about $^1/_8$ inch from the edges.

2. **Trim away the excess lining fabric and batting that extend beyond the edges of the pillow top.**

3. **Using the all-purpose thread, begin stitching the piping around the edges of the pillow top front. Begin stitching at the center of one side, leaving a 2-inch tail of piping hanging free.**

4. **When you approach a corner, stop stitching ¹/₄ inch from the corner. Clip into the seam allowance of the piping *close to, but not through,* the stuffed area of the piping.**

   This eliminates the bulk that would have resulted at the corners if you had tried to turn them without stopping and clipping. By clipping the seam allowances, you get nice, pointed corners.

5. **Turn the corner and resume stitching. When you arrive back at your starting point, overlap the remaining piping and the tail you left at the starting point and stitch across them.**

   The layers of fabric and batting are a bit bulky. Stitch slowly so that you don't break your needle. Trim the excess tails of the piping so that they are only about ¹/₂ inch long.

6. **Place the completed pillow top against the piece of backing fabric, right sides together. Pin the two pieces together to keep them from shifting while stitching.**

7. **Stitch the pillow top to the backing along the same line of stitches you used to attach the piping, leaving a 10-inch opening along the bottom edge for turning.**

8. Clip the corners close to the stitching line, *but not through it,* to eliminate bulk at the corners.

9. Turn the pillow top right side out.

10. Insert the pillow form or stuff firmly.

11. Tuck the seam allowances of the open area into place and hand stitch the turning opening closed, using the ladder stitch.

To launder the pillow simply pop the whole thing into the washer on a delicate setting and then air dry. No need to remove the covers. The stuffing in the pillow forms is polyester and is completely machine washable.

Half-Size Quilting Pattern

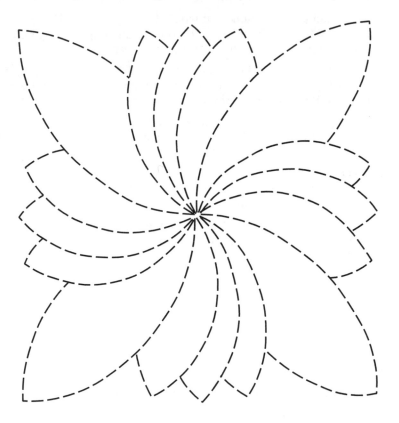

Double the size (200 percent) for a full-size pattern.

Project 1A

Trapunto Mini-Pillow

• •

Finished size: 7 inches x 7 inches

• •

Trapunto is a fancy style of hand quilting in which certain areas are stuffed for added loft. In other words, certain parts of the quilt's design are puffier than others because you carefully insert extra materials into those areas to make them stand out.

Although it's a bit more time-consuming than standard hand quilting, Trapunto is very easy to do, and the results are gorgeous! This technique traditionally has been used in white-on-white bridal quilts and other *whole-cloth quilts* (quilts that are quilted only, with no appliqué or piecing).

The following sections tell you how to create a beautiful Trapunto Mini-Pillow.

Stashing Your Materials

The following list describes the fabrics and notions you need to make the Trapunto Mini-Pillow:

- 1 $5^{1}/_{2}$-inch x $5^{1}/_{2}$-inch square of off-white solid fabric for pillow center
- $^{1}/_{4}$ yard print fabric for outer borders (a *fat-quarter* works nicely here)
- 1 8-inch x 8-inch square of off-white solid fabric for lining
- 1 8-inch x 8-inch square of print fabric for pillow backing
- Off-white all-purpose thread
- Off-white hand-quilting thread and "between" needle

    ✔ 1 yard of purchased piping to coordinate with the border fabric

    ✔ 1 bag of polyester stuffing (fiberfill) for stuffing the pillow (pillow forms are not available in this small size)

    ✔ Off-white rug-weight yarn (available at any fabric shop) and large-eyed needle

Preparing the Pillow Top for Quilting

1. **Fold the 5¹/₂-inch off-white pillow center square into quarters and press it. Unfold the square and lay it flat.**

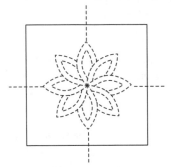

2. **Using the crease lines as a guide, transfer the quilting pattern at the end of this project to the center of the square by tracing or using dressmakers' carbon and a sharp pencil.**

You don't want to press at this point as it may set the markings permanently; I don't recommend pressing when transferring designs except for appliqué (in which case, the lines are covered by the fabric appliqués). Not pressing will not interfere with quilting the fabric because handling will cause the creases to fall out.

3. **From the print yardage, cut two 1¹/₂-inch x 5¹/₂-inch strips of print fabric for upper and lower borders, and cut two 1¹/₂-inch x 7¹/₂-inch strips of print fabric for side borders.**

Using the all-purpose thread and a ¹/₄-inch seam allowance, stitch the upper and lower borders to the square.

Press the seam allowances toward the borders.

4. **Repeat Step 3 to add the two side borders.**

5. Layer the pillow top with the batting and the lining piece, which acts as the backing for the quilted portion of the pillow. Baste the three layers together in preparation for quilting.

Quilting the Pillow Top

1. Thread a quilting needle (a "between") with a length of quilting thread no longer than your arm. Starting wherever you feel like on the quilting design (this is a feel-good project), bury the knot in the batting (see Chapter 12 on hand quilting), and begin quilting.

   Take small, evenly spaced stitches.

2. Hand quilt around each border $\frac{1}{4}$ inch away from either side of the seamline.

3. **Stipple quilt the entire off-white area outside the quilting design (refer to Chapter 10 for information on stipple quilting), taking small, meandering stitches.**

   This stipple quilting will help "raise" the main quilting motif by squishing down the areas surrounding it.

4. **Turn the pillow top over so that the wrong side (the lining) is facing you.**

Stuffing the Pillow Top

Here's how to stuff your pillow:

1. **Thread a large-eyed needle with a doubled length of the rug yarn.**

2. **Starting at the center end of a channel (which resulted from quilting the design in the center of the pillow top), insert the needle between the batting and the lining fabric. Do not go through the front!**

   When doing Trapunto, you need to keep the yarn between the batting and the lining. Otherwise, you'll see the yarn through the top layer of fabric. Also, instead of being a smoothly filled channel, the channel will be bumpy.

3. Pull the needle out of the fabric at the tip of the petal and pull the yarn until only ¹/₂ inch of the yarn is still peeking out at the starting point. Then insert the needle into the hole you just came out of and run it through the channel to the other end, pulling the needle out when you reach the end.

4. Trim the yarn close to the hole and at your starting point.

5. Repeat Steps 2 through 4 in the channels of all eight petals.

6. With a small pair of scissors, carefully cut a small slit in the lining fabric at the center of each petal, but do not cut through the batting or through to the front.

    It need only be ¹/₂-inch long or less.

7. Using the large-eyed needle or some other sharp object, push a small amount of stuffing (about the size of a pea) into the slit.

    Repeat with small bits of stuffing until you fill the petal.

8. Carefully whip-stitch the slit closed using all-purpose thread that matches the lining fabric.

9. After you stuff all the petals, machine stitch very close (about ¹/₈ inch) to the raw edges of the pillow top; then trim away the excess lining fabric and batting that extends beyond the edges of the pillow top.

Assembling the Pillow

Follow these steps to assemble the pillow:

1. **Using the all-purpose thread, begin stitching the piping around the pillow top at the center of one edge, leaving a 2-inch "tail" of piping hanging free.**

2. **When you approach a corner, stop stitching ¹/₄ inch away from the corner.**

3. **Clip into the seam allowance of the piping close to _but not through_ the stuffed area of the piping.**

   This eliminates the bulk that would have resulted at the corners if you had tried to turn them without stopping and clipping. (That creates rounded, icky corners rather than nice, pointed ones.)

4. **Turn the corner and resume stitching.**

   Repeat Steps 2 and 3 at each corner.

5. **When you return to your starting point, overlap the remaining piping and the tail you left at the starting point and stitch across the overlapped tails to completely stitch the piping in place. Trim the excess from the tails to ¹/₂ inch.**

   The fabric and piping thicknesses will be a bit bulky. Stitch slowly so that you don't break your needle.

6. **Pin together the completed pillow top and the piece of backing fabric, right sides together, to keep them from shifting while stitching.**

7. **Stitch the pillow top to the backing along the same stitching line as your piping, leaving a 10-inch opening along the bottom edge for turning.**

8. Clip the corners close to the stitching line *(but not through it)* to eliminate bulk at the corners.

9. Turn the pillow top right side out.

10. Stuff the little pillow pocket firmly.

11. To finish the project, tuck the seam allowances into the turning-opening and hand stitch the opening closed, using the ladder stitch.

Full-Size Quilting Pattern

Project 2

Appliquéd Bluebirds Breakfast Set

● ●

Finished size of pillow: 14 inches x 14 inches

Finished size of placemat, napkin, and kitchen towel: varies by manufacturer

● ●

*T*his plump little bluebird adds cheer to four different projects. Three of the projects are absolute no-brainers because they use pre-purchased items! These projects prove that you can use appliqué on many different objects, whether they're made from scratch or purchased items. Have fun!

Stashing Your Materials

This list describes the materials you need to create a pillow, placemat, napkin, and kitchen towel:

- ✔ ³/₄ yard of off-white print fabric
- ✔ ¹/₄ yard of dark blue fabric (lower bodies)
- ✔ ¹/₄ yard of medium blue fabric (wings)
- ✔ ¹/₈ yard of light blue fabric (heads)
- ✔ Scraps of golden yellow fabric (beaks)
- ✔ 1 15-inch x 15-inch square of off-white solid fabric (pillow lining)
- ✔ 2 yards of purchased blue piping (for pillow)
- ✔ Medium-blue all-purpose thread for pillow assembly
- ✔ 3 shades of blue rayon thread or all-purpose thread to match the blue fabrics for the appliqués, plus a golden yellow for the beaks for machine appliqué
- ✔ 1 15-inch x 15-inch square of low-loft quilt batting (pillow)
- ✔ 1 yard of 18-inch-wide paper-backed fusible webbing

✔ 1 yard of 18-inch-wide tear-away stabilizer

✔ 1 off-white kitchen towel, prewashed

✔ 1 off-white cotton placemat with matching napkin

✔ 1 14-inch pillow form or stuffing

✔ 2 $^3/_4$-inch-diameter dark blue buttons (bird eyes on pillow and placemat)

✔ 3 $^1/_2$-inch-diameter dark blue buttons (bird eyes on napkin and kitchen towel)

Making the Pillow

Follow these steps to make the pillow:

Note: All seam allowances on the pillow assembly are $^1/_4$ inch.

1. **Referring to Table BB-1, cut the border, center, and backing pieces.**

Table BB-1	Pillow Border, Center, and Backing Pieces		
Piece	*Fabric*	*Measurements*	*Quantity*
Backing	Off-white print	15" x 15"	1
Center (A)	Off-white print	7$^1/_2$" x 8$^1/_2$"	1
Side border (B)	Off-white print	2$^1/_2$" x 10$^1/_2$"	2
Upper/lower border (C)	Off-white print	2$^1/_2$" x 14$^1/_2$"	2
D	Yellow	1$^1/_2$" x 8$^1/_2$"	1
Side border E	Dark blue	1$^1/_2$" x 8$^1/_2$"	2
Upper/lower border F	Dark blue	1$^1/_2$" x 10$^1/_2$"	2

2. **Stitch the yellow D strip to one short side of the rectangular A piece to make a square.**

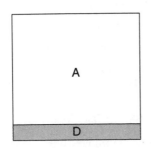

3. Trace the four pieces for the large bluebird on the paper side of the fusible webbing using the full-size appliqué patterns at the end of this project.

4. Roughly cut out all the shapes.

   You will cut them neatly after fusing them onto the fabrics.

5. Fuse the beak to the wrong side of the golden yellow fabric. Fuse the head to the wrong side of the light blue fabric. Fuse the wing to the wrong side of the medium blue fabric. Fuse the lower body to the wrong side of the dark blue fabric.

6. Neatly cut out all the shapes you fused in Step 5.

7. Referring to the patterns at the end of this project, lightly trace the bird and its legs onto the square you created in Step 2.

   This makes a bird block.

8. Remove the paper backings from the bird parts (all four pieces) and arrange them on the square, using your markings as a guide.

   Overlap the pieces slightly so that none of the off-white fabric shows between the pieces (refer to the appliqué pattern).

9. Fuse the pieces in place with an iron set on "cotton" (or about halfway between medium and high).

10. Cut a piece of stabilizer just slightly larger than the bird and pin it to the back (wrong) side of the square, behind the bird.

11. Machine appliqué all the pieces in place with the matching threads.

    The width of the satin stitch should be about 2 to 3 mm wide (about $^1/_8$ inch).

12. Using the same width of satin stitch, stitch along the leg markings to machine embroider the legs.

    When you have finished appliquéing all pieces in place, remove the pins and tear away the stabilizer from the block.

13. Stitch the blue E strips to the sides of the bird block.

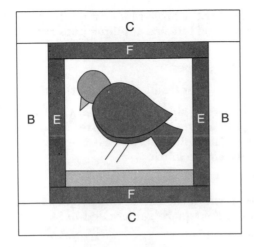

14. Stitch the blue F strips to the top and bottom of the block. (Refer to the figure in Step 13.) Press the E and F strips outwards.

15. Stitch the off-white B strips to the sides of the block. (Refer to the figure in Step 13.)

16. Stitch the off-white C strips to the top and bottom of the block. (Refer to the figure in Step 13.) Press the B and C strips outwards.

17. Layer the pillow top with the batting and the off-white solid lining piece and hand or pin baste the layers together.

18. Quilt the pillow top as you like.

19. Machine stitch very close to the raw edges of the pillow top and then trim away the excess batting and backing that extends beyond the edges of the pillow top.

20. Stitch the piping around the edges of the pillow top, clipping at the corners to avoid rounded corners. Clip close to, but not through, the cord.

21. **Place the pillow top to the pillow backing right sides together and stitch around all four sides, leaving an 8-inch opening along the bottom edge for turning.**

22. **Clip the corners close to, but not through, the stitching. (Refer to the figure in Step 21.)**

    This eliminates the bulk in the corners, giving you pointed instead of rounded corners.

23. **Turn the pillow cover right side out.**

24. **Hand stitch one large button eye on the bird's head.**

25. **Insert the pillow form or stuffing and then hand stitch the turning opening closed.**

Appliquéing the Placemat

Follow these steps to appliqué the placemat:

1. **Trace the four pieces for the large bluebird on the paper side of the fusible webbing using the full-size appliqué patterns.**

2. **Roughly cut out all the shapes.**

    You will cut them neatly after fusing them onto the fabrics.

3. **Fuse the beak to the wrong side of the golden yellow fabric. Fuse the head to the wrong side of the light blue fabric. Fuse the wing to the wrong side of the medium blue fabric. Fuse the lower body to the wrong side of the dark blue fabric.**

4. **Carefully cut out all the shapes.**

5. **Referring to the patterns at the end of this project, lightly trace the bird and the legs onto the lower-right corner of the placemat (refer to photo in color section if necessary).**

6. **Remove the paper backings from the bird parts (all four pieces) and arrange them on the placemat, using your markings as a guide.**

   Overlap the pieces slightly so none of the placemat fabric shows between the pieces (refer to the pattern).

7. **Fuse the pieces in place with an iron set on "cotton" (or about halfway between medium and high).**

8. **Cut a piece of stabilizer just slightly larger than the bird itself and pin it to the back (wrong) side of the placemat, behind the bird.**

9. **Machine appliqué all the pieces in place with the matching threads.**

   The width of the satin stitch should be about 2 to 3 mm wide (about $1/8$ inch).

10. **Using the same width of satin stitch, stitch along the leg markings to machine embroider the legs.**

    Remove the pins and tear the stabilizer from the back side of the appliqués.

11. **To finish the placemat, hand stitch a large button eye on the bird's head.**

Appliquéing the Napkin

Follow these steps to appliqué the napkin:

1. **Reverse the pattern for the small bluebird and trace the four pieces on the paper side of the fusible webbing using the full-size appliqué patterns.**

   The bluebird will face left when appliquéd.

2. **Roughly cut out all the shapes.**

   You will cut them neatly after fusing.

3. **Fuse the beak shape to the wrong side of the golden yellow fabric. Fuse the head to the wrong side of the light blue fabric. Fuse the wing to the wrong side of the medium blue fabric. Fuse the lower body to the wrong side of the dark blue fabric.**

4. **Carefully cut out all the shapes.**

5. **Referring to the patterns at the end of this project, lightly trace the bird and the legs onto a corner of the napkin.**

6. **Remove the paper backings from the bird parts (all four pieces) and arrange them on the napkin, using your markings as a guide.**

   Overlap the pieces slightly so none of the napkin fabric shows between the pieces (refer to the appliqué pattern).

7. **Fuse the bird to the napkin using an iron set on "cotton" (or about halfway between medium and high).**

8. **Cut a piece of stabilizer just slightly larger than the bird and pin it to the back (wrong) side of the napkin, behind the bird.**

9. **Machine appliqué all the pieces in place with the matching threads.**

   The width of the satin stitch should be about 2 to 3 mm wide (about $1/8$ inch).

10. **Using the same width of satin stitch, stitch along the leg markings to machine embroider the legs. Remove the pins and tear the stabilizer from the backs of the appliqués.**

11. **To finish the napkin, hand stitch a small button eye on the bird's head.**

Appliquéing the Kitchen Towel

Follow these steps to appliqué the kitchen towel:

1. **Trace the four pieces for the small bluebird on the paper side of the fusible webbing.**

2. **Reverse the small bluebird pattern and repeat Step 1 so that you have two birds facing opposite directions.**

3. **Roughly cut out all of the shapes.**

   You will cut them neatly after fusing.

4. **Fuse the beaks to the wrong side of the golden yellow fabric. Fuse the heads to the wrong side of the light blue fabric. Fuse the wings to the wrong side of the medium blue fabric. Fuse the lower bodies to the wrong side of the dark blue fabric.**

5. **Carefully cut out all the shapes.**

6. **Referring to the patterns at the end of this project, lightly trace the birds and their legs onto the center of one end of the kitchen towel.**

   Remember that the birds should face in opposite directions.

7. **Remove the paper backings from the bird parts (all eight pieces) and arrange them on the towel, using your markings as a guide.**

   Overlap the pieces slightly so none of the towel shows between the pieces (refer to the pattern).

8. **Fuse the birds to the towel using an iron set on "cotton" (or about halfway between medium and high).**

9. **For each bird, cut a piece of stabilizer just slightly larger than the bird itself and pin it to the back (wrong) side of the towel, behind the bird.**

10. **Machine appliqué all of the pieces in place with the matching threads.**

    The satin stitch should be about 2 to 3 mm wide (about 1/8 inch).

11. **Using the same width of satin stitch, stitch along the leg markings to machine embroider the legs.**

12. **To finish the towel, hand stitch a small button eye to each bird's head.**

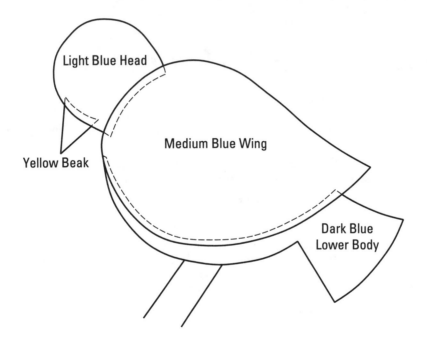

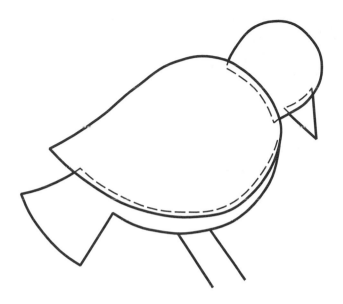

Double the size (200 percent) for a full-size pattern.

Project 3

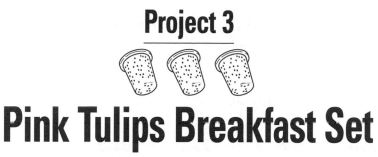

Pink Tulips Breakfast Set

Finished block size: 4 inches x 8¹/₂ inches

Finished size of placemat: 20 inches x 15¹/₂ inches

Finished size of hotpad: 8 inches x 10¹/₂ inches

Finished size of napkin: 18 inches x 18 inches

*N*ot all quilt blocks are square! This breakfast set is based on a rectangular-shaped, odd-sized block. The floral block in fresh Spring pinks and bright green is perfect whether it's lined up in threes for placemat centers or standing on its own in a hotpad (the napkin is left plain). If pink's not your color, try making the tulip portion of the blocks in yellow, purple, or red — anything tulip-ish!

The top area of the block uses a set-in seam.

Stashing Your Materials

The lists in this section describe the fabrics and notions you need to make two napkins, two placemats, and one hotpad:

- ✔ 1 yard of white print fabric (includes fabric needed for backings)
- ✔ ¹/₃ yard each of two different pink print fabrics
- ✔ ¹/₄ yard each of two different green fabrics (either solids or prints work fine)
- ✔ ¹/₄ yard yellow fabric (either solid or print works fine)
- ✔ White, pink, and yellow all-purpose threads

Additional materials needed for two placemats

- ✔ 2 24-inch x 18-inch pieces of cotton batting
- ✔ 5 yards of yellow bias binding

Additional materials needed for one hotpad

- ✔ 2 10-inch x 12-inch pieces of cotton batting
- ✔ 1¼ yards of yellow piping
- ✔ Scrap of pink ribbon for hanging loop

Always use cotton batting on hotpads, placemats, or anything else that may be subjected to the heat of a warmed dish — polyester batting will melt!

Materials needed for two napkins

- ✔ 2 19-inch x 19-inch squares of pink fabric for the napkins (use a coordinating print or a solid, depending on whether you want your napkins to match or contrast)
- ✔ All-purpose thread to match the fabric

Assembling the Quilt Blocks

This section explains how to construct the quilt blocks that are used in the placemats and the hotpad.

1. **Make a template for each pattern piece shown in the figure that follows.**

   Rev. means to reverse the block.

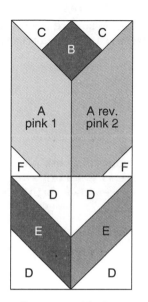

If you need help creating templates, see Chapter 4. Template patterns are at the end of this project's instructions.

Be sure to label each template and include the grainline markings.

Note: All seam allowances are ¹/₄ inch and are included in the template patterns.

2. **Referring to Table PTBS-1, trace and then cut out the appropriate quantities of each block piece.**

Be sure to mark the corner dots on pieces A and B.

Table PTBS-1	Quilt Block Pieces		
Piece	*Fabric Color*	*Quantity*	*Size in Inches*
A	Pink print #1	7	
A	Pink print #2	7 reversed	
B square	Yellow	7	
C triangle	White print	14	
D triangle	White print	28	
E	Green #1	7	
E	Green #2	7 reversed	
F triangle	White print	14	

3. **Stitch two white C triangles to a yellow B square to create a top unit. Repeat to make seven top units. Press seam allowances towards the yellow fabric.**

4. **Stitch one F triangle to the shortest edge of a pink A piece to create a petal unit. Repeat to make seven pink #1 petal units and seven pink #2 petal units. Press the seam allowances towards the pink fabrics.**

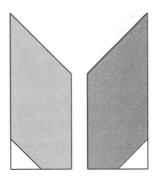

5. **Right sides together, stitch a left petal unit to a right petal unit, as shown.**

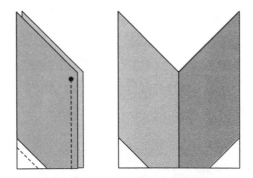

Stitch only from the dot at the center top of the petals so that you can "set in" the top portion of the block in the next step. This dot is located $1/4$ inch from the edges of the pieces.

6. **Stitch a top unit to the left petal unit, as shown. Start stitching at the top-left corner, and stop stitching at the dot. This is a "set-in" seam, so you must stop stitching at the dot indicated on template B (which is $1/4$ inch from the corner). End your stitching and cut the thread. Then stitch the top unit to the right petal in the same manner, starting at the dot and ending at the outside tip. Make seven of these flower sections.**

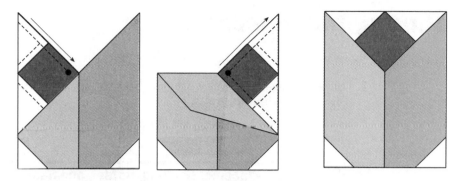

7. Stitch two white D triangles to each green E piece. Make seven left leaf sections and seven right leaf sections. Then stitch one left and one right leaf section together to make a leaf unit. Repeat this step until you have seven leaf units.

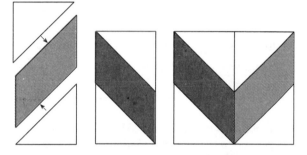

8. Stitch one flower section (created in Steps 3 through 6) to a leaf unit to create a block. Make seven of these blocks.

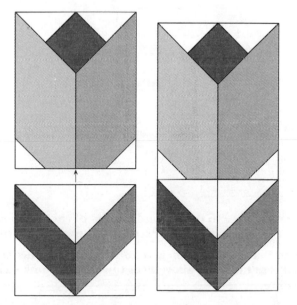

Making the Placemats

Follow these steps to create the two placemats:

1. **Following the steps in the previous section, construct six quilt blocks (three for each placemat).**

2. **Referring to Table PTBS-2, cut the placemat borders and backing pieces for each placemat.**

Table PTBS-2	Placemat Backing, Border, and Sashing Pieces		
Piece	*Fabric*	*Measurements in Inches*	*Quantity*
Backing	White print	24 x 18	1 for each placemat
Strip 1	White print	1¹/₂ x 9	4 for each placemat
Strip 2	White print	1¹/₂ x 16¹/₂	2 for each placemat
Strip 3	Pink print #1	1 x 16¹/₂	2 for each placemat
Strip 4	White print	2¹/₂ x 16¹/₂	2 for each placemat
Strip 5	White print	2¹/₂ x 16	2 for each placemat

3. **Alternate four white sashing strips (Strip 1) with three quilt blocks and stitch together to form a placemat center. Press the seam allowances towards the blocks. Repeat this step to form the other placemat.**

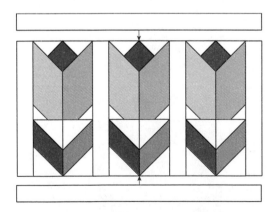

4. **Stitch white #2 strips to the top and bottom of each placemat center. (Refer to the preceding figure.) Press strips towards the blocks.**

5. **Stitch pink #3 strips to the top and bottom of each placemat section, as shown. Press the seam allowances towards the pink strips.**

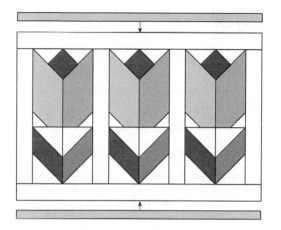

6. Stitch white #4 strips to the top and bottom of each placemat section. Press the seam allowances outwards towards the white strips.

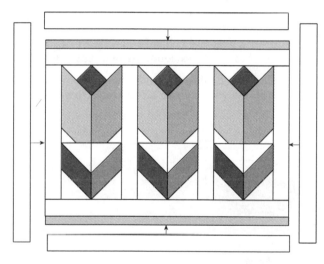

7. Stitch white #5 strips to the left and right sides of each placemat section. (Refer to the preceding figure.) Press the seam allowances outwards towards the white strips.

8. Layer a placemat top, right side up, with a piece of batting and a piece of backing fabric, right side down. Repeat for the other placemat. Then hand or pin baste the layers together and quilt them any way you wish. Repeat for the second placemat sandwich.

9. After you quilt the placemat tops, machine stitch very close to their raw edges and trim away the excess batting and backing fabric.

10. Bind the placemats with the yellow bias binding.

Making the Hotpad

Follow these steps to create the hotpad:

1. **Following the steps in the section "Assembling the Quilt Blocks," assemble one quilt block.**

2. **Referring to Table PTBS-3, cut the backing and border pieces for the hotpad.**

Table PTBS-3	Hotpad Backing and Border Pieces		
Piece	*Fabric*	*Measurements in Inches*	*Quantity*
Backing	White print	10 x 12	1
Strip 1	White print	2½ x 9	2
Strip 2	White print	1½ x 8½	2

3. **Stitch a white Strip 1 to the left side of a flower block. Repeat on the right side of the block. Press seam allowances towards the block.**

4. **Stitch a white Strip 2 to the top of the flower block. Repeat on the bottom of the block. Press seam allowances towards the block.**

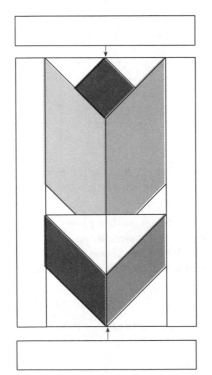

5. **Stitch the piping around the edges of the hotpad.**

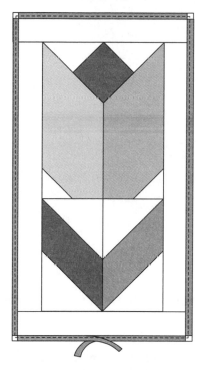

Begin stitching at the center of one side, leaving a 2-inch tail of piping hanging free. When you approach a corner, stop stitching ¹/₄ inch from the corner. Clip into the seam allowance of the piping *close to, but not through,* the stuffed area of the piping. This eliminates the bulk that would have resulted at the corners if you had tried to turn them without stopping and clipping. By clipping the seam allowances, you get nice, pointed corners.

Turn the corner and resume stitching. When you arrive back at your starting point, overlap the remaining piping and the tail you left at the starting point and stitch across them. Because the layers of fabric and batting are a bit bulky, so stitch slowly so that you don't break your needle. Trim the excess tails of the piping so that they are only about ¹/₂-inch long.

6. **Pin the double layer of batting to the wrong side of the backing piece.**

7. **Place the backing piece and the hotpad top together, right sides facing.**

8. **With the wrong side of the block facing up, stitch around the edges of the hotpad top along the piping stitching lines, leaving a 3-inch opening at the top edge for turning.**

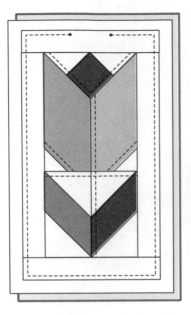

9. **Trim the excess batting and backing fabric, clip the corners, and turn the hotpad right side out.**

10. **Fold the scrap of ribbon in half to form a loop.**

11. **Tuck the ends of the ribbon loop in the center of the turning opening at the top to create a hanging loop. Then hand stitch the turning opening closed, catching the ends of the ribbon loop in your stitching as you go.**

12. **Quilt the hotpad in any manner you choose to finish the project.**

Making the Napkins

These napkins are a breeze to make. Simply hem the two 19-inch x 19-inch pink fabric squares following these two steps:

1. **Fold each edge of a pink square under $1/4$ inch and press. Then fold each edge under another $1/4$ inch and press again.**

   Turning under $1/4$ inch twice on each napkin creates a doubled-hem. Doing this keeps the hem from fraying during laundering.

   Repeat the step on the other fabric square.

2. **Stitch the hems in place with pink all-purpose thread, stitching around all four sides closest to the first $1/4$-inch fold (a scant $1/4$ inch from the actual edges of the napkin).**

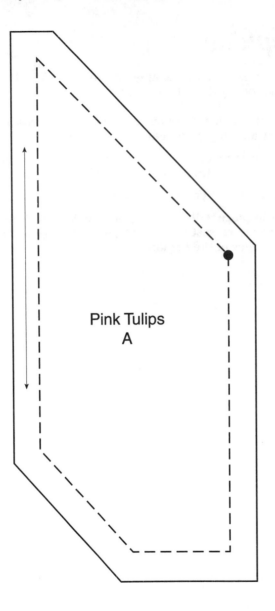

Pink Tulips
A

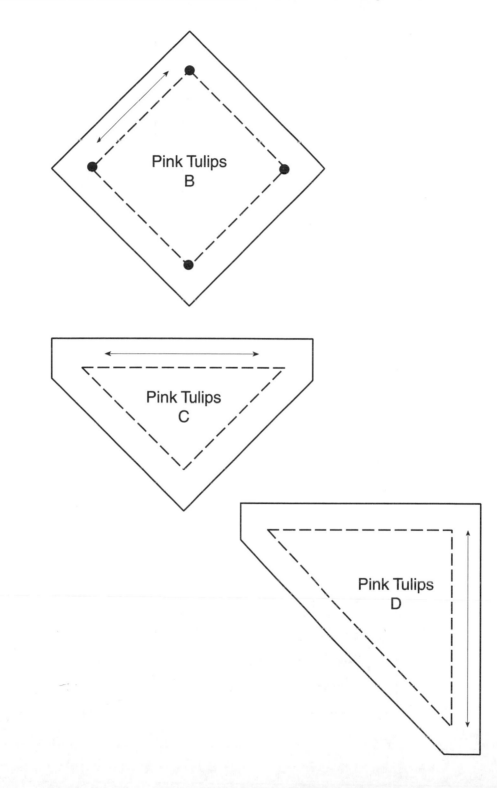

Pink Tulips
B

Pink Tulips
C

Pink Tulips
D

Templates

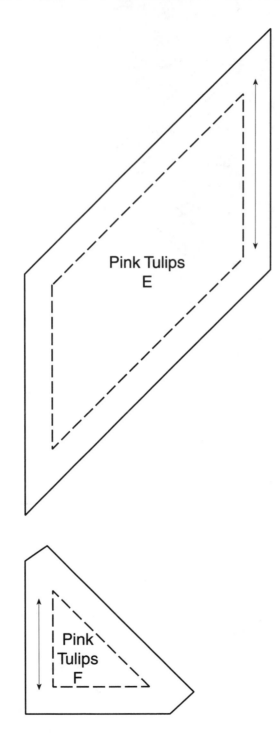

Pink Tulips
E

Pink
Tulips
F

Project 4

Blue Star Placemat and Hotpad Set

Finished size of placemat: 14 inches x 18 inches

Finished size of hotpad: 10 inches x 10 inches

Finished size of napkin: 18 inches x 18 inches

*T*his project is fun as well as versatile. Why? For starters, you can practice your rotary cutting skills and whip this out in a flash, and the placemats are actually miniature quilts!

Try making just one placemat as a wallhanging, or make several for your table. You can make the matching hot pad and napkins quickly, too.

Stashing Your Materials

I list the materials that you need to make *one* of each item. Because the placemat fabrics require a *fat quarter,* which is 18 inches x 22 inches, you can easily figure the yardage needed for additional placemats — ¹/₂ yard of fabric makes two placemats, 1 full yard makes four placemats, and so on.

Be sure to use cotton batting in this project. Polyester batting often melts when exposed to high temperatures.

Note: All seam allowances are ¹/₄ inch and are included in the given measurements.

Materials for one placemat

- ✔ 1 18-inch x 22-inch piece of blue print fabric for the star blocks (fat quarter)
- ✔ 1 18-inch x 22-inch piece of tan print fabric for the blocks and inner borders (fat quarter)
- ✔ 1 8-inch x 20-inch piece of blue paisley print for the outer borders
- ✔ 1 16-inch x 20-inch piece of cotton batting
- ✔ 1 16-inch x 20-inch piece of fabric for the backing
- ✔ 2 yards of dark blue quilt binding, $1/2$-inch finished width
- ✔ All-purpose thread to match the fabrics

Materials for one hotpad

- ✔ 1 7-inch x 10-inch piece of blue print fabric for the block
- ✔ 1 10-inch x 20-inch piece of tan print fabric for the block and inner borders
- ✔ 1 12-inch x 7-inch strip of blue paisley fabric for the outer borders
- ✔ 2 11-inch x 11-inch pieces of cotton batting
- ✔ 1 11-inch x 11-inch piece of fabric for the backing
- ✔ $1^1/2$ yards of dark blue quilt binding, $1/2$ inch finished width
- ✔ All-purpose thread to match the fabrics

Materials for one napkin

- ✔ 1 19-inch x 19-inch square of blue paisley fabric
- ✔ All-purpose thread to match the fabric

Putting Together a Placemat

Follow these steps to make one placemat:

1. **Cut out the pieces for this project, following the measurements listed in Table BS-1.**

Table BS-1	Pieces to Cut to Make One Placemat		
Fabric Color	*Piece*	*Amount*	*Size in Inches*
Tan print	Inner border strip	4	$2^1/_2$ x 14
	Piece	1	14 x 10
	Square	24	$1^1/_2$ x $1^1/_2$
Blue print	Piece	1	14 x 10
	Square (star center)	6	$2^1/_2$ x $2^1/_2$
Blue paisley print	Outer border strip	2	$1^1/_2$ x $16^1/_2$
	Outer border strip	2	$1^1/_2$ x $14^1/_2$

2. **Mark a grid of 24 squares measuring $1^7/_8$ inches x $1^7/_8$ inches on the wrong side of the 14-inch x 10-inch tan piece. Draw a diagonal line through each square.**

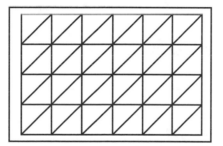

3. **Place the marked tan piece and the 14-inch x 10-inch blue piece together, right sides facing. Pin them together around the outside edges, placing the pins out of the way of stitching lines (diagonal lines). Stitch $^1/_4$ inch from each side of the diagonal line. Cut out the 24 squares.**

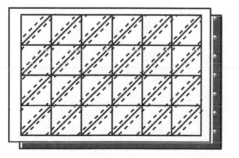

4. Remove the pins. Cut the squares in half along the diagonal lines to form 48 doubled triangles.

5. Open each doubled triangle to form a two-colored square. Press the squares open, with the seam allowances toward the blue fabric.

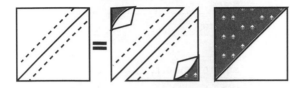

6. Stitch together two of the two-colored squares. Make 24 of these strips.

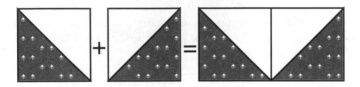

7. Stitch a tan 1¹/₂-inch square to one end of 12 of the strips that you made in Step 6. Then stitch another tan square to the opposite end of the same 12 strips.

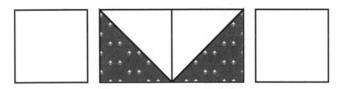

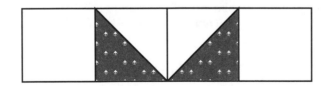

8. **Stitch two of the remaining strips that you made in Step 6 to opposite sides of each of the six 2¹/₂-inch blue center squares. Make six of these units.**

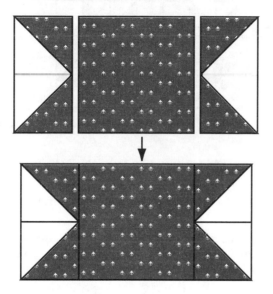

9. **Stitch two of the strips that you made in Step 7 to one of the strips that you made in Step 8. Make six of these star blocks.**

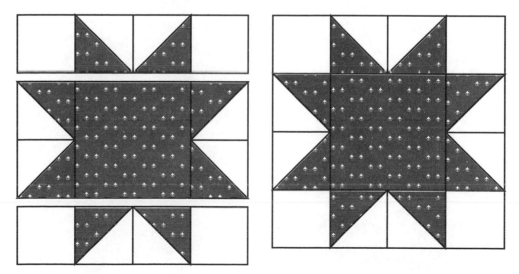

10. **Stitch three of the star blocks together horizontally to form one row. Make two of these rows.**

11. **Stitch the two rows together along one long edge to make the placemat center.**

12. **Stitch one $2^1/_2$-inch x 14-inch tan strip to each of the two long sides of the placemat center. Trim the ends.**

13. **Stitch the remaining two tan strips to the sides of the placemat, and trim the ends.**

14. **Stitch the two $1^1/_2$-inch x $16^1/_2$-inch blue paisley strips to the two long sides of the placemat center. Stitch the two $1^1/_2$-inch x $14^1/_2$-inch blue paisley strips to other two sides of the placemat center.**

15. **Layer the placemat top with the batting and backing. Pin-baste the layers together.**

16. **Quilt as desired.**

    I quilted the color insert sample in a 1-inch grid with contrasting thread.

17. **Trim the excess batting and backing fabric.**

18. **Bind the placemats with the dark blue binding.**

Assembling a Hotpad

Follow these steps to make a hotpad:

1. **Cut out the pieces for the hotpad, following the measurements listed in Table BS-2.**

Table BS-2	Pieces to Cut to Make One Hotpad		
Fabric Color	*Piece*	*Amount*	*Size in Inches*
Tan print	Square	1	7 x 7
	Inner border strip	2	$2^1/_2$ x $4^1/_2$
	Inner border strip	2	$2^1/_2$ x $8^1/_2$
	Square	4	$1^1/_2$ x $1^1/_2$
Blue print	Square (star center)	1	$2^1/_2$ x $2^1/_2$
Blue paisley	Outer border strip	2	$1^1/_2$ x $8^1/_2$
	Outer border strip	2	$1^1/_2$ x $10^1/_2$

2. **On the wrong side of the 7-inch x 7-inch tan square, mark four $1^7/_8$-inch x $1^7/_8$-inch squares. Draw a diagonal line through each square.**

3. **Place the tan square and the 7-inch x 7-inch piece of blue print fabric together, right sides facing. Pin them together as for the placemat instructions. Stitch $^1/_4$ inch from each side of the diagonal lines, and then cut out the four squares.**

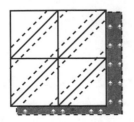

4. Cut the squares in half along the diagonal lines to form eight doubled triangles.

5. Open each doubled triangle to form a two-colored square. Press the squares open, with the seam allowances toward the blue fabric.

6. Stitch together two of the two-colored squares. Make four of these units.

7. Stitch one tan 1^1/$_2$-inch square to one end of each of the two of the units that you made in Step 7. Then stitch another tan square to the opposite end of the same two units.

8. Stitch the two remaining units that you made in Step 7 to opposite sides of the 2^1/$_2$-inch blue center square.

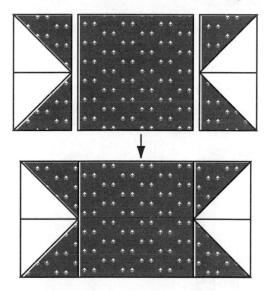

9. Stitch two units that you made in Step 8 to the unit that you made in Step 9 to make one star block.

10. Stitch the tan inner borders to the star block, stitching the shorter strips to opposite sides and the longer strips to the two remaining sides. Repeat with the blue paisley outer borders to complete the hot pad top.

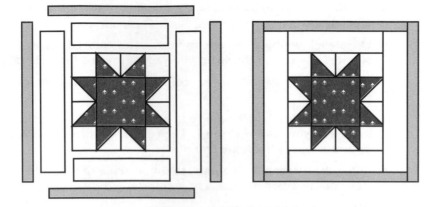

11. **Layer the hot pad top on top of both pieces of batting and the wrong side of the backing fabric.**

12. **Quilt as for the placemats.**

13. **Trim away the excess batting and backing fabric.**

14. **Bind the hot pad with the dark blue binding (as you did for the placemats), leaving one 6-inch tail at one corner.**

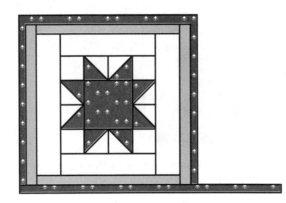

15. **Tuck in the raw edges on the end of the binding and fold the tail towards the back of the hot pad to form a loop. Hand stitch the loop in place at the corner to finish the hotpad.**

Making a Napkin

To make one napkin, turn under the raw edges of the 19-inch x 19-inch square of blue paisley fabric $1/4$ inch *twice* and stitch in place with matching thread to hem.

Project 5

Pastel Nine-Patch Wallhanging

- -

Finished size: 21 inches x 21 inches square

- -

*H*ere's a project so simple and quick that you can make it in one day —
no kidding! It's based on simple nine-patch blocks set on point.

Be sure to use a large floral print in this project, and experiment with it. In
the quilt that's shown in the color insert, I used the heaviest, busiest section
of the floral fabric right in the center of the quilt top, and the least busy
areas of the fabric in the sides and corners. This layout is a great way to use
a large-scale print effectively because you can balance the quilt, making
sure that all the busy areas don't end up on one side while the other side
remains plain.

Stashing Your Materials

- ✔ ¹/₄ yard of light yellow solid for the blocks
- ✔ ¹/₄ yard of light blue solid for the block centers and border corner-stones
- ✔ ¹/₃ yard of light pink print for the blocks and borders
- ✔ ¹/₃ yard of blue large-scale floral print for the center areas surrounding the blocks
- ✔ 1 24-inch x 24-inch piece of batting
- ✔ 1 24-inch x 24-inch piece of coordinating fabric for the backing
- ✔ All-purpose threads to match the fabrics (light yellow, light blue, light pink, and blue floral)
- ✔ 3 yards of quilt binding

Assembling the Quilt Top

Follow these steps to assemble the top. *Note:* All seam allowances are ¼ inch and are included in all the given measurements.

1. **Cut out the pieces of the quilt per the measurements in Table NP-1.**

   Use a rotary cutter to cut all the pieces for the best results (nice straight edges). You may also use scissors if desired.

Table NP-1	Pieces to Cut		
Fabric	*Piece*	*Quantity*	*Size in Inches*
Light yellow solid	Square	16	2½ x 2½
Light blue solid	Square	8	2½ x 2½
Light pink print	Border strip	4	2½ x 17½
	Square	16	2½ x 2½
Blue floral print	Square	2	5 x 5
	Square	1	9 x 9
	Square	1	6½

2. **To make the nine-patch blocks, stitch one yellow square to one side of a pink square, and then stitch another yellow square to the opposite side of the same pink square. Make eight of these units.**

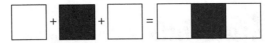

3. **Stitch one pink square to one side of a light blue solid square, and then stitch another pink square to the opposite side of the same blue square. Make four of these units.**

4. **Assemble one nine-patch block by stitching together one of the units in Step 3 to two of the units made in Step 2. Make four of these blocks.**

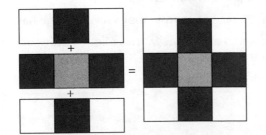

5. Cut the two 5-inch x 5-inch blue print squares diagonally in half to form four A triangles.

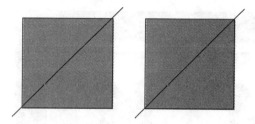

6. Cut the 9-inch x 9-inch square twice diagonally into quarters to make four of the B triangles.

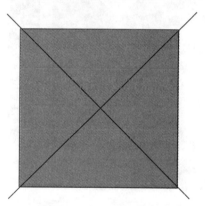

7. Assemble the quilt center area as shown in the following figure.

8. **Stitch two of the pink print border strips to the top and bottom edges of the quilt center and trim.**

9. **Stitch one of the four remaining $2^1/_2$-inch blue squares to the short ends of the two remaining pink print border strips. Stitch these strips to the side edges of the quilt center.**

Quilting and Completing the Project

Follow these steps to complete your quilt:

1. **Layer the quilt top on top of the batting and the wrong side of the backing. Hand or pin baste the layers together to prepare them for quilting. (See Chapter 12.)**

2. **Hand or machine quilt as desired. (See Chapter 13.)**

3. **Stitch $^1/_8$ inch away from the raw edges of the quilt top and trim away the excess batting and backing even with the edges of the quilt top.**

4. **Bind the quilt to finish. (See Chapter 14.)**

Project 6

Pieced Flower Pots Wallhanging

• •

Finished size of quilt: 25 inches x 33 inches

Finished block size: 9 inches x 13 inches

• •

Not all quilt blocks are square! This just-too-easy pieced flower pot quilt is a beginner's dream. It looks involved, but it's actually very simple to construct and is made of only strips and squares — no triangles with bias edges to worry about.

To speed up the cutting process, use your rotary cutter, and when stitching, be sure to keep your $\frac{1}{4}$-inch seam allowance accurate.

Stashing Your Materials

You need the following materials to complete the Pieced Flower Pots wallhanging:

- ✔ 1 yard of green print fabric
- ✔ $\frac{1}{2}$ yard of tan print fabric
- ✔ $\frac{1}{3}$ yard each of blue print and yellow print fabrics
- ✔ $\frac{1}{4}$ yard of peach print fabric
- ✔ $\frac{1}{2}$ yard of rust print fabric
- ✔ 1 28-inch x 36-inch piece of coordinating fabric for the backing
- ✔ 1 28-inch x 36-inch piece of traditional-weight quilt batting
- ✔ 4 yards of quilt binding to coordinate with fabrics
- ✔ Matching all-purpose threads

Assembling the Quilt Top

To assemble the four blocks of this quilt, you make two blocks in each colorway (or color arrangement) — one colorway consists of a block with two yellow flowers and one blue flower (block 1), and the second is the opposite — two blue flowers and one yellow (block 2). There are two blocks of each colorway in this quilt.

Because the leaf and pot areas of all the blocks are identical, and the colors of the flowers are the only things that are reversed, I show only block 1 in the following diagrams. The assembly is so simple, you won't need diagrams to guide you through making the second colorway.

Note: All seam allowances are $^1/_4$ inch and are included in the given measurements. Remember to press all the seam allowances toward the darker color.

Follow these steps to assemble your quilt top:

1. **Cut out the quilt pieces, following the measurements listed in Table PF-1.**

Table PF-1	Pieces to Cut		
Fabric Color	*Piece*	*Amount*	*Size in Inches*
Green print	Upper/lower Borders	2	$2^1/_2$ x $19^1/_2$
	Side Borders	2	$2^1/_2$ x $27^1/_2$
	D square	36	$1^1/_2$ x $1^1/_2$
Tan print	A strip	8	$1^1/_2$ x $4^1/_2$
	B piece	8	$2^1/_2$ x $3^1/_2$
	C strip	28	$1^1/_2$ x $2^1/_2$
	D square	52	$1^1/_2$ x $1^1/_2$
	E square	8	$2^1/_2$x $2^1/_2$
	F strip	12	$1^1/_2$ x $3^1/_2$
Blue print	C strip	26	$1^1/_2$ x $2^1/_2$ (use 8 for borders and 18 for blocks)
	D square	12	$1^1/_2$ x $1^1/_2$
Yellow print	C strip	18	$1^1/_2$ x $2^1/_2$
	D square	12	$1^1/_2$ x $1^1/_2$
	Cornerstones	4	$2^1/_2$ x $2^1/_2$
Peach print	F strip	4	$1^1/_2$ x $3^1/_2$

Fabric Color	Piece	Amount	Size in Inches
	G strip	4	$2^1/_2$ x $5^1/_2$
Rust print	Sashing (vertical) #1	6	$1^1/_2$ x $13^1/_2$
	Sashing (horizontal) #2	3	$1^1/_2$ x $21^1/_2$
	H strip	4	$1^1/_2$ x $7^1/_2$

2. To make row 1 of block 1, stitch together one blue D square to two tan A strips. Repeat with the second colorway for block 2, using the yellow D square. Make two strips of each colorway.

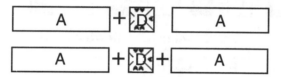

3. To make row 2 of block 1, stitch together two tan B pieces, two blue C strips, and one yellow C strip. Reverse the blue and yellow colorway for block 2 and make two of each strip.

You're getting the hang of it now.

4. For row 3, make two rows in each colorway, as shown in the following figure.

5. For row 4, make two rows in each colorway, as shown in the following figure.

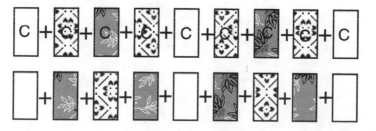

6. For row 5, make two rows in each colorway, as shown in the following figure.

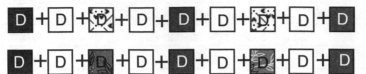

7. To make row 6, stitch five tan D squares to four green D squares, alternating each square. Make four of these strips.

8. Make four of row 7, as shown in the following figure.

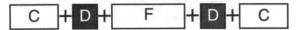

9. Make four of row 8, as shown in the following figure.

   This is the pot rim row.

10. Make four of row 9, as shown in the following figure.

11. Make four of row 10, as shown in the following figure.

12. To assemble block 1, stitch together rows 1 through 10 of colorway 1. Make two of these blocks.

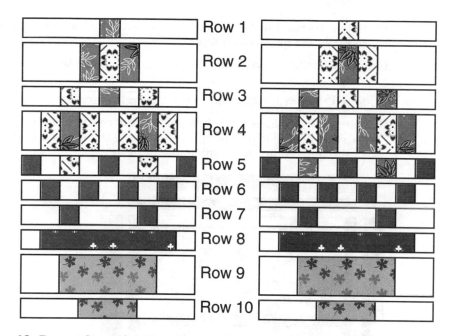

Row 1
Row 2
Row 3
Row 4
Row 5
Row 6
Row 7
Row 8
Row 9
Row 10

13. Repeat Step 12 with colorway 2 to assemble block 2.

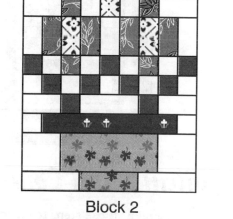

Block 1   Block 2

You now have four flowerpot blocks — two of block 1 and two of block 2.

14. Stitch three sashing #1 strips alternately with one block 1 and one block 2 to make a row. Repeat with the three remaining sashing #1 strips and the remaining two blocks, reversing the placement of the blocks.

15. Stitch the two block rows alternately with the three sashing #2 strips to make the quilt center. Press.

16. Stitch one blue C strip to each of the ends of the border #1 and #2 strips.

17. Stitch the border #2 strips to the left and right sides of the quilt center.

18. Stitch one $2^1/_2$-inch x $2^1/_2$-inch yellow square to each short end of the two border #1 strips. Stitch these strips to the top and bottom edges of the quilt center to complete the quilt top.

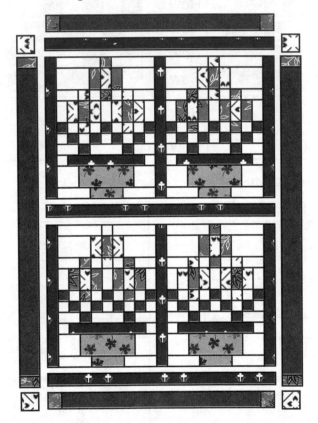

Quilting and Completing the Project

Follow these steps to finish your project:

1. Layer the quilt top right side up, with the batting and the wrong side of the backing fabric. Hand or pin baste the layers together to prepare it for quilting.

2. Hand or machine quilt as desired.

3. Finish the quilt by stitching the quilt binding around the edges.

Project 7

Pieced Hearts Wallhanging

• •

Finished size of quilt: 25 inches wide x 32 inches long

Finished block size: 6 inches x 6 inches

• •

This fun little quilt is a "strippy" quilt — the blocks are assembled in vertical rows that are separated by other strips. Constructing the quilt is very easy, and the plain band down the center gives you a nice spot to show off your new quilting skills!

The following sections guide you through the construction of the Pieced Hearts Wallhanging, from choosing fabrics to preparing the quilt for display.

Stashing Your Materials

The following list describes the fabrics and notions you need to make this quilt:

- ✔ ½ yard of solid tan fabric (blocks and center strip)
- ✔ ½ yard of blue paisley fabric (outer borders)
- ✔ ⅓ yard of red print fabric 1 (hearts)
- ✔ ⅓ yard of red print fabric 2 (hearts)
- ✔ ⅓ yard of blue print fabric 1 (hearts)
- ✔ ⅓ yard of blue print fabric 2 (hearts)
- ✔ ⅓ yard of solid light red fabric (sashing)
- ✔ 1 29-inch x 36-inch piece of fabric for the backing
- ✔ 1 29-inch x 36-inch piece of low-loft or traditional-weight quilt batting
- ✔ 4 yards of quilt binding
- ✔ All-purpose threads to match fabrics and binding

Cutting the Pieces

In this section, I walk you through cutting the pieces required for the quilt top. (See Table PH-1 for a quick run-down of the specifications for each piece.) All of the templates and measurements that are given in these instructions include the standard $1/4$-inch seam allowances.

Table PH-1		Pieces to Cut	
Piece	*Fabric*	*Quantity*	*Size in Inches*
A	Red print 1	Cut 2, cut 2 more with template reversed	
A	Red print 2	Cut 2, cut 2 more with template reversed	
A	Blue print 1	Cut 2, cut 2 more with template reversed	
A	Blue print 2	Cut 2, cut 2 more with template reversed	
B	Tan solid	Cut 16	
C	Tan solid	Cut 32	
Center strip	Tan solid	Cut 1 strip	$3^{1}/_{2} \times 24^{1}/_{2}$
Vertical sashing	Light red solid	Cut 4	$1^{1}/_{2} \times 24^{1}/_{2}$
Horizontal sashing	Light red solid	Cut 2	$1^{1}/_{2} \times 19^{1}/_{2}$
Border 1	Blue paisley	Cut 2	$3^{1}/_{2} \times 26^{1}/_{2}$
Border 2	Blue paisley	Cut 2	$3^{1}/_{2} \times 25^{1}/_{2}$

1. **Place the A template on the wrong side of red print 1, aligning the grainline arrows on the template with the grain of the fabric. Trace the template twice with a washable pencil. Next, flip over the template and trace it two more times. Repeat this procedure for red print 2. Cut out the pieces along the cutting lines.**

   By reversing the template, you create the left halves of the hearts. (If you don't flip the template, you're stuck with 16 lonely right heart halves.)

2. **Repeat Step 1 with blue print 1 and blue print 2.**

   Don't forget to reverse the template for half of the tracings.

3. **From the tan fabric, cut the quilt's center strip according to the measurements provided in Table PH-1.**

4. **On the wrong side of the remaining tan fabric, trace template B 16 times and trace template C 32 times.**

   Mark a diagonal line on the wrong side of each C square as indicated on the template.

5. **From the light red fabric, cut the vertical and horizontal sashing strips according to the measurements provided in Table PH-1.**

   Cut four vertical sashing strips and two horizontal sashing strips.

6. **From the blue paisley fabric, cut the four border strips according to the measurements provided in Table PH-1.**

   Cut two border 1 strips and two border 2 strips.

Assembling the Quilt Top

After you cut the quilt top pieces, you're ready to stitch them together. The following steps explain how:

1. **Stitch one tan triangle (B) to a red or blue piece (A), as shown in figure below, having the right sides of the pieces facing each other.**

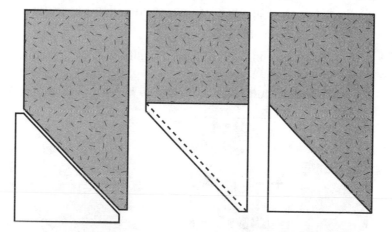

   Press the seam allowance toward the red or blue fabric.

   Repeat this step with each of the red or blue A pieces to create 16 rectangular units: 8 for the left sides of the heart and 8 for the right sides.

2. **Place one tan C square in the top-left corner (on the read and blue fabrics, *not* the tan!) of a unit you created in Step 1, and then place another C square in the top-right corner of the same unit. The right sides of the pieces will be facing each other.**

Do you see the direction of the marked lines on the little C squares? Place yours the same way.

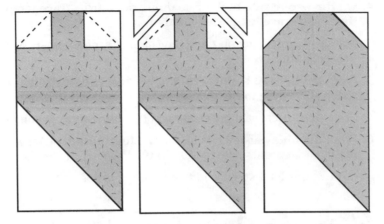

3. **Stitch both C squares onto the rectangular unit along the marked lines.**

   Repeat Steps 2 and 3 for each of the 16 rectangular units you created in Step 1.

4. **Trim away the excess fabric from the C squares — cutting ¼ inch from the stitching line, as shown in Step 2 — and discard it.**

   Press the seam allowances toward the red or blue print fabric.

   This creates one-half of a heart unit.

   Repeat this step for each of the 16 units — 8 for the left sides and 8 for the right sides.

5. **Stitch a heart left to a heart right to make one complete heart block.**

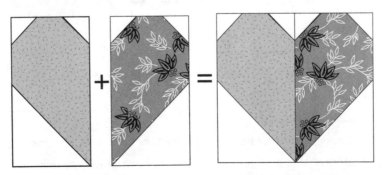

6. **Construct two heart blocks from each of the following fabric combinations, as shown in the following figure: red 1/blue 1, blue 1/red 1, red 2/blue 2, blue 2/red 2.**

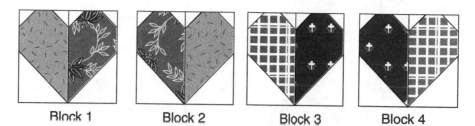

| Block 1 | Block 2 | Block 3 | Block 4 |

7. **Stitch the eight heart blocks together in groups of four to form two vertical rows, arranging the blocks in the order shown in the following figure.**

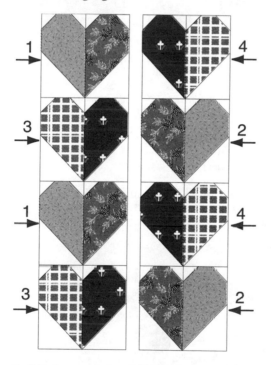

8. **Stitch one strip of the light red vertical sashing to the left side of one heart block row. Repeat on the right side of that heart block row. Press the seam allowances toward the light red sashing strips. Repeat this step for the other heart block row.**

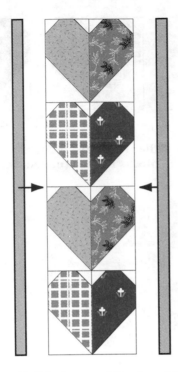

9. **Stitch one of the heart block strips to the left side of the tan center strip, and then stitch the other heart block strip to the right side of the tan center strip.**

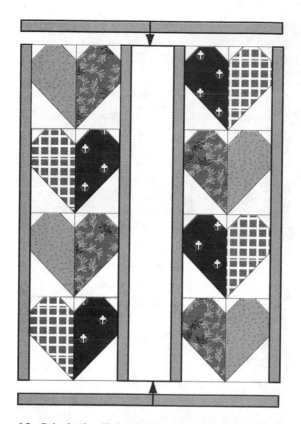

10. Stitch the light red horizontal sashing strips to the top and bottom of the quilt center. (Refer to the illustration in Step 9.)

11. As shown in the following figure, stitch a blue paisley border 1 strip to the left side of the quilt center. Stitch the other blue paisley border 1 strip to the right side of the quilt center.

12. **As shown in the preceding figure, stitch a blue paisley border 2 strip to the top of the quilt center. Stitch the other blue paisley border 2 strip to the bottom of the quilt center.**

Quilting and Finishing the Project

The quilt top looks great, but you need to complete a few more steps before your Pieced Hearts Wallhanging is ready for display:

1. **Mark the desired quilting patterns on the quilt top.**

   Transfer the heart pattern that follows or use any other pattern you like.

This heart quilting pattern looks particularly attractive when repeated on the center strip.

2. **Layer the quilt top with the batting and the backing fabric, and hand or pin baste the layers of the quilt together to prepare it for quilting.**

3. **Hand or machine quilt as desired. (The sample was machine-quilted.)**

4. **Stitch within ¹/₄ inch of the raw edges of the quilt top around all four sides. Trim away the excess batting and backing that extends beyond the edges of the quilt top.**

5. **Bind the quilt to complete.**

Template Patterns

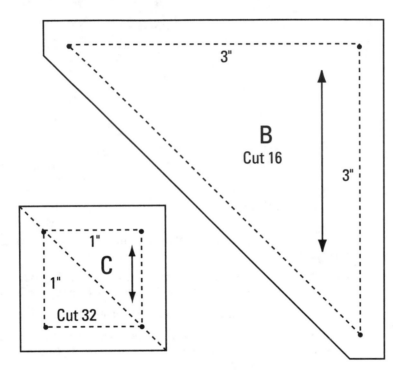

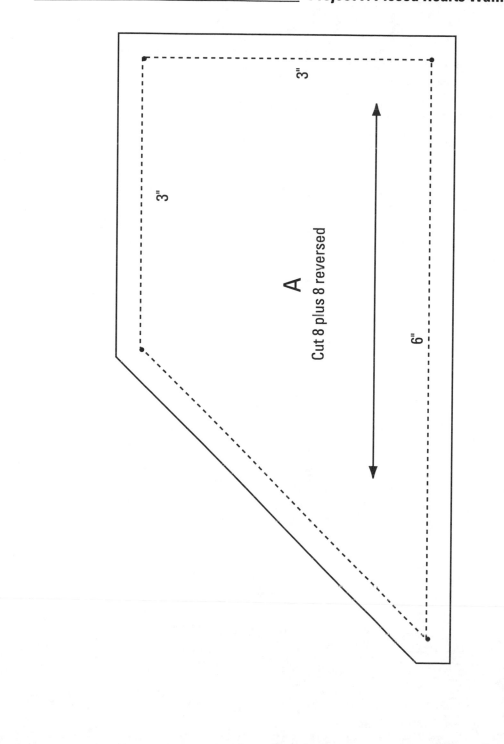

3"

3"

A

Cut 8 plus 8 reversed

6"

Project 8

May Baskets Wallhanging

Finished size of quilt: 33 inches x 28 inches

Finished size of block: 8 inches x 10 inches

*H*ere is a simple, yet elegant project that works up quickly. The plain-Jane tan and rose fabrics are spiffed up through the use of a colorful floral print in the narrow inner borders and the binding. Although this quilt has been machine quilted, the outer borders and tan basket squares have been accented with hand quilting in contrasting brown thread to make them stand out. The flowers have a ring of French knots hand embroidered around their centers. Ribbon bows complete the look.

Stashing Your Materials

The list in this section describes the fabrics and notions you need to make the May Baskets Wallhanging:

- ⅓ yard of off-white print fabric for the background of the handle portion of the blocks
- ½ yard of light brown print fabric for the basket squares and outer borders
- ¾ yard of medium brown print fabric for the baskets and handles
- ⅓ yard of green print fabric for the sashing
- ⅓ yard of floral print on white for the inner borders and binding
- 6 4 inch-x 4-inch scraps of assorted pink fabrics for the flowers
- 12 3-inch x 3-inch scraps of assorted green fabrics for the leaves
- 6 2-inch x 2-inch squares of assorted yellow fabrics for the flower centers
- 35-inch x 30-inch piece of coordinating fabric for the backing
- 35-inch x30-inch piece of low-loft or traditional weight quilt batting

- 6-strand cotton embroidery floss in light pink and dark pink (optional)
- All-purpose threads to match fabrics (pink, yellow, green, and light brown)
- 12-inch x 36-inch piece of waxed freezer paper
- 2 yards of yellow $1/2$-inch-wide satin ribbon for bows on handles

Cutting the Strips

Table MB-1 provides a quick summary of the number and sizes of the pieces you will cut for this project. All seam allowances are the standard $1/4$ inch and are included in the given measurements and template patterns.

Table MB-1	Quick Cutting Guide		
Fabric Color	*Piece*	*Amount*	*Size in Inches*
Off-white print	Rectangle A	6	$5^1/2 \times 8^1/2$
Medium brown print	B	18	$1^1/2 \times 8^1/2$
	C Strip 1	6	1×22
Light brown	C Strip 2	5	$1^1/2 \times 22$
Green	Sashing D	8	$1^1/2 \times 10^1/2$
	Sashing E	3	$1^1/2 \times 28^1/2$
Multicolored floral print	Border F	2	$1 \times 23^1/2$
	Border G	2	$1 \times 29^1/2$
Light brown print	H	2	$2^1/2 \times 29^1/2$
	I	2	$2^1/2 \times 28^1/2$

Tracing the Basket Handles

Follow these steps to trace the basket handles:

1. **From the off-white print fabric, cut six rectangles $5^1/2$ inches x 8-1/2 inches for rectangle A.**

2. **Fold each A rectangle in half as shown and press to mark the center with a crease.**

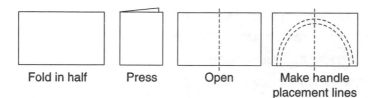

Fold in half   Press   Open   Make handle
placement lines

3. **Enlarging the pattern at the end of this project at 200 percent, trace the basket handle on each of the A rectangles as shown in the illustration that follows Step 2.**

   This is your stitching guide for the basket handles, which you will cut and apply later.

Making the Basket Blocks

Follow these steps to make the basket blocks:

1. **Cut the following strips from the medium brown print:**

   - Six strips 1 inch x 22 inches (the finished width of the strips is only $^1/_2$ inch).

     Set these aside to make the C #1 strips.

   - 18 strips measuring $1^1/_2$ inches x $8^1/_2$ inches for unit B.

2. **Cut the following strips from the light brown print:**

   - Five strips measuring $1^1/_2$ inches x 22 inches.

     Set these strips aside to make the C #2 strips.

   - Two strips measuring $2^1/_2$ inches x $29^1/_2$ inches for the upper and lower borders (H).

   - Two strips measuring $2^1/_2$ inches x $28^1/_2$ inches for the side borders (I).

3. **Make the C strips:**

   - Stitch the six medium brown C #1 strips alternately with the five light brown C #2 strips.

   - Press the seam allowances toward the medium brown strips.

   - Using a rotary cutter and ruler, cut twelve $1^1/_2$-inch-wide C strips.

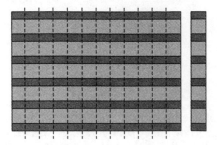

4. **Stitch two C strips alternately with three B strips to create the basket bottoms. Make six of these units.**

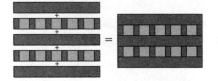

5. **From the remaining medium brown fabric, cut six strips *on the bias,* measuring 1 inch x 13 inches, to create the basket handles.**

13"

6. **Place one of the bias basket strips face down on your ironing board; the wrong side (WS) will be facing you. Then fold the two long sides to meet in the center and carefully press them without stretching the bias strip.**

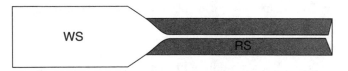

WS

RS

7. **Carefully pin one of these strips to the marked A rectangles from the "Tracing the Basket Handles" section. Pin the inside edge of the handle first, as the outside edge will stretch to accommodate the curve of the handle.**

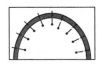

8. **Hand appliqué the handles in place using matching thread and the blind stitch. Stitch one basket handle unit to one basket bottom.**

Make six of these basket blocks.

Making the Flowers

Follow these steps to make the flowers:

1. **On the wrong sides of each pink square, trace one flower using the solid *outside* lines on the pattern found at the end of this project. Repeat with the leaves using the assorted green scraps, and with the flower centers using the yellow scraps.**

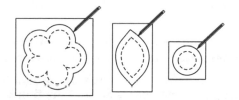

2. **Cut out the appliqués along the marked line.**

3. **On the non-shiny side of the freezer paper, mark six flowers, six flower centers, and 12 leaves using the *dashed inside* lines on the pattern.**

4. **Cut out the shapes.**

5. **Using a hot iron, press one paper flower to the center of each fabric flower (on the wrong side), having the shiny side of the freezer paper towards the flower fabric. Repeat with the leaves and flower centers.**

Freezer paper at center of each shape

6. **Using matching yellow thread for the flower center, stitch a line of running stitches in the fabric surrounding the circle of paper.**

   Pull the end of the thread to gather the fabric around the circle. Fasten off the thread and press the circle, using a little bit of spray starch.

   Repeat for all six flower centers.

7. **Using matching green thread, gather the seam allowances around the leaves in the same manner described in Step 6. Press and add a bit of spray starch.**

8. **To gather the seam allowances around the flowers, first clip into the inward points on each petal. Then, using matching pink thread, gather the petal edges in the same way that you gathered the edges of the leaves and the flower centers in Steps 6 and 7. Press, adding a bit of spray starch.**

Assembling the Quilt Top

1. **Using matching threads and the blind stitch, applique one flower, two leaves, and one flower center to the left sides of three basket blocks and to the right sides of the remaining three blocks.**

   Place the flowers near the area where the basket handle meets the lower basket section.

2. **Cut a length of the light pink six-strand floss the length of your arm. Separate this strand into two lengths having three strands each.**

3. **Thread a large-eyed needle with one of the three-strand lengths and hand embroider a ring of French knots around the flower centers of the three darkest pink flowers.**

4. **Repeat Step 3 using the dark pink floss in the same manner on the remaining three flowers.**

5. **From the green fabric, cut the sashing strips: cut eight strips $1^1/2$ inches x $10^1/2$ inches for D and cut three strips $1^1/2$ inches x $28^1/2$ inches for E.**

6. **Stitch three blocks alternately with four D strips to make a block row. Make two of these blocks rows.**

7. **Stitch the two block rows alternately with the three E strips to make the quilt center.**

8. **From the multicolored floral print cut the inner border strips: Cut two strips 1 inch x $23^1/2$ inches for the side borders (Border F) and cut two strips 1 inch x $29^1/2$ inches for the upper/lower borders (Border G).**

9. Stitch the side borders to the quilt center, followed by the upper and lower borders.

10. Press the seam allowances towards the floral print fabric.

11. Use the remaining floral fabric to cut the strips for the quilt binding.

12. Stitch the side and upper/lower borders cut in Step 8 to the quilt center, stitching the upper and lower borders in place first, followed by the side borders.

This completes the quilt top.

Completing Your Quilt

1. Layer the quilt top with the batting and backing fabric.

2. Hand or pin baste the layers together to prepare it for quilting.

3. Quilt as desired by hand or machine.

4. When you have completed the quilting, stitch very close to the raw edges of the quilt top by machine.

5. Trim away the excess batting and backing fabric that extends beyond the edges of the quilt top.

6. Bind your quilt.

7. Cut the yellow satin ribbon into six equal pieces.

8. Tie each piece of ribbon into a bow and hand-stitch one bow to each basket handle, using matching thread to finish the quilt.

Half-Size Basket Handle Guide and Full-Size Templates

Double the size of the basket handle (200 percent) for a full-size pattern.

Templates

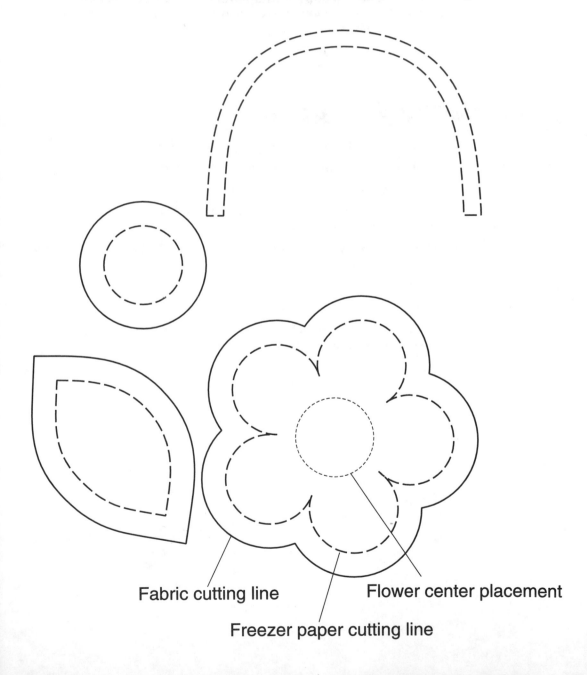

Fabric cutting line

Flower center placement

Freezer paper cutting line

Project 9

Traditional Basket Wallhanging

• •

Finished size: approximately 24 inches x 24 inches

• •

*T*his little wallhanging is made in a very traditional style, but with a modern twist. The appliqué style mimics time-consuming hand appliqué but utilizes machine stitching and clear nylon monofilament.

With this project, I also include an optional quilting pattern that you can hand or machine quilt into the dark blue triangles on the quilt.

Stashing Your Materials

Because this is a scrap-basket project, I list the following pieces according to their measurements rather than by the yard. If you can't find just the right piece in your own scrap basket, I suggest raiding your mother's or a friend's.

- 1 14^{1}/$_{2}$-inch x 14^{1}/$_{2}$-inch square of light-tan fabric for the center square
- 2 11-inch x 11-inch squares of dark-blue fabric for the large triangles
- 4 2^{1}/$_{2}$-inch x 20-inch strips of red-checkered fabric for the borders
- 4 2^{1}/$_{2}$-inch x 2^{1}/$_{2}$ squares of deep-yellow fabric for the cornerstones
- 1 12-inch x 12-inch square of medium-brown print for the basket appliqué
- 2 3-inch x 5-inch scraps each of light-green, medium-green, and dark-green fabrics for the leaves
- 4 5-inch x 7-inch scraps of assorted colors for the flower appliqués
- 4 3-inch x 4-inch scraps of assorted colors for flower-center appliqués
- 26-inch x 26-inch piece of fabric for the backing that coordinates with the others
- 3 yards of dark-blue quilt binding

✔ 1 26-inch x 26-inch piece of low-loft or traditional-weight batting

✔ All-purpose thread for assembly to match fabrics

✔ Clear nylon monofilament thread for the machine appliqué

✔ Wax-coated freezer paper

Creating Appliqué Shapes

Follow these steps to create your appliqué shapes:

1. **Trace all the appliqué shapes at the end of this project — six leaves, four flowers, four flower centers, and a basket — onto the unwaxed side of the freezer paper. Cut out all the shapes with scissors; be sure to use the ones reserved for paper or other uses — don't use your fabric-cutting scissors.**

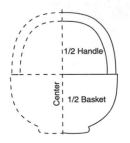

For the basket, join the basket handle to the basket base and then trace it. Reverse the pattern and trace the other half of the basket so that you have the full pattern.

2. **Start pressing! Press the cut-out leaf shapes to the wrong sides of the green appliqué fabrics, press the cut-out flowers to the wrong sides of the flower fabrics, press the flower centers to the wrong sides of the fabric for the flower centers, and press the basket pieces to the wrong side of the fabric for the basket. Be sure to leave at least ¹/₂ inch to 1 inch between the paper pieces.**

Although you can use freezer paper many different ways, as explained in previous chapters, use it here with the waxed (shiny) side pressed to the wrong sides of the fabrics. See Chapter 7 for more on pressing.

3. **Using scissors, cut out each shape ¹/₄ inch to ¹/₂ inch from the edges of the freezer paper.**

If you're uncomfortable with eyeballing this distance, feel free to draw a line around each shape ¹/₄ inch to ¹/₂ inch from the edges.

4. **To prepare the leaf, flower, and flower-center pieces for appliqué, turn the seam allowances to the wrong sides of the appliqué and secure them in place. Thread a hand-sewing needle with thread to match the colors of the different appliqués, and carefully stitch near the edges of the seam allowances using a long running stitch. Pull the thread gently to gather the seam allowances around the paper shapes.**

The thread should be stitched through the fabric only — not through the paper.

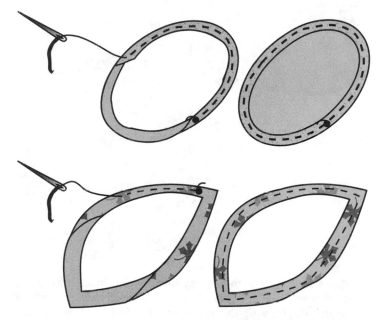

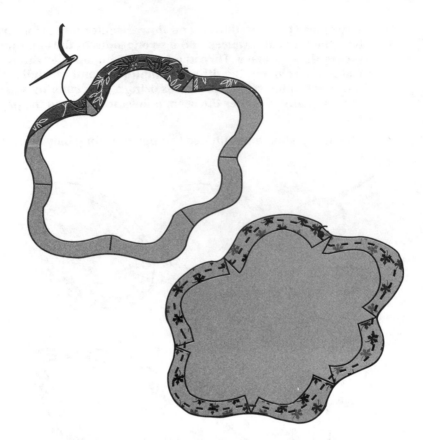

5. **Mist the shapes with a spray bottle containing water and press them until they're dry. Carefully remove the freezer paper from the appliqués, leaving the running stitches intact (hence the reason for the matching shade of thread).**

6. **Repeat Steps 4 and 5 with the basket, now that you have the hang of it.**

Appliquéing the Shapes

Follow these steps to appliqué the shapes onto your quilt top:

1. **Arrange the pressed appliqué shapes on the light-tan center square as in the following figure.**

Feel free to alter the arrangement to suit yourself.

2. **Pin or baste the pieces in place on the center square to prepare them for machine appliqué.**

3. **Load light tan thread in your machine's bobbin case and load clear nylon thread throughout the machine. Set your machine for the blindstitch.**

4. **Test sew a length of blindstitch on a scrap of fabric to test your stitch.**

   If you notice that the bobbin thread is being pulled to the top of the fabric, loosen the tension of the upper thread slightly until the problem is corrected.

5. **Machine appliqué the pieces to the light tan square using a blindstitch, placing the straight-stitch portion of the stitch off the edge of the appliqué, and the zigzag portion of the stitch so that it just catches the appliqué.**

   Remember that you want the thread to hide close to the edge of the appliqué where you can't see it. Then everyone will think that you hand appliquéd the project, and you'll be a quilting hero.

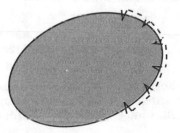

6. **After appliquéing all your shapes in place, remove your pins or basting stitches.**

Assembling the Quilt Top

Follow these steps to assemble your quilt top:

1. **Cut each of the two 11-inch x 11-inch dark-blue squares in half on the diagonal. Fold each triangle in half and press the fabric to mark the center of the long bias edge.**

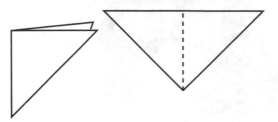

   You make two large triangles from each square — four triangles total. Because this may be the first time you've ever attempted this, I have built in a fudge factor for you to ensure you end up with accurate squares.

2. **Find the center of a side of the tan center square and align it with the center crease of a blue triangle. Stitch the blue triangle to the side of the tan square.**

3. **Repeat Step 2 with the other three blue squares; then press all the seam allowances towards the blue fabric.**

   Your triangles may look a little rough, or downright crooked even. That's okay. Remember the fudge factor? In the next step, you tidy up those rough edges.

4. **Trim the blue triangles with a rotary cutter and ruler so that the triangles extend just ¼ inch from the center points of the tan square, as shown on the opposite page.**

   Be sure to stay squared!

5. **Measure across the entire quilt center from one end to the other widthwise.**

6. **Trim the red-checkered border strips to match your measurement from Step 5. Stitch one red-check strip to each side of the quilt center.**

7. **Stitch a cornerstone to the short ends of the two remaining red-checkered border strips and stitch them to the top and bottom edges of the quilt. Press the seam allowances toward the border strips.**

   This step completes the quilt top.

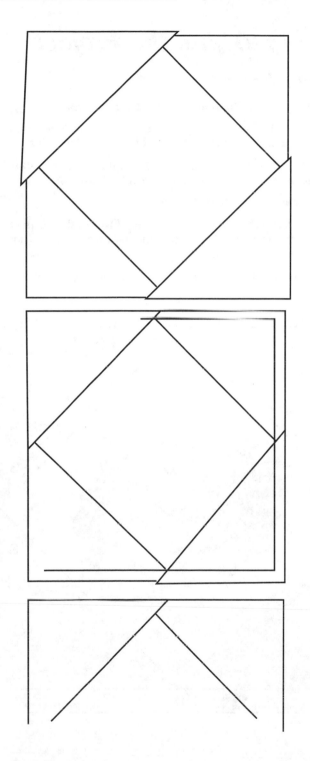

Quilting and Finishing the Project

Follow these steps to complete your project:

1. **Transfer your quilting markings to the quilt top.**

   If you want, you can double the size of the quilting pattern (included with this project) and use it in each of the blue triangles.

2. **Layer the quilt top with the batting and backing, and hand or pin baste the layers together to prepare it for quilting.**

3. **Hand or machine quilt as desired.**

4. **Machine stitch close to the raw edges of the quilt top in straight stitch; then trim away the excess batting and backing that extends beyond the edges of the quilt top.**

5. **Bind the quilt with the binding to complete the project.**

Half-Size Quilting Pattern and Full-Size Templates

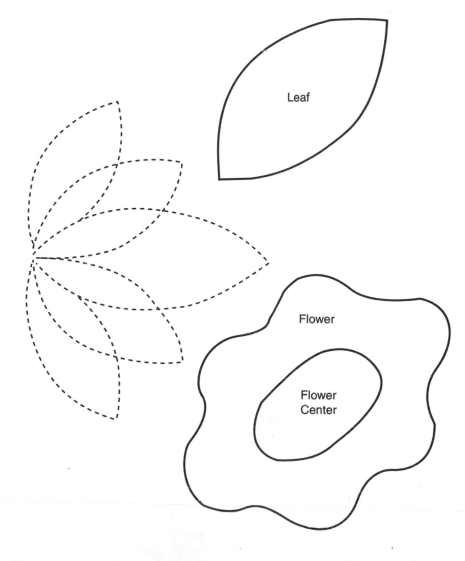

Leaf

Flower

Flower
Center

Templates

Double the size of the quilting pattern (200 percent) for a full-size pattern.

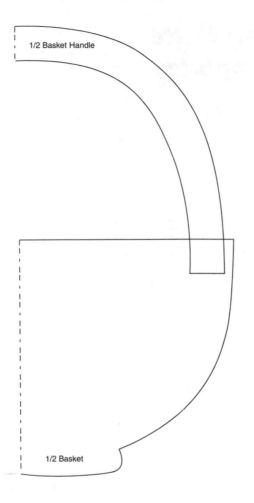

1/2 Basket Handle

1/2 Basket

Double the size (200 percent) for a full-size pattern.

Project 10

Pieced Blossoms Lap Quilt

- -

Finished size: 36 inches x 51 inches

Finished block size: 8 inches x 13 inches

- -

*T*he pieced blossoms lap quilt has a "controlled" scrappy look to it. You can stitch this quilt in a multitude of bright, cheery spring pastels or perhaps choose some spunky primary tones for a real splash of color.

This quilt utilizes template-free rotary cutting techniques, and you can complete the project quickly and effortlessly. Although you trim and discard small bits of fabric, this quilt is not at all wasteful, and you'll love the speed-piecing techniques. No need to trace those tedious pattern pieces with this one!

For best results, use a multitude of different pink fabrics — the more the better! The yardage requirements listed below are approximate, due to the fact that you may want to add to or scale down the number of pinks used in the project according to your own preferences.

Stashing Your Materials

You will need the following materials for the Pieced Blossoms Lap Quilt:

- 🡒 $^3/_4$ yard of cream-colored fabric for the background
- 🡒 $^1/_2$ yard of multicolored print or floral fabric for the outer borders
- 🡒 $^1/_4$ yard *each* of six to eight different shades of pink print fabric for the flowers
- 🡒 $^1/_4$ yard *each* of six to eight different shades of green print fabric for the leaves

✔ Scraps of assorted yellow prints (as many as you would like) for the flower centers

✔ ¹⁄₃ yard of yellow fabric for the inner borders

✔ 1 40-inch x 55-inch piece of coordinating fabric for the backing

✔ 1 40-inch x-55-inch piece of quilt batting, any loft except high-loft

✔ All-purpose threads to match the fabrics (cream, pink, green, and yellow)

✔ 6 yards of green quilt binding

Cutting the Pieces

For best results, use a rotary cutter and ruler to cut the pieces. Not only will you get more accurate cutting edges, but you'll also save a tremendous amount of time!

1. **Cut the strips for the borders and sashing per Table PB-1, and then set them aside.**

Table PB-1	Cutting the Border and Sashing Strips		
Fabric Color	*Piece*	*Amount*	*Size in Inches*
Multicolored print	Border A	2	$3^1/_2$ x $45^1/_2$
	Border B	2	$3^1/_2$ x $36^1/_2$
Yellow	Border C	2	$1^1/_2$ x $43^1/_2$
	Border D	2	$1^1/_2$ x $28^1/_2$
Cream	Sashing E	12	$1^1/_2$ x $13^1/_2$
	Sashing F	4	$1^1/_2$ x $28^1/_2$

2. **Cut the pieces for the blocks according to Table PB-2, keeping in mind that each block requires two different shades of pink and green.**

   I broke down one block into individual units so you can get a better visual idea of what pieces you need for each block.

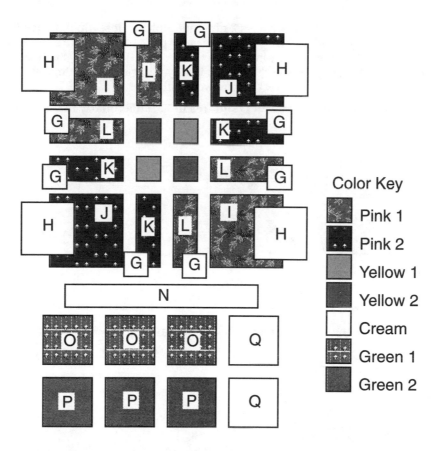

Color Key

Pink 1
Pink 2
Yellow 1
Yellow 2
Cream
Green 1
Green 2

Table PB-2	Cutting the Pieces for the Nine Blocks		
Fabric	**Piece**	**Amount**	**Size in Inches**
Cream	G — Small squares (8 per block)	72	$1^{1}/_{2}$ x $1^{1}/_{2}$
	H — Large squares (4 per block)	36	$2^{1}/_{2}$ x $2^{1}/_{2}$
Pink	I — Pink square #1 (2 per block)	18	$3^{1}/_{2}$ x $3^{1}/_{2}$
	J — Pink square #2 (2 per block)	18	$3^{1}/_{2}$ x $3^{1}/_{2}$
	K — Pink strip #1 (4 per block)	36	$1^{1}/_{2}$ x $3^{1}/_{2}$
	L — Pink strip #2 (4 per block)	36	$1^{1}/_{2}$ x $3^{1}/_{2}$
Yellow print	M — Yellow centers (4 per block)	72	$1^{1}/_{2}$ x $1^{1}/_{2}$
Cream	N — Block band (1 per block)	9	$1^{1}/_{2}$ x $8^{1}/_{2}$
Green	O — Green unit #1 (3 per block)	27	$2^{7}/_{8}$ x $2^{7}/_{8}$
	P — Green unit #2 (3 per block)	27	$2^{7}/_{8}$ x $2^{7}/_{8}$
Cream	Q — Cream units (2 per block)	18	$2^{7}/_{8}$ x $2^{7}/_{8}$

NOTE: Each block uses 2 different pink fabrics, which I have labeled as pink 1 and pink 2. Cut all pieces for pink 1 from the first pink fabric, and cut all pieces for pink 2 from the second pink fabric. Each block uses a different pink 1 and 2 (which is why you can have as many different pinks in this project as you would like!).

3. **Cut all the O, P, and Q squares in half diagonally to make triangles.**

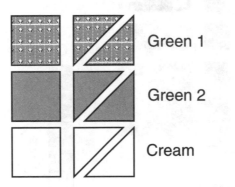

Green 1

Green 2

Cream

4. **On the *wrong side* of each of the cream G and H pieces, mark a diagonal line.**

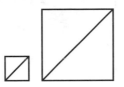

Do not cut this line! This will become a stitching line.

Assembling the Quilt Top

Note: All seam allowances are $1/4$ inch and are included in all the given measurements.

After you cut and prepare all the block pieces, you need to stitch the blocks together and assemble the quilt top:

1. **Place a marked H piece on one corner of each pink I piece, with their right sides facing.**

   Stitch along the diagonal lines of each H piece.

   Trim the excess from the corners of the pieces, $1/4$ inch from the stitching lines, and then discard the excess.

   Press the corners open to make square petal units You will have 18 of these H/I units.

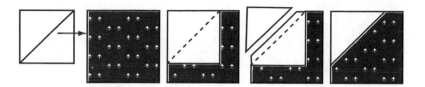

2. Repeat Step 1 using the J pieces and the remaining H pieces You will also have 18 of these H/J units.

3. Stitch one G piece to one K piece, stitching along the marked line on the G piece. Trim the excess ¹/₄ inch from the stitching line and discard this excess. Press the unit open.

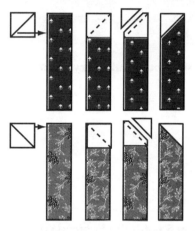

Make 18 of these right-facing petal strips — two for each block.

4. With the remaining G and K pieces, make 18 left-facing petal strips — which are the reverse of the petal strips that you made in Step 3.

5. Repeat Steps 3 and 4 with the L pieces and the remaining G pieces.

You end up with 18 left-facing petal strip units for both pink 1 and pink 2, and 18 right-facing petal strip units for both pink 1 and pink 2. (36 left and 36 right.)

6. **Stitch a yellow M piece to the bottom of every *right-facing* petal strip.**

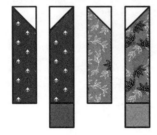

7. **Stitch a petal strip from Step 6 (with the M piece attached) and a left-facing petal strip to each petal unit that you made in Steps 1 through 3.**

   Be sure to stitch petal strips from pink 1 to the petal units from pink 1 and vice versa. You will have 18 petals made from pink 1 and 18 from pink 2.

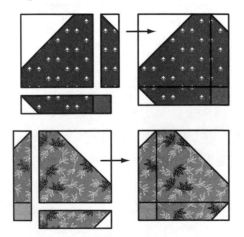

8. Stitch two petal squares of each fabric together to form a flower block. Make nine of these flowers.

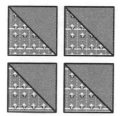

9. Referring to the diagrams, stitch four O triangles to four P triangles to form a leaf section.

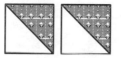

10. Stitch two O triangles to two Q triangles to form a leaf section.

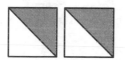

11. Stitch two P triangles and two Q triangles to form a leaf section.

12. Stitch together the eight leaf sections from Steps 9 through 11 to make the leaf unit.

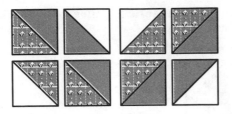

13. Stitch an N strip to the top edge of the leaf unit you just made in Step 12.

14. Repeat Steps 9 through 13 to create nine leaf units.

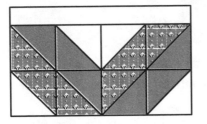

15. Stitch the nine completed leaf units to the nine completed flowers to make the nine blocks.

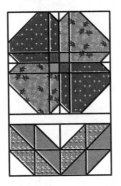

16. Stitch three blocks alternately with four of the cream E sashing strips. Press seam allowances toward the sashing strips. Make three of these block rows.

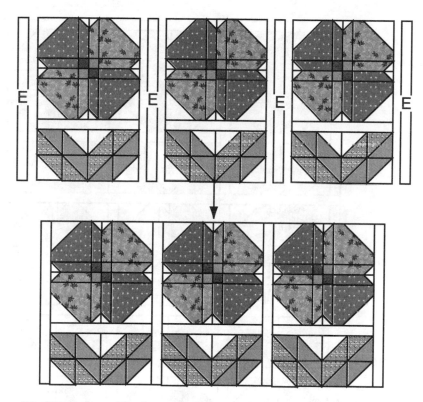

17. Stitch three block rows alternately with the four cream F sashing strips to make the quilt center, shown on the following page.

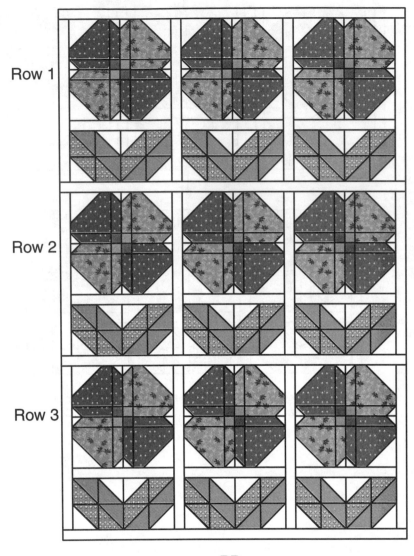

Row 1

Row 2

Row 3

PB

18. Stitch the two yellow C borders to the sides of the quilt center. Stitch the two yellow D borders to the top and bottom of the quilt center.

19. Repeat Step 18 with the two A and two B borders.

Quilting and Finishing Your Quilt

To finish your quilt:

1. Layer the quilt top with the batting and backing and hand or pin baste the layers together to prepare it for quilting.

2. Hand or machine quilt as desired.

3. To finish the quilt, stitch close to the raw edges of the quilt top. Trim away the batting and backing that extends beyond the edges of the quilt top.

4. Bind the quilt to complete the project.

Project 11

Winter Holly Lap Quilt or Wallhanging

Finished block size: $8^1/_2$ inches x $8^1/_2$ inches

Finished size of quilt: 36 inches x 36 inches

*U*se an assortment of green scraps to give your quilt a charming, old-fashioned look. You can even use this pattern to create a Charm Quilt by trading green fabric pieces with your friends and using a different green for each leaf.

Stashing Your Materials

You will need the following materials for the Winter Holly Lap Quilt or Wallhanging:

- 1 yard of tan fabric for the block background areas
- $^3/_4$ yard *total* of at least 6 different green fabrics for the leaves — the more the better!
- $^1/_2$ yard of red-print fabric for the bows
- 1 yard of paper-backed fusible webbing for the bows
- 1 40-inch x 40-inch piece of coordinating fabric for the backing
- 1 40-inch x 40-inch piece of traditional or lightweight batting
- All-purpose threads to match the fabrics (tan, green, and red)
- $4^1/_2$ yards of dark green quilt binding
- 1 $^7/_8$-inch-diameter button (for the center of quilt)
- 4 $^3/_4$-inch-diameter red buttons (for the side blocks)

Cutting the Pieces

Follow these steps to cut out the pieces of your quilt. Note: All seam allowances are $1/4$ inch and are included in all the given measurements.

1. **Create templates from the full-size leaf and bow patterns.**

2. **Cut the border strips, sashing strips, and block pieces according to the measurements in Table WH-1, and then set them aside.**

Table WH-1		Pieces to Cut	
Fabric	*Piece*	*Quantity*	*Size in Inches*
Tan	Border A	2	$2^1/2$ x $36^1/2$
	Border B	2	$2^1/2$ x $32^1/2$
	Border E	2	$2^1/2$ x $30^1/2$
	Border F	2	$2^1/2$ x $26^1/2$
	Sashing G	2	$1^1/2$ x $26^1/2$
	Sashing H	6	$1^1/2$ x $8^1/2$
	Piece I	4	$4^1/2$ x $8^1/2$
	Piece J	4	$4^1/2$ x $4^1/2$
	Squares	24	$2^7/8$ x $2^7/8$
Red	Border C	2	$1^1/2$ x $32^1/2$
	Border D	2	$1^1/2$ x $30^1/2$

3. **Cut the tan squares in half diagonally to make 48 triangles.**

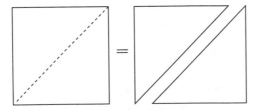

4. **From the green fabrics, cut a total of 48 pieces using the leaf template at the end of this project.**

For faster cutting, cut your green fabrics into 2-inch-wide strips, stack them, and cut through all the layers at once using your rotary cutter and see-through ruler. These strips can be any length; they can be the entire length if you're working with yardage, or smaller lengths if you decide to pull fabrics from your scrap bag.

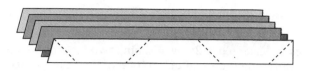

5. Trace four bow shapes in pencil onto the paper side of the fusible webbing.

6. Fuse the four bow shapes to the wrong side of the remaining red fabric and then cut them out neatly with your fabric-only scissors.

Assembling the Quilt Center

Follow these steps to assemble the quilt center:

1. Assemble a leaf section by stitching one tan triangle to a green leaf piece. Create 48 leaf sections.

2. Stitch two leaf sections together to form a leaf square. Repeat this step until you have 24 leaf squares.

   It doesn't matter which green fabrics you stitch together to form the leaf squares. The squares can be as scrappy or as orderly as you like.

3. Assemble the following three blocks that are used in this quilt (for the sake of convenience, I call them blocks 1, 2, and 3):

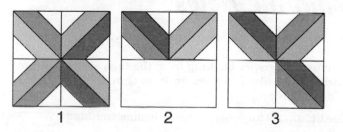

1   2   3

- **Block 1:** Make one block 1 by stitching four of the leaf squares together. Block 1 is the center block of the quilt.

- **Block 2:** Make block 2s by stitching two leaf squares together and then stitching the 2-leaf unit to one of the I pieces. You need four of these center-side blocks.

- **Block 3:** You need four block 3s, which you make by stitching two leaf squares together and one leaf square to one J piece. Stitch the two-leaf section to the one-leaf section to make a block. These are called the corner blocks.

4. **Stitch the blocks into a horizontal row by stitching two block 3s and one block 2 alternately with two of the H sashing strips. Form two of these rows.**

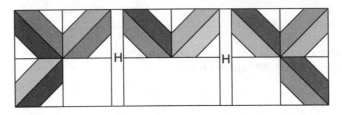

5. **Stitch two block 2s and the block 1 alternately with the two remaining H sashing strips.**

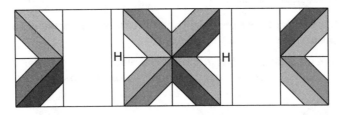

6. **Stitch the three rows together with the two G sashing strips between them.**

You have now completed construction of the quilt center and are ready to begin the appliqué process.

Appliquéing the Bows

Follow these steps to appliqué the bows on your quilt top:

1. **Remove the paper backing from the bow shapes and fuse one bow to each corner block of your quilt, as shown in the figure at the beginning of this project.**

See Chapter 9 for more on using fusible webbing.

2. Machine appliqué the bows in place using red thread and a medium-width machine satin stitch.

Quilting and Finishing the Project

Follow these steps to finish your project:

1. Complete the quilt top by adding the borders to the quilt center. Stitch the tan F and E strips first, then stitch the red D and C strips, and finish with the tan B and A strips.

2. Layer the quilt top with the batting and backing fabric, and then hand or pin baste the layers of the quilt sandwich together to prepare your project for quilting.

3. Hand or machine quilt as desired.

   I machine quilted the sample in this book's color insert in a large, meandering stipple pattern.

4. Machine straight stitch $1/8$ inch from the raw edges of the quilt top.

5. Using your fabric scissors or your rotary cutter and ruler, trim away the excess batting and backing fabric that extends beyond the edges of the quilt top.

6. Bind the quilt with the green binding.

7. Hand stitch the large button to the center square with red thread. Stitch the smaller buttons to the center-side squares in the same manner — they're the holly berries!

Your quilt is now complete!

Leaf Template and Half-Size Appliqué Pattern

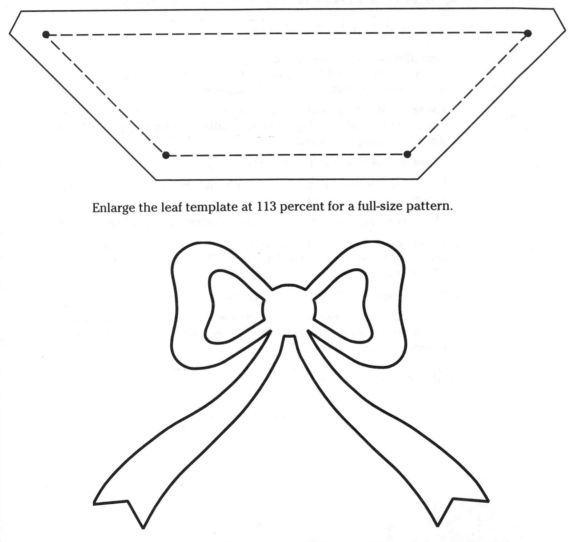

Enlarge the leaf template at 113 percent for a full-size pattern.

Double the size of the bow pattern (200 percent) for a full-size pattern.

Project 12

Scrappy Pines Lap or Nap Quilt

Finished size of quilt: 79 inches x 50 inches

Finished size of tree block: 6 inches x 10 inches

1 love scrap basket projects! They have such a warm and inviting look to them. Pull lots of different green and brown fabrics from your stash to make this quilt. If you find yourself low on a particular color, trade fabrics with a friend.

Also, in this quilt, you can play with some of your machine's decorative or utility stitches. Refer to your owner's manual for instructions on setting up the machine for decorative stitching, if needed.

You see some of the stitches used in the illustration that follows. Feel free to experiment with your machine's stitch repertoire!

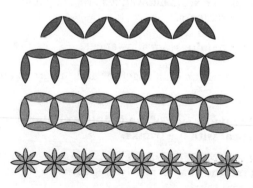

Of course, you can substitute satin stitch appliqué for the decorative stitching, if desired.

Stashing Your Materials

The list in this section describes the fabrics and notions you need to make the Scrappy Pines Lap or Nap Quilt:

- ✔ 20 rectangles of assorted tan fabrics measuring 6^1/$_2$ inches x 10^1/$_2$ inches for the tree block rectangles
- ✔ 20 5-inch x 8-inch pieces of assorted green fabrics for the tree appliqués
- ✔ 20 1-inch x 2-inch pieces of assorted brown fabrics for the trunk appliqués
- ✔ ^{1}/$_2$ yard of tan fabric for the sashing
- ✔ ^{1}/$_3$ yard rust print fabric for the block borders
- ✔ 2 yards green print fabric for the outer borders
- ✔ 2 yards of 18-inch-wide paper-backed fusible webbing for appliqué
- ✔ 20 5-inch x 9-inch pieces of tear-away stabilizer for appliqué
- ✔ All-purpose threads to match fabrics, including green, brown, and tan
- ✔ 1 85-inch x 55-inch piece of coordinating fabric for the backing
- ✔ 1 85-inch x 55-inch piece of low- to medium-loft quilt batting
- ✔ 8 yards of rust-colored quilt binding

Appliquéing the Quilt Blocks

As for all quilts in this book, the seam allowances are ^{1}/$_4$ inch and are included in the given measurements.

The appliqué pieces do not require seam allowances.

Use the tan thread for stitching the quilt together and the green and brown threads for the appliqué:

1. **Trace 20 trees on the paper side of the fusible webbing. Cut out the shapes roughly. Repeat with the trunks.**

2. **Fuse the trees to the wrong sides of the 20 pieces of green fabric for the appliqués. Cut out the shapes neatly. Repeat with the trunks and the 20 pieces of brown fabric.**

3. **Remove the paper backings from the appliqués and arrange one tree and trunk on the center of each of the 20 block rectangles.**

   Tuck the top edge of the trunk just under the tree bottom to conceal the raw edge under the tree.

4. **Fuse the tree and trunk pieces in place on the blocks with your hot iron (refer to the insert that accompanied your fusible webbing for iron settings).**

5. **Pin a piece of tear-away stabilizer to the wrong side of each tree block.**

   Place the pins at the corners to keep them away from the stitching areas.

6. **Using the brown thread, machine appliqué the trunks in place on all blocks using different decorative or utility stitches. Change the thread to green and repeat with the trees.**

When you have completed the stitching, remove the pins and tear away the paper stabilizer from the blocks.

Assembling the Quilt Top

After you cut and prepare all the block pieces, you need to stitch the blocks together and assemble the quilt top. *Note:* All seam allowances are $1/4$ inch and are included in all the given measurements.

1. **From the rust fabric, cut 40 strips measuring 1 inch x $10^1/2$ inches for the side block borders (the finished size of these strips is a mere $1/2$ inch).**

2. **Also from the rust fabric, cut 40 strips measuring 1 inch x $7^1/2$ inches for the upper/lower block borders.**

3. **Stitch the side block borders to the blocks.**

4. **Press the seam allowances toward the rust strips.**

5. **Stitch the upper and lower borders to the blocks and press in the same manner.**

6. From the tan fabric, cut six strips $2^1/_2$ inches x $38^1/_2$ inches for the horizontal sashing strips.

7. From the same tan fabric, cut 25 strips measuring $2^1/_2$ inches x $11^1/_2$ inches for the vertical sashing strips.

8. Stitch five of the vertical sashing strips alternately with four of the appliquéd blocks to make a row. Make five of these rows.

9. Stitch the five rows alternately with the six horizontal sashing strips to make the quilt center.

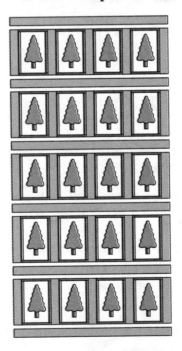

10. From the green fabric, cut two side-border strips measuring $6^1/_2$ inches x $67^1/_2$ inches and two strips (one each) for the upper/lower border strips measuring $6^1/_2$ inches x $50^1/_2$ inches.

11. Stitch the side borders to the sides of the quilt center.

12. Press the seam allowances towards the green fabric.

13. Stitch the upper/lower borders to the top and bottom edges of the quilt center.

14. Press as for the side borders.

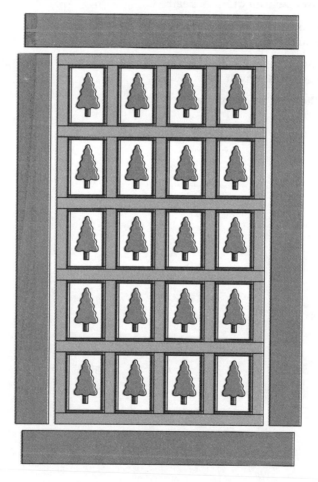

Quilting Your Quilt

To finish your quilt:

1. **Layer the quilt top with the batting and backing.**

2. **Hand or machine quilt as desired.**

3. **When you have completed the quilting, stitch close to the raw edges of the quilt top.**

4. **Trim away the excess batting and backing fabric that extends beyond the edges of the quilt top.**

5. **Bind the quilt to complete it.**

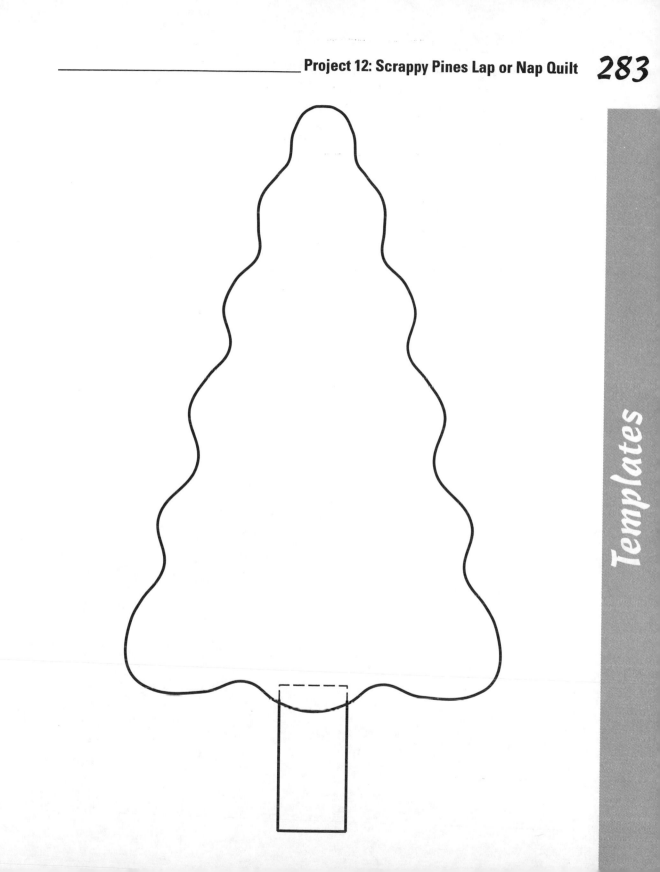

Project 13

Rosy Wreath Quilt

Finished size of quilt: 39 inches x 39 inches

Finished size of block: 15 inches x 15 inches

*H*ere's a fun and easy quilt that combines strip-piecing, hand appliqué, and hand embroidery. Don't let the combination of techniques scare you! The strip-piecing is a breeze and is great practice when learning to use your cutter.

This project works up quickly and with little effort. After assembling the rose units, prepare the leaf shapes and take the project along on your commute or vacation.

Stashing Your Materials

The list in this section describes the fabrics and notions you need to make the Rosy Wreath Quilt:

- ⚐ ³/₄ yard of white solid fabric for blocks and sashing
- ⚐ ¹/₃ yard of dark pink print for flowers
- ⚐ ¹/₃ yard of medium pink print for flowers
- ⚐ ¹/₂ yard of green print for leaves and outer borders
- ⚐ ¹/₃ yard of golden yellow print for flower centers and inner borders
- ⚐ 1 45-inch x 45-inch piece of coordinating fabric for the backing

✔ 1 45-inch x 45-inch piece of low- or traditional-loft quilt batting

✔ $\frac{1}{2}$ yard of 12-inch-wide, wax-coated freezer paper

✔ All-purpose threads in white and green to match the green fabric

✔ 6-strand cotton embroidery floss to match the green fabric

✔ 5 yards of pink quilt binding

All seam allowances are the standard $\frac{1}{4}$ inch and are included in the given measurements or directions.

Cutting the Pieces

For best results, use a rotary cutter and ruler to cut the pieces. Not only will you get more accurate cutting edges, but you'll also save a tremendous amount of time!

1. **Cut the strips for the flower units according to Table RW-1.**

Table RW-1	Cutting the Flower Units	
Fabric Color	*Size in Inches*	*Amount*
Dark pink	$2\frac{1}{2}$ x 44	2
Medium pink	$2\frac{1}{2}$ x 44	2
White	$1\frac{1}{2}$ x 44	4

2. **Cut the sashing and border strips according to Table RW-2 and set them aside for later use.**

Table RW-2	Cutting the Border and Sashing Strips		
Fabric Color	*Piece*	*Size in Inches*	*Amount*
White	Vertical sashing	$1\frac{1}{2}$ x $15\frac{1}{2}$	6
White	Horizontal sashing	$1\frac{1}{2}$ x $33\frac{1}{2}$	3
Golden yellow	Inner border	$1\frac{1}{2}$x $33\frac{1}{2}$	2
Golden yellow	Inner border	$1\frac{1}{2}$ x $35\frac{1}{2}$	2
Green	Vertical outer border	$2\frac{1}{2}$ x $35\frac{1}{2}$	2
Green	Horizontal outer border	$2\frac{1}{2}$ x $39\frac{1}{2}$	2

3. Cut the remaining pieces from the leftover fabrics, using Table RW-3.

Table RW-3	Cutting the Remaining Pieces		
Fabric Color	*Piece*	*Size in Inches*	*Amount*
White squares	Block centers and leaf blocks	$5^1/_2$ x $5^1/_2$	20
Golden yellow	Squares for flower centers	$1^1/_2$ x $1^1/_2$	16

Creating the Flower Squares

Follow these steps to create the flower squares:

1. **Stitch one of the white strips from Table RW-1 to one long side of each pink strip, having their right sides together.**

   You will have two medium-pink 2-strip units and two dark-pink 2-strip units. Press the seam allowances towards the pink fabric.

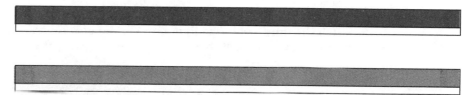

2. **Cut sixteen $2^1/_2$-inch units from each dark and medium pink strip that you assembled in Step 1.**

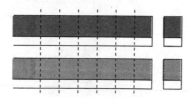

   These are the petal units. You will have 32 units of each color, measuring $2^1/_2$ inches x $3^1/_2$ inches.

3. **Follow Steps 4 through 7 to create flower square units.**

   You will stitch together one golden yellow $1^1/_2$-inch square, two medium-pink petal units, and two dark-pink petal units.

4. **Stitch one yellow center square to one of the medium pink petal units: Place the right sides together and stitch only halfway across the yellow center square as shown. Press the yellow square outwards to prepare it for the next petal.**

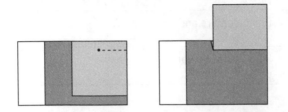

5. **Stitch the next petal (dark pink) to the resulting unit as shown, stitching down the entire length this time. Press the petal unit outwards.**

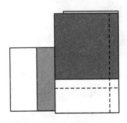 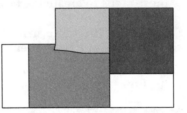

6. **Stitch the third petal (medium pink) to the unit in the same manner, pressing the petal outwards.**

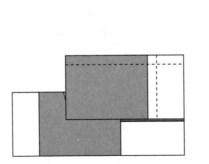 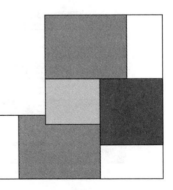

7. **Stitch the fourth and final petal (dark pink) to the unit in two steps.**

First, stitch the final petal to the previous petal as you did for the previous two in Steps 4 and 5. Press the petal outwards.

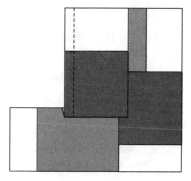 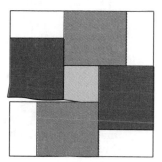

Second, fold the resulting unit so that the edges of the two unstitched sides are together, right sides facing. Stitch across this edge and end your stitching at the center square's halfway point (where you began your stitching).

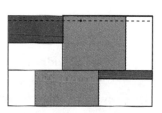 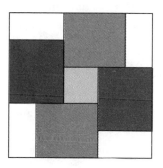

This completes a flower square.

8. **Make 15 additional flower squares.**

Creating the Leaf Squares

To create the leaf squares:

1. **On each of the white squares you cut using Table RW-3, trace the leaf shape and stem using the full-size appliqué pattern at the end of this project.**

Use a water-soluble pencil or chalk and trace very lightly.

2. **Using the leaf template at the end of this project, trace 16 leaves along the outer (solid) line, on the wrong side of the remaining green fabric. Cut out the leaves along the marked lines.**

3. **On the paper side (not the shiny side) of the freezer paper, trace 16 leaf shapes *without* seam allowances.**

   You'll be tracing the leaves along the dotted lines. Cut out the paper leaves along the marked lines.

4. **Iron one paper leaf shape, shiny (wax) side down, on the wrong side of each green-fabric leaf shape.**

   The wax coating will stick to the fabric easily.

5. **Turn under the seam allowances (¹/₄ inch) on all of the leaves and baste them down by hand with a needle and thread, stitching only through the seam allowance and not through to the right side of the leaf.**

6. **Gently pull your sewing thread to gather the seam allowance around the leaves, so the seam allowance will be on the underside (wrong side) of the leaf.**

   The figure that follows illustrates Steps 4 through 6.

   Press the leaves using a starch spray so that the edges of the leaves hold a nice crease.

7. **Carefully remove the freezer paper from the center of one leaf.**

   Be gentle so you don't mess up the creased leaf shape.

8. **Hand appliqué one leaf to each square marked in Step 1 using the tracing lines as a guide. Stitch the leaf in place using matching thread and the blind-stitch. Repeat for all 16 leaf squares.**

9. **Cut a length of the green six-strand embroidery floss as long as your arm. Divide the floss into two lengths, each having three strands, and thread a large-eyed needle with one three-strand section of floss.**

10. **Hand-embroider the stem line and tendril in stem-stitch. Repeat for all 16 leaf squares.**

Assembling the Quilt Top

1. Stitch one flower square to each side of the of the four remaining white squares from Table RW-3, as shown. Make four of these single-flower row units.

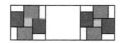

2. Stitch one leaf square to each side of one flower square, as shown. Make eight of these double-flower row units. Note the directional placement of the stems and leaves.

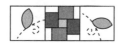

3. Stitch one double-flower row alternately with two single-flower rows, as shown, to complete a block. Make four of these blocks.

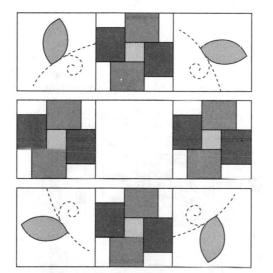

4. Stitch two blocks along with three white vertical sashing strips from Table RW-2. Make two of these block rows.

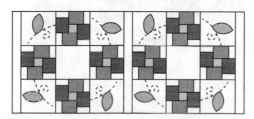

5. **To complete the quilt center, stitch the two block rows to the three horizontal sashing strips cut from Table RW-2. Trim excess sashing.**

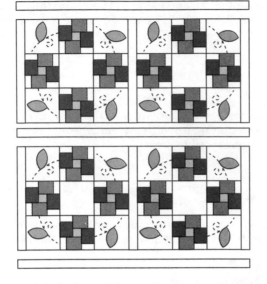

6. **Stitch the golden yellow inner border strips to the quilt center. Stitch the side borders first, followed by the upper and lower borders. Trim any excess. Press the seam allowances towards the border fabrics. Repeat with the green outer border strips to complete the quilt top.**

Quilting Your Quilt

To finish your quilt:

1. Layer the quilt top with the batting and backing.

2. Hand or pin baste the layers together to prepare it for quilting.

3. Hand or machine quilt as desired.

4. When you have completed the quilting, stitch very close to the raw edges of the quilt top and trim away the excess batting and backing that extends beyond the edges of the quilt top.

5. Bind the edges of the quilt to complete.

Full-Size Stem Diagram

Project 14

Scrappy Bloomers Wallhanging or Lap Quilt

- -

Finished size of quilt: 35 inches x 42 inches

- -

*T*his chapter tells you everything you need to know to create my Scrappy Bloomers quilt. Machine blanket stitch appliqué makes the quilt quick to construct, and the project's size makes it versatile — display the quilt as a decorative wallhanging or use it as a cozy lap quilt. This is a great project for using up all those scrap-basket fabrics that are just too pretty to throw away. The maximum size of scrap material needed is a mere 5 inches square, so save all those little bits and pieces!

To make your assortment of scraps even more interesting, swap scraps with your friends, or purchase a bunch of fat quarters.

Don't forget to prewash all fabrics before beginning this project.

Stashing Your Materials

In addition to basic supplies such as a pencil, ruler, pins, and scissors or a rotary cutter, you also need the following materials to create this quilt:

- ✔ ³/₄ yard of off-white fabric for the background blocks
- ✔ ¹/₂ yard of multi-colored floral print fabric for sashing and outermost border
- ✔ ¹/₃ yard of blue floral print fabric for the wide border
- ✔ ¹/₃ yard of medium green fabric for the leaves

✔ Assorted medium-toned pastel fabric scraps for the flowers (you'll need 20 pieces, each no smaller than 5 inches x 5 inches)

✔ ¼ yard of solid tan fabric for the flower centers

✔ 2 yards of paper-backed fusible webbing, 16-18 inches wide

✔ 20 6-inch x 6-inch pieces of tear-away stabilizer

✔ All-purpose thread for assembly in a neutral color, such as off-white

✔ Dark brown buttonhole twist or topstitching-weight thread for appliqué

✔ 5 yards of off-white quilt binding, either purchased ready-made or homemade according to the instructions in Chapter 13

✔ 1 37-inch x 44-inch piece of coordinating fabric for the backing

✔ 1 37-inch x-44-inch piece of traditional-weight batting

The following sections tell you how to create this project from start to finish. Please note that all seam allowances are the standard 1/4 inch and are included in all of the given measurements. The appliqués do not require seam allowances.

Preparing the Appliqué Pieces

The first step in creating the Scrappy Bloomers quilt is to prepare the flower appliqué shapes. The following steps explain this process:

1. **Using the full-size applique patterns at the end of this project, trace 20 flowers, 20 centers, and 20 sets of leaves onto the paper side of the fusible web using a regular pencil.**

   Because these flower pieces will be machine appliquéd onto blocks rather than pieced together, you don't need to add seam allowances when you trace the appliqué shapes onto the fusible webbing.

2. **Roughly cut out the fusible webbing pieces.**

3. **Using an iron, fuse these fusible webbing pieces to the wrong sides of their respective fabrics.**

   Fuse the leaf shapes to the green fabric, the flower center shapes to the tan fabric, and the flower shapes to the assorted scraps of fabric, referring to the insert that accompanied your brand of fusible webbing for iron settings.

4. **Cut out the web-backed fabric shapes, carefully following the outlines of the fusible web shapes.**

Appliquéing the Quilt Blocks

After you prepare your flower shapes, you're ready to appliqué them to the quilt blocks. The following steps tell you how:

1. **Cut out the pieces for the quilt top (see Table SB-1 for the dimensions and quantities of each piece).**

   Set aside all the sashing and border pieces. You only need the 20 off-white blocks right now.

Table SB-1		Quilt Top Pieces	
Piece	*Number of Pieces*	*Fabric*	*Size in Inches*
Block	20	Off-white	$6^1/_2$ x $6^1/_2$
Sashing A	25	Floral print	$1^1/_2$ x $6^1/_2$
Sashing B	6	Floral print	$1^1/_2$ x $29^1/_2$
Border C	2	Blue print	$1^1/_2$ x $36^1/_2$
Border D	2	Blue print	$1^1/_2$ x $31^1/_2$
Border E	2	Floral print	$2^1/_2$ x $38^1/_2$
Border F	2	Floral print	$2^1/_2$ x $35^1/_2$

2. **Remove the paper backings from the applique shapes. Arrange one flower and one set of leaves on each of the $6^1/_2$-inch off-white blocks. Fuse each set of appliqués to off-white blocks.**

3. **Draw stems with a washable pencil or tailor's chalk by drawing a straight line from the flower to the leaves.**

   You can do this freehand or use a ruler. You'll be stitching along the stem later.

4. **Place a piece of stabilizer against the wrong side of each block. Pin it in place at the corners with straight pins.**

5. **Load the buttonhole-weight thread in the upper part of your machine; wind a bobbin with the all-purpose thread and insert it in the machine's bobbin case.**

   The top (buttonhole-weight) thread is the one that will appear around each applique as the top-stitching thread.

6. **Stitch a sample of your machine's blanket stitch on a scrap of fabric.**

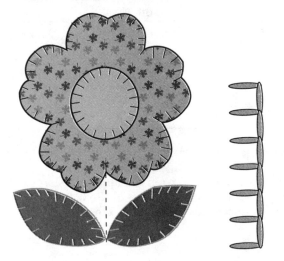

   If the bobbin thread is pulled through the fabric and onto the top surface of the sample, loosen the tension of the upper thread slightly (refer to your machine's owner's manual for help).

7. **Machine appliqué each piece on each block using your machine's blanket stitch.**

   The machine blanket stitch adds a decorative accent while also holding down your appliqué pieces.

   Stitch along the stem lines in a straight stitch using the same thread as for the appliqués — buttonhole twist in the top and all-purpose in the bobbin.

8. **Remove the pins holding the stabilizer in place and tear off the stabilizer from the back of the appliquéd block.**

Assembling the Quilt Top

After you appliqué your quilt blocks, you're ready to assemble the quilt top. Get out your sashing and border strips and follow these steps:

1. **Stitch five A sashing strips alternately with four appliquéd blocks to make a horizontal row. Press the seam allowances towards the sashing strips.**

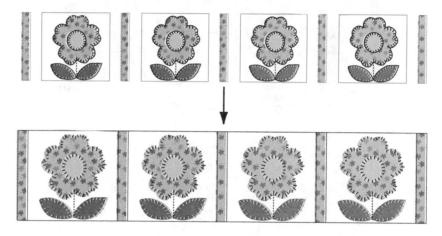

Make a total of five of these block rows.

2. **Stitch the five rows alternately with the B sashing strips to make the quilt center.**

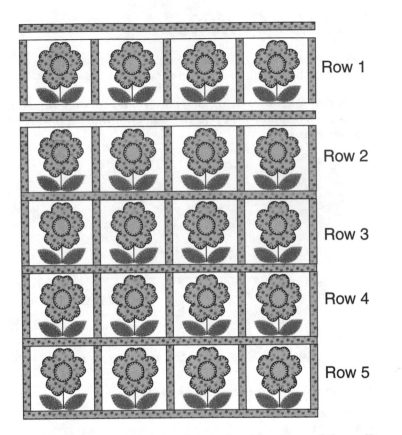

Row 1

Row 2

Row 3

Row 4

Row 5

3. **Stitch the C border strips to the side edges of the quilt center. Press the seam allowances toward the border strips. Then stitch the D border strips to the top and bottom edges of the quilt center. Press the seam allowances toward the border strips.**

4. Stitch the E border strips to the side edges of the quilt top. Press the seam allowances toward the border strips. Then stitch the F border strips to the top and bottom edges of the quilt top and press the seam allowances toward the border strips.

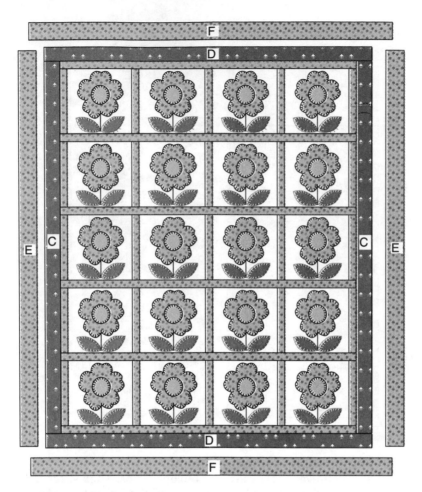

This completes the quilt top.

Quilting and Finishing the Project

You're in the home stretch now! The following steps explain how to quilt and finish your Scrappy Bloomers wallhanging:

1. **Layer the quilt top with the batting and backing and hand or pin baste the layers together for quilting.**

2. **Hand or machine quilt as desired.**

3. Stitch close to the raw edges (within $1/4$ inch to $1/8$ inch) of the quilt top and trim away any excess batting or backing fabric that extends beyond the edges of the quilt top.

4. Bind the quilt to finish the project.

Templates

Project 15

Snow Crystals Pieced and Appliquéd Lap Quilt

Finished size of quilt: 46 inches x 46 inches

peedy rotary-cutter techniques and machine blanket-stitch appliqué make this quilt quicker to assemble than it appears. The appliqué method that you use to make this quilt requires buttonhole-weight or topstitching-weight thread. Both of these threads are heavier than all-purpose thread and are used only for the appliqués. You assemble everything else with all-purpose thread.

If you don't care much for blanket stitch, try satin-stitch appliqué instead. For other ideas, refer to Chapter 9. Keep in mind, however, that for speed, blanket stitch beats satin stitch.

Stashing Your Materials

You will need the following materials to complete your Snow Crystals project:

- 2³/₄ yards of blue print or solid fabric (main color) for all areas
- 1¹/₄ yards of white cotton solid fabric for the snowflakes and the pieced border
- ³/₄ yard of mustard-yellow print or solid fabric for the block sashing and cornerstones
- 1¹/₂ yards of 16-to-18-inch-wide paper-backed fusible webbing

✔ 9 10-inch x 10-inch squares of tear-away stabilizer

✔ 1 50-inch x 50-inch square of traditional-weight batting

✔ 1 50-inch x 50-inch square of fabric for the backing

✔ All-purpose thread in colors to match fabrics (blue, white, and mustard-yellow)

✔ Buttonhole-weight mustard-yellow thread for appliqué

✔ $5^1/_2$ yards of bias binding

Cutting the Pieces

Follow these steps to cut out the quilt pieces:

1. **Cut out all the pieces of the project per the specifications in Table SC-1. For the best results, cut the pieces in the order that they're listed in this table.**

   To be sure that you have enough fabric for this project, cut out all the pieces across the width of the fabric (from selvage to selvage). For instance, to cut the C strips, cut three $2^1/_2$-inch x 44-inch strips of fabric, and then recut each 44-inch strip into $10^1/_2$-inch lengths (you'll get four C strips for each strip of fabric that you cut this way).

Table SC-1		Pieces to Cut	
Fabric	*Piece*	*Quantity*	*Size in Inches*
Blue	Blocks	9	$10^1/_2$ x $10^1/_2$
	A strip	4	$2^1/_2$ x $42^1/_2$
	B strip	4	$2^1/_2$ x $38^1/_2$
	C strip	12	$2^1/_2$ x $10^1/_2$
	D-1 piece	1	14 x 29
White	D-2 piece	1	14 x 29
Mustard-yellow	E strip	36	1 x 11
	F square	12	$2^1/_2$ x $2^1/_2$

2. **Using a regular pencil (a #2 is fine here!), trace nine snowflake shapes on the paper side of the fusible webbing, directly over the full-size pattern.**

   Because you fuse these shapes in place and use machine appliqué, the snowflakes don't require seam allowances.

3. **Fuse the snowflakes to the remaining piece of white fabric. Cut out the snowflake shapes neatly with scissors.**

4. **Remove the paper backings from the snowflakes and fuse one snowflake to the center of each of the 10$\frac{1}{2}$-inch blue blocks.**

Appliquéing the Snowflakes

Follow these steps to appliqué the snowflakes to your quilt blocks:

1. **Pin a piece of tear-away stabilizer to the backside of each snowflake block to prepare it for machine appliqué. Position the pins so that they won't interfere with your stitching — about $\frac{1}{2}$ inch from the appliqués is a good distance.**

   The tear-away stabilizer keeps the blocks from being shoved down into the machine's throat plate and jammed by the actions of the needle and feed dogs — growl!

2. **Load the top of the machine with the buttonhole-weight mustard-yellow thread. Use blue or white all-purpose thread in the bobbin case.**

3. **Using a scrap of fabric, test sew a sample of your machine's blanket stitch.**

   You want to be certain that your machine is making a well-formed blanket stitch before you begin your machine appliqué — it's better to test now than to rip out the threads later!

   If you notice that the bobbin thread is being pulled through the fabric onto the top surface, slightly loosen the tension for the upper thread. If you find yourself encountering difficulty, refer to Chapter 10 and consult your machine's owner's manual.

4. **Machine appliqué the snowflakes to the blocks and then remove the stabilizer.**

Assembling the Quilt Top

Note: All seam allowances are $1/4$ inch and are included in all the given measurements.

Follow these steps to assemble the top of your quilt:

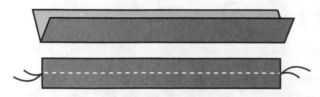

1. **Fold each of the mustard-yellow E strips in half lengthwise, wrong sides facing, and then press the strips.**

2. **Place one pressed E strip along one edge of a block, aligning the double raw edges of the strip with the raw edge of the block. Using matching all-purpose thread, stitch the strip in place using a scant**

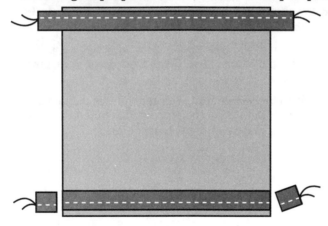

   (slightly less than) $1/4$**-inch seam allowance and then trim the excess overhang. Repeat this process with the other three sides of the block.**

3. **Repeat Step 2 to stitch four E strips to each of the nine blocks.**

4. **Stitch three of the completed blocks alternately with four of the C strips to make one row. Repeat to make a total of three rows.**

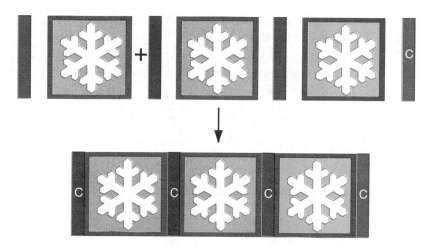

5. Stitch the three rows alternately with the four blue B strips to make the quilt center.

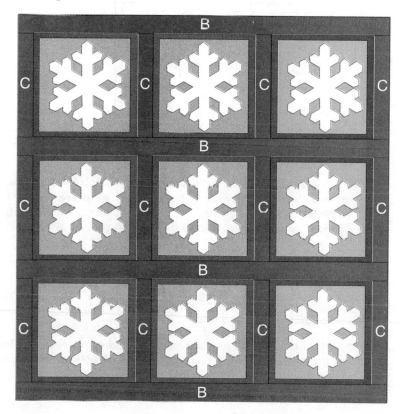

6. On the *wrong* side of the white D-2 piece, mark 36 $2^7/_8$-inch x $2^7/_8$-inch squares. Mark a diagonal line through each square.

7. Place the marked D-2 piece and the unmarked blue D-1 piece together, right sides facing, and pin them together to keep them from shifting during sewing.

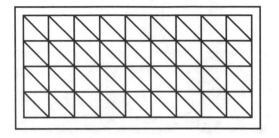

8. Stitch $^1/_4$ inch away from each side of the marked diagonal.

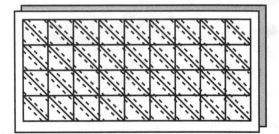

9. Cut out the individual squares, and then cut each square in half along its diagonal line.

10. Open all the triangles to form squares, which I refer to as half-square units because they're made from half of a square. (Some books call these half-triangles.) Press the seam allowances toward the blue fabrics. You will have a total of 72 half-square units.

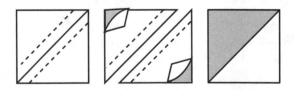

11. Stitch nine of the half-square units together to form one long strip. All the units should be facing the same direction. Make four of these strips.

12. Stitch nine more of the half-square units together. These units face the opposite direction as the ones that you made in Step 11. Make four of these strips.

13. Stitch one of each type of strip to opposite sides of a mustard-yellow F square. Make four of these strips. Stitch one strip to the top and one strip to the bottom edges of the quilt center, reserving the remaining two strips for the next step.

14. Stitch one mustard-yellow F square to each end of two strips left over from Step 1. Stitch these two strips to the remaining two sides of the quilt center.

15. Stitch a blue A strip to the top and bottom edges of the quilt center. Stitch a mustard-yellow F square to each end of the remaining two A strips, and stitch these strips to the remaining two sides of the quilt center. Press everything.

You have now completed the quilt top.

Quilting and Finishing the Project

Follow these steps to complete your quilt:

1. Layer the quilt top with the batting and backing and hand or pin baste the layers together to prepare it for quilting.

2. Hand or machine quilt as desired.

3. Machine straight stitch close to the raw edges of the quilt top (about $1/4$ inch from the edges) and trim away the excess batting and backing fabric that extends from beyond the edges of the quilt top.

4. Bind the quilt to complete.

Half-Size Snowflake Pattern

Double the size (200 percent) for a full-size pattern.

Project 16

Caribbean Dream Quilt

· ·

Finished size: 62 inches wide x 90 inches long; fits a twin-size bed with a deep drop.

Finished block size: 12 inches x 12 inches

· ·

*B*ecause it's so lively and colorful, I call this quilt "Caribbean Dream." The vibrant colors remind me of tropical fruits and those neat frozen drinks with umbrellas sticking out of them. I can almost hear the steel drums as I look at this quilt!

Feel free to tone down this project a bit by choosing softer colors for your fabrics. Just keep in mind that the fabrics' coordinating colors, patterns, and textures are what give an otherwise simple block complexity and movement.

If you're a bit nervous about choosing the right mix of fabrics, eliminate the guesswork by looking for collections of fabrics put together by fabric companies. (You should be able to find the various fabrics in a particular collection next to one another at the fabric store.)

The following sections walk you through the construction of the Caribbean Dream quilt, from choosing your materials to finishing the project. Enjoy!

Stashing Your Materials

You will need the following materials to make the Caribbean Dream Quilt:

- ✔ 3 yards of blue print fabric (outer border, sashing squares, and block centers)
- ✔ 2¹/₂ yards of red print fabric (block squares and innermost border)
- ✔ 2 yards of multi-colored floral print fabric (small block squares and middle border)

- 1 yard of yellow print fabric (sashing strips)
- 1 yard of green print fabric (large block triangles)
- $3/4$ yard of white solid fabric (small block triangles)
- Backing fabric measuring at least 70 inches x 98 inches
- 81-inch x 90-inch (full-size) quilt batting
- All-purpose sewing thread to coordinate with fabric colors
- 9 yards of solid white quilt binding

Cutting the Pieces

This section tells you the sizes and quantities of the pieces you need to cut for this quilt.

Note: All seam allowances are $1/4$ inch and are included in all the given measurements.

1. **Cut the block pieces according to the specifications in Table CD-1.**

Table CD-1		Block Pieces	
Piece	*Fabric*	*Size in Inches*	*Quantity*
A	Blue print	$4^1/2$ x $4^1/2$	15
B	Red print	$4^1/2$ x $4^1/2$	60
C	Green print	$4^7/8$ x $4^7/8$	30
D	White solid	$2^7/8$ x $2^7/8$	60
E	Multicolor print	$2^1/2$ x $2^1/2$	60

2. **Cut the border pieces according to the specifications in Table CD-2.**

Table CD-2		Border Pieces	
Border #	*Fabric*	*Size in Inches*	*Quantity*
1a	Red print	$72^1/2$ x $2^1/2$	2
1b	Red print	$47^1/2$ x $2^1/2$	2
2	Multicolor floral	44 x $2^1/2$	8 (will be pieced later to create borders 2a and 2b)
3a	Blue print	$80^1/2$ x $7^1/2$	2
3b	Blue print	$62^1/2$ x $7^1/2$	2

3. Cut the sashing pieces according to the specifications in Table CD-3.

Table CD-3		Sashing Pieces	
Piece	*Fabric*	*Size in Inches*	*Quantity*
F	Yellow	2½ x 12	38
G	Blue	2½ x 2½	24

Assembling the Quilt Blocks

After you cut the pieces required for this quilt, you're ready build the quilt blocks. The following steps walk you through this construction:

1. **Cut each green square (C) in half diagonally to create two triangles. This creates 60 large green triangles.**

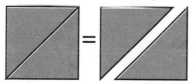

2. **Cut each white square (D) in half diagonally to create two triangles. This creates 60 small white triangles.**

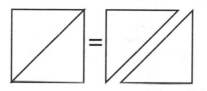

3. **Stitch two small white triangles (created in Step 2) to a multicolored square (E). Repeat this step until you have 60 of these units.**

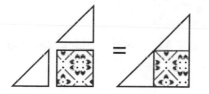

4. **Stitch one large green triangle (created in Step 1) to each unit created in Step 3. Repeat this step until you have 60 of these units.**

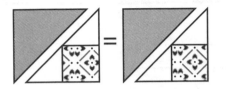

5. **To assemble rows 1 and 3 of the block, stitch one of the units you made in Step 4 to the left side of a red square (B). Stitch another one of the units made in Step 4 to the right side of the red square (B). Assemble 30 of these strips.**

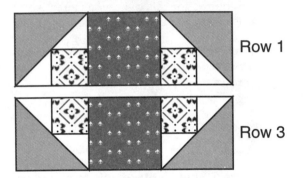

Row 1

Row 3

Note: Rows 1 and 3 are identical — you just turn row 3 upside down when you assemble the block.

6. **Create row 2 by stitching two red squares to a blue square: stitch one red square (B) to the left side of a blue square (A); then stitch another red square (B) to the right side of the blue square (A). Assemble 15 of these strips.**

Row 2

7. **Stitch together rows 1, 2, and 3 to create a block. Assemble 15 of these blocks.**

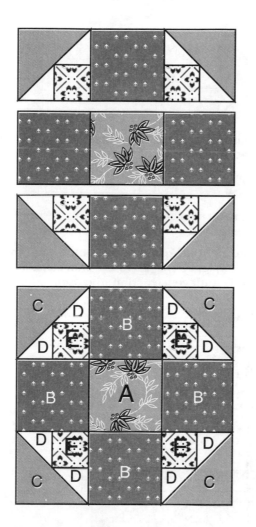

Assembling the Quilt Top

After you put together the quilt blocks, you're ready to combine the blocks with the sashing strips and the borders to create the quilt top. The following steps tell you how:

1. **Stitch four yellow sashing strips (F) alternately with three of the blocks you assembled in Step 7 of the previous section to create the row shown in the following figure. Assemble five of these rows.**

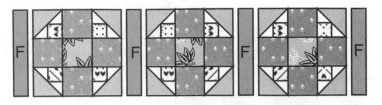

2. **Stitch four blue squares (G) alternately with three yellow strips (F) to create a sashing row. Assemble six of these rows.**

3. **Stitch the five block rows alternately with the six sashing rows to assemble the quilt center.**

4. **Stitch borders 1a and 1b to the quilt center: Stitch 1a to the two long sides of the quilt center, and strips 2b to the short sides, in the order shown in the following quilt construction diagram.**

5. Stitch together two of the multicolored strips along their short ends to make one long strip. Assemble four of these strips.

6. Having the seam at the center of the strips, trim down two of the strips created in Step 5 to measure $2^1/_2$ inches x $76^1/_2$ inches, creating the two 2a border pieces.

7. Trim down the remaining two strips to measure $2^1/_2$ inches x $52^1/_2$ inches, creating the two 2b border pieces, as you did in the previous step.

8. Stitch the four border pieces to the quilt center, stitching the longer strips to the sides first, followed by the shorter strips on the top and bottom edges as shown in the quilt construction diagram following Step 4.

9. Stitch border 3 to the quilt center in the same manner as the previous border.

10. The quilt top is now complete.

Quilting and Finishing the Project

After the quilt top assembly is complete, you're in the home stretch! Follow these steps to quilt and finish your Caribbean Dream quilt and get it ready for the bed:

1. Layer the quilt top with the batting and backing and hand-baste the layers together. Quilt as desired.

2. Trim away the excess batting and backing fabric.

3. Bind the quilt to finish the project.

Part V
The Part of Tens

The 5th Wave   By Rich Tennant

In this part . . .

Once you start quilting, I know you'll be hooked on it. And this part gives you tens of suggestions for how to expand your outlook on this uniquely personal, practical, and artistic craft. View some of America's best quilt collections, shop for quilting supplies on the Internet and chat with folks who share your interest, display your own quilt art, and develop time-saving techniques with the tips I give you in this quilting cornucopia.

Chapter 14

Ten Museums with Great Quilt Exhibits

▶ Museum quality quilting across the country

*Q*uilting has become both an art and a craft. Some quilt artists today produce fabric creations that bear no resemblance to traditional patchwork. Instead, they take their inspiration from the works of the Great Art Masters and contemporary artists. Traditional quilt designs are also valued for their artistic and historical value. For a look at the best in quilt design and construction through the ages, check out the permanent or rotating exhibits at the following great museums.

Museum of the American Quilter's Society

215 Jefferson Street
Paducah, Kentucky 42002
Telephone: 502-442-8856
E-mail: maqsmus@apex.net
Web site: www.aqsquilt.com
Contacts: Dorisanna Conne, Curator; Victoria Faoro, Executive Director
Hours:
Monday through Saturday: 10 a.m. – 5 p.m.
Sunday: 1 p.m. – 5 p.m. April – October only
Closed holidays
Admission:
$5.00 adults; $3.00 students; group rates available

A must-see for every quilter, the Museum of the American Quilter's Society is the only national quilt museum honoring today's quilter. This nonprofit museum, associated with the American Quilter's Society, has three exhibit galleries with three or more antique and contemporary quilt exhibits on display, plus temporary exhibits on loan. A book and gift shop is on the premises. The museum hosts workshops, educational programs, and special events.

San Jose Museum of Quilts

110 Paseo de San Antonio
San Jose, California 95112
Telephone: 408-971-0323
Web site: www.folkart.com/~latitude/museums/m_amqt.htm
Contact: Robin Treen, Exhibits Director
Hours:
Tuesday through Sunday: 10 a.m. – 5 p.m.
Thursday: open until 8 p.m.
Closed Mondays
Admission:
$5 adults; $4 seniors/students; kids under 13 free
Special: Free admission offered on first Thursday of every month
Group tours available

Regularly changing exhibits feature both historical and contemporary quilts from around the world. The museum also has a permanent collection of 19th and 20th century quilts, textiles, and garments. In addition, the museum provides educational outreach for 5th grade students, which includes a 45-minute presentation that relates U.S. history through the art of quilting. Additional programs, workshops, and lectures are also available. Contact the museum for more information.

International Quilt Study Center University of Nebraska, Lincoln

234 HE Building, P.O. Box 830802
Lincoln, Nebraska 68583
Telephone: 402-472-2911
E-mail: cducey@unl.edu
Web site: www.ianr.unl.edu/tcd/quilts/homepage.htm
Contact: Carolyn Ducey, Curator, Dept. of Textiles, Clothing and Design
Hours: By appointment only

The center has one of the largest and most comprehensive quilt collections in the world, featuring 950 antique and contemporary quilts donated by Ardis and Robert James. Call the center for current information on exhibits, as they change often. The center also offers monthly tours of the facility by appointment. Group size is 10 to 15 people. Tours include its state-of-the-art storage facility and some of the quilts from the collection. A question-and-answer session led by the curator or an intern follows the tour. Additionally, in order to support the center's work, an Adopt-A-Quilt program allows individuals, groups, and corporations to participate in quilt conservation and educational efforts.

Museum of American Folk Art

2 Lincoln Square
Columbus Avenue between 65th and 66th Streets
New York, New York 10023
Telephone: 212-977-7170
E-mail: info@folkartmuse.org
Web site: www.folkartmuse.org/toc.html
Contact: Susan Flamm, Publicity
Hours:
Tuesday through Saturday: 11:30 a.m. – 7:30 p.m.
Closed Mondays
Admission: Free; suggested donation of $3

Together with a permanent collection gallery and rotating exhibits, the museum sponsors a yearly quilt show. Membership options include "The Quilt Connection," a special membership level for quilters, quilt collectors, and quilt enthusiasts. Members receive a newsletter that covers quilt and textile research, interviews with quilters and collectors, news of quilt exhibitions and museum programs, and a calendar of selected quilt events around the country.

Rocky Mountain Quilt Museum

1111 Washington Avenue
Golden, Colorado 80401
Telephone: 303-277-0377
E-mail: RMQM@worldnet.att.net
Web site: www.rmqm.org/
Hours:
Tuesday through Saturday: 10 a.m. – 4 p.m.
Sunday: noon – 4 p.m.
Closed Mondays
Admission: $2 adults; members and kids under 6 free

Presents six different quilt exhibits each year, each with a different style, theme, history, or technique. Includes traditional, contemporary, and art quilts. Reference library available for quilt-related research and has a gift shop with new and old quilts, quilt-related books, and gifts.

DAR Museum (Daughters of the American Revolution Museum)

1776 "D" Street NW
Washington, DC 20006
Telephone: 202-879-3241
Contact: Nancy Tuckhorn, Curator of Textiles
Hours:
Monday through Friday: 8:30 a.m. – 4 p.m.
Sunday: 1 p.m. – 5 p.m.
Closed Saturdays, holiday weekends, and holiday Mondays
Admission: Free and open to the public

A permanent display of quilts rotates at least twice a year. Quilts are on exhibit in four of the 33 period exhibition rooms and are seen by guided tour only. A 1½ hour program is held the first Thursday of most months from 1– 3 p.m. The curator will attempt to identify any pre-20th century American-made textile that visitors bring in. Advance reservations are required for this service, as well as a fee of $10 per object.

The New England Quilt Museum

18 Shattuck Street
Lowell, MA 01852
Telephone: 978-452-4207
E-mail: mps@tiac.net
Web site: www.tiac.net/users/mps/
Contacts: Jennifer Gilbert, Curator; Pat Stuart, Director
Hours:
Tuesday through Saturday: 10 a.m. – 4 p.m.
Sunday: noon – 4 p.m. (May through November)
Closed Mondays
Admission: $4 adults; $3 seniors/students; free to museum members

Exhibits quilts from contemporary quilt artists, as well as antique quilts. Offers workshops, classes, demonstrations and lectures, as well as quilt-related activities for children.

Virginia Quilt Museum

301 South Main Street
Harrisonburg, Virginia 22801
Telephone: 540-433-3818
E-mail: ceknightt@postoffice.worldnet.att.net
Web site: www.folkart.com/~latitude/museums/m_vqm.htm
Contact: Joan Knight, Director
Hours:
Monday, Thursday, Friday, and Saturday: 10 a.m. – 4 p.m.
Sunday: 1 p.m. – 4 p.m.
Closed Wednesdays
Admission: $4 adults; $3 seniors/students; $2 6-12 years old; under 6 free

The Virginia Quilt Museum is open to the public as a resource center for the study of the role of quilts and quilting in the cultural life of society. The museum offers opportunities to view significant work by both early and contemporary quilt artisans, and encourages documentation and conservation of quilts by maintaining the records of the Virginia Quilt Project. It also offers educational programs, classes, and special publications, along with a museum gift shop. Free Group rates are available.

Michigan State University Museum

East Lansing, Michigan 48824
Telephone: 517-432-3800 quilt line
E-mail: quilts@museum.cl.msu.edu
Web site: www.museum.cl.msu.edu
Contacts: Elizabeth Donaldson, Quilt Collections Assistant; Marsha MacDowell, Ph.D., Curator of Folk Arts
Hours:
Monday through Friday: 9 a.m. – 5 p.m.
Saturday: 10 a.m. – 5 p.m.
Sunday: 1 p.m. – 5 p.m.
Admission: Free; suggested donation $2

The museum provides Quilt Collection Tours of its collection of about 500 quilts, which includes the collections of Mary Schafer, Merry Silber, the Michigan Quilt Project, African-American quilts, and Native American quilts. The museum is also host to the 20th annual travelling "American Quilt Study Group" 1999 seminar. The home of the on-going Michigan Quilt Project, which features more than 4,000 documented and databased quilts available for research, the museum trains quilt guilds to do oral histories as part of the Alliance for the American Quilts' Boxes Under the Bed Program. The museum also has a store and provides a newsletter for Great Lakes quilt lovers.

The Kentucky Museum Quilt Collection

The Kentucky Museum
Western Kentucky University
Bowling Green, Kentucky 42101
Telephone: 502-745-2592
E-mail: library.web@wku.edu
Web site: www2.wku.edu/library/museum/quilts.htm
Contact: Donna Parker, Associate Professor, Exhibit Curator
Hours:
Tuesday through Saturday 9:30 a.m. – 4 p.m.
Sunday: 1 p.m. – 4 p.m.
Closed Monday
Admission: $2 adults; $1 students; $5 families; children under 5 free; no charge on Sunday

Having both permanent and rotating exhibits, the museum's approximately 130 examples of Kentucky quilts made between the years 1850 and 1900 includes piecework, applique, white-on-white, and stuffed work. The collection includes 27 crazy-quilts and 9 log cabin variations. Hosts educational activities for students, teacher workshops, and group tours.

Chapter 15

Top Ten Cyber-Sites for Shoppers

In This Chapter

▶ Cheryl's favorite supply sites

*1*n line with quilting's steady march through history, today's quilters can access a wealth of information, education, and supplies online. Computer quilting is also developing quite a following. The following are great Web sites for buying quilting supplies and getting tips, tricks, and a variety of freebies geared to all levels of quilting.

Thread and Thimble
Web site: www.threadandthimble.com/
E-mail: karenm@threadandthimble.com
Location:
4507 East Oregon Street
Bellingham, Washington 98226
Fax order line: 360-734-2275

This online catalog features fabrics, books, patterns, notions, and clearance items. This site is a breeze to navigate. It includes tips on fabric care and a list of links. Minimum fabric cut is $1/4$ yard. MasterCard and Visa accepted. Free shipping provided on orders of $50 or more of regularly priced merchandise (and oh, how we fabri-holics know how quickly those orders add up!).

Country Stitches
Web site: www.countrystitches.com/visit.html
E-mail: stitches@voyager.net
Location:
2200 Coolidge Road
East Lansing, Michigan 48823
Telephone: 800-572-2031

Calling itself the "largest quilting shop in the United States," Country Stitches features more than 6,000 bolts of prints and solids in 100 percent cotton, hundreds of books, threads, rulers, and needles. Pattern of the month and some kits, fabric packets, and other products are available through their online catalog. Listing of events and classes and a cyber quilt-show. MasterCard, Visa, and Discover accepted.

Common Threads Quilt Shop
Web site: www.members.aol.com/commonthd/
E-mail: commonthd@aol.com
Location:
142 West Main Street
Mesa, Arizona 85201
Telephone: 602-668-0908
Fax: 602-668-9828

This wonderful shop is one of my top picks to visit in person as well. It features all the best in fabrics for quilters, a block-of-the-month program, books, end-of-month specials, and a newsletter. The site also includes links to other quilting sites. Visa, MasterCard, Discover, and American Express accepted.

TreadleArt
Web site: www.treadleart.com
E-mail: treadleart@treadleart.com
Locations (2):

25834 Narbonne Avenue	1965 Mendocino Avenue
Lomita, California 90717	Santa Rosa, California 95401
Telephone: 310-534-5122	707-523-2122
Fax: 310-534-8372	707-523-2144

TreadleArt stocks a very large selection of books in all categories as well as a delightful assortment of patterns for quilters and threads, notions, tools, and specialty items. They're often at major sewing expositions and their book is always a big hit. I recommend an in-person visit to their shops or exposition booths. You can e-mail them for a catalog. MasterCard, Visa, American Express, and Discover accepted.

The Quilt Gallery
Web site: www.cyberport.net/quiltgallery/index.html
E-mail: quiltgal@cyberport.net
Location:
1710 Highway 93 South
Kalispell, Montana 59901
Phone/fax: 406-257-5799

The Quilt Gallery is another one of my top picks to visit in person as well as on the Web. It offers approximately 4,000 bolts of fabric from top manufacturers, as well as specialty fabrics and flannels. It also carries a large selection of books, patterns, and notions. Fabric packets and kits, a newsletter, and online order forms are available. Visa, MasterCard, Novus, Bernina, and American Express accepted.

Animas Quilts
Web site: www.animas.com
E-mail: AnimasQuilts@animas.com
Location:
600 Main Avenue
Durango, Colorado 81301
Telephone: 800-770-2523
Fax: 970-247-2569

This shop has been a Mecca for quilters for as long as I can remember, and is a must-see if you're in the Durango area (home of the all-time baseball great, Jackie Robinson). Featuring an online catalog with secure ordering, Animas carries books, kits, and block-of-the-month patterns, as well as a listing of favorite links. MasterCard, Visa, and Discover accepted.

The Icehouse Quilt Shop
Web site: www.theicehousequiltshop.com/
E-mail: icehouse@freeway.net
Location:
509 Norway Street
Grayling, Michigan 49738
Telephone: 517-348-4821
Fax: 517-348-7745

This site has an online newsletter and online catalog featuring a wonderful assortment of books, patterns, notions, and kits. It also has a cyber "shop tour." I recommend a live visit if you're in the area; you'll find a map online. Visa, MasterCard, Discover, and American Express accepted.

Quiltropolis
Web site: www.quiltropolis.com/
E-mail: info@quiltropolis.com
Telephone: 804-730-0672
Fax: 804-730-8829

This online catalog features fabrics, battings, software, books, patterns, and notions. This site even offers a club, chat room, and online sewing classes, as well as an internal search feature and a toll-free ordering number of 1-888-831-2360. Orders to APO, FPO, and other countries are welcome.

Stitchin' Heaven
Web site: www.stitchinheaven.com/index.htm
E-mail: stitchin@stitchinheaven.com
Location:
502 East Goode
Quitman, Texas 75783
Telephone: 903-763-5048

Stitchin' Heaven offers a nice assortment of quilting supplies, as well as a newsletter and calendar of upcoming events, and a block-of-the-month club. It ships outside the country, too! Visa, MasterCard, Discover, and American Express accepted.

The Country Peddler Quilt Shop
Web site: www.countrypeddler.com/
E-mail: quilts@countrypeddler.com
Location:
2230 Carter Avenue
Saint Paul, Minnesota 55108
Telephone: 612-646-1756

This is another place you just have to visit if you're in the area! It offers a great selection of fabrics, books, patterns, kits, and notions, along with several different block-of-the-month options. The Web site has an online gallery and a printable order form. Visa and MasterCard only accepted.

Chapter 16

Ten Time-Saving Quilting Tips

*T*hroughout this book, I give you time-saving ideas and tips to help you progress in your stitching progress more quickly and smoothly. Here are a few more tips I'd like to pass along:

✔ **Keep your machine clean, oiled, and in top condition.** Nothing wastes time faster than having to restitch a seam because the needle is skipping, adjust the tension during a project, or pick lint out of a seam because the machine wasn't cleaned before use.

✔ **Set up an efficient workspace.** The "kitchen triangle" that interior designers insist upon works for quilting, too! Instead of a "sink, stove, work surface," set up a "machine, pressing, work surface" triangle. Position everything so you only have to take a few steps in between. This saves time and energy when working on large projects.

✔ **When piecing, choose one neutral thread color that works well with all fabrics.** This saves the hassle of changing thread color for every fabric.

✔ **Divide the work into manageable units that can be completed in 10 to 15 minutes time.** Then you can work on them when you know you have some wait-time ahead of you, such as when waiting for a phone call.

✔ **When working on small units, finger-press the pieces open rather than running to the ironing board each time.** To do this, simply run your fingernail over the seamline of the opened unit to press the seam allowance open. You can press the pieces at the ironing board later.

✔ **Chain-piece whenever possible.** You can cut the units apart later, perhaps while watching television or helping the youngsters with homework. Likewise, trim all thread tails at once.

✔ **Work in shifts.** Divide your time by cutting out all of the pieces at once, followed another time by stitching units together, then the units into blocks, and finally the blocks into a quilt top.

✔ **Stitch on the run.** Are you working on a project which requires hand appliqué or hand piecing? Pack a resealable plastic bag with your fabric, thread, extra needles, and a small pair of scissors so you can work on your project just about anywhere. Tote your project with you during those endless lobby loungings at the dentist's or doctor's office. Keep it in the car and work on it while waiting outside the schoolyard during carpool duty.

If you're bringing your project along on vacation or an overnight visit, bring a 75-watt light bulb along so you know you'll always be stitching in good light. Hotels are notorious for using low-wattage light bulbs.

✔ **When doing hand appliqué, piecing, or quilting, keep several needles threaded at all times.** Threading needles is a great job for the kids.

If you're interested in measuring the amount of thread you put into a quilt, a great time to measure is when you thread your needles. Simply cut enough one-yard lengths of the thread at one time for any number of needles (working in 10s would help). Thread the needles and place them in a pincushion. Keep track of the number of yards cut in your notepad. Hey, some quilters go in for this stuff!

✔ **Buy prepackaged binding rather than making your own.** Binding is usually sold in 2- to 3-yard units.

Chapter 17

Ten Tips for Displaying Your Art

In This Chapter

▶ Creating hangers for your quilts

▶ Securing large quilts

▶ Using other display methods

*B*ecause quilted items are practical as well as decorative, you may be showing off your quilt as a bedcovering on your bed or a placemat on your table. But you can also display your quilting as decorative art.

Following are ten tips to help you display your masterpiece safely and to its best advantage. I start with four ways to hang your quilts:

✔ **Pin your quilt to the wall.** Using those nice, skinny straight pins — the same kind used for pinning fabric together when sewing — insert a pin in the *backing* on each upper corner of the quilt, about $\frac{1}{2}$ inch from the corner, pushing the pin into the wall at an angle upwards about $\frac{1}{2}$ inch. (By inserting the pin in the backing, you can actually hide the pin *behind* the quilt, and no one will be the wiser.) Do the same thing with the lower corners, but angle the head of the pin downwards so that the ends of the quilt won't "crawl" up the pin.

Pinning doesn't work well for quilts larger than, say, 36 inches x 36 inches. Quilts beyond that size are too heavy for the pins to hold up properly.

✔ **Use a wooden quilt hanger.** Wooden quilt hangers are available in many quilt shops and quilting catalogs. However, they are very easy to make, so you may want to enlist your favorite handy-person to make one for you. The hangers consist of two pieces of wood that are placed on top of one another, sandwiching the top edge of the quilt between them. This method cuts off the top edge of your quilt from view. To correct this, consider hand-stitching a *dummy strip* of fabric to the top-back edge of your quilt. Insert this strip between the boards instead of the binding. (Of course, if you remove the quilt from the hanger to use as a table covering or lap quilt, remove this dummy strip.)

✔ **Attach a dowel sleeve.** To use this popular quilt-hanging method, attach a sleeve to the upper backside of the quilt and insert a dowel or lath strip into the sleeve. To hang your quilt, place a cord through the dowel sleeve and hang it over the nail you previously banged into the wall. You can also cut the dowel an inch or two longer than the quilt is wide and attach finials to the ends of the dowel for a decorative look.

✔ **Use a café curtain rod and the accompanying brackets.**

Here are six more display ideas:

✔ **Use the quilt as a table topper.**

✔ **Drape the quilt over the back of a chair.**

✔ **Fold and stack several quilts in an open cupboard (very "country-looking").**

✔ **Arrange a quilt so that it appears to spill out of a big basket or trunk.**

✔ **Fold the quilt and place it at the foot of the bed or on the back of the sofa.**

✔ **Drape the quilt over the stair rail. Quilts look wonderful hanging from the landing railing!**

Use your imagination to come up with additional ways to show off your quilted art!

Hanging large-sized quilts

To hang a large quilt, make a sleeve as for a smaller quilt, but cut the strip of fabric the width of the quilt x 12 inches. For example, if the width of your quilt is 60 inches, cut your sleeve fabric 60 inches x 12 inches. Finish and attach the sleeve as you would for smaller quilts, but instead of inserting a dowel, use a length of closet rod cut the exact width of the quilt. Insert a heavy-duty screw eye into each end and insert the rod into the sleeve. To hang, cut a length of heavy-gauge wire 6 inches longer than the length of the closet rod and insert one end into each screw eye; secure by twisting. Hang the quilt on a nail that has been pounded into a wall stud.

Resources for Quilters

● ●

*Q*uilting opens a whole new world of fabulous fabrics, creative patterns, and a range of notions and other necessities to warm the heart of anyone who once stared starry-eyed at the colorful variety of pencils and tablets and stuff arrayed in the grade school supply store.

What follows are lists of my favorite suppliers, along with a selection of books and magazines that will help expand your quilting horizons. You'll develop more of your own favorites as you proceed. And don't forget to hook up with your local Quilting Guild and fabric stores to develop your quilting style in the best quilting tradition — community.

Quilting Supplies

If you need assistance locating supplies for quilting, contact the following manufacturers. They can tell you where their products are available in your area or recommend a mail-order source. Many of these manufacturers also support quilting contests and guild activities, provide free patterns or giveaways, or have other resources available to quilters. Be sure to check out their Web sites!

Fabrics

Fabric Traditions and Classic
Traditions
1530 Broadway, Suite 2106
New York, NY 10018
800-538-0668
Web site:
www.fabrictrad.com

Marcus Brothers Textiles
1460 Broadway
New York, NY 10036
800-548-8295
Web site: www.marcusbrothers.com

P&B Textiles
1580 Gilbreth Road
Burlingame, CA 94010
800-852-2327
Web site: www.pbtex.com

RJR Fabrics
13748 S. Gramercy Place
Gardena, CA 90249
800-422-5426
Web site:
www.rjrfabrics.com

Robert Kaufman Co., Inc.
P.O. Box 59266
Los Angeles, CA 90059
800-877-2066

Springs "Quilter's Only"
420 West White Street
Rock Hill, SC 29730
Web site: www.quiltersonly.com

VIP Fabrics
469 Seventh Avenue
New York, NY 10018
800-847-4064
Web site: www.cranstonvillage.com

Batting (B), stuffing (St), and pillow forms (PF)

Buffalo Batt & Felt
3307 Walden Avenue
Depew, NY 14043
B, St, PF

Fairfield Processing
P.O. Box 1130
Danbury, CT 06813
800-980-8000
Web site: www.poly-fil.com
B, St, PF

Hobbs Bonded Fibers
P.O. Box 2521
Waco, TX 76702
B

Morning Glory Products
302 Highland Drive
Taylor, TX 76574
800-234-9105
B, St, PF

Mountain Mist
100 Williams Street
Cincinnati, OH 45215
800-345-7150
Web site: www.palaver.com/mountainmist/
B, St, PF, as well as quilting stencils and patterns

Fusible transfer webbing (FW) and stabilizer (Sb)

Handler Textile Corporation
60 Metro Way
Secaucus, NJ 07094
877-448-2669
Web site: www.htc-handler.com
FW, Sb

Pellon/Freudenberg Nonwovens
20 Industrial Avenue
Chelmsford, MA 01824
FW, Sb

Threads

Coats & Clark
Two Lakepointe Plaza
4135 South Stream Blvd.
Charlotte, NC 28217
Consumer services: 704-329-5800
Web site: www.coatsandclark.com
All-purpose, rayon and buttonhole twist threads, as well as needles (both hand and machine), embroidery floss, and ready-made bias tape.

Quilt frames (F), hoops (H), display racks (DR), and other items (O)

Grace Quilting Frames
P.O. Box 27823
Salt Lake City, UT 84127
800-264-0644
F

Hinterberg Design, Inc.
2805 E. Progress Drive
West Bend, WI 53095
800-443-5800
H, F, DR

Jasmine Heirlooms
500Fairview Drive
Greenville, SC 29609
800-736-7326
H, F, DR

Quilting software

The Electric Quilt Company
419 Gould Street, Suite 2
Bowling Green, OH 43402
800-356-4219
Web site: www.wcnet.org/
ElectricQuiltCo/

Quilt-Pro Systems, Inc.
P.O. Box 560692
The Colony, TX 75056
800-884-1511
Web site: www.quiltpro.com

Notions, rotary cutting supplies, and fun stuff

Clover Needlecraft Products
1007 E. Dominguez St, #L
Carson, CA 90746
800-233-1703
All sorts of quilting tools:
scissors, thimbles, marking
pencils, and more

EZ International
95 Mayhill Street
Saddlebrook, NJ 07662
Rotary cutting supplies,
marking pencils, thimbles, and
other goodies

Heirloom Woven Labels
P.O. Box 428
Moorestown, NJ 08057
Web site: members.aol.com/
heirlooml
Personalized, custom-woven
labels for quilting and other
crafts projects

Master Piece Products
10481 NW 107th Avenue
Granger, IA 50109
Rotary cutting supplies

Prym-Dritz Corporation
P.O. Box 5028
Spartanburg, SC 29304
800-845-4948
Rotary cutting supplies, marking pencils,
thimbles, and other goodies

Recommended Reading

Country Living's Country Quilts
By the editors of *Country
Living Magazine*
Hearst Books

Fast, Fun & Fabulous Quilts
By Suzanne Nelson
Rodale Press

The Joy of Quilting
By Joan Hanson and
Mary Hickey
That Patchwork Place

Quick Classic Quilts
By Marsha McCloskey
Leisure Arts

Quilter's Complete Guide
By Marianne Fons and Liz Porter
Leisure Arts

The Quilting Sourcebook
By Maggi McCormick Gordon
Trafalgar Square

Quiltmaking Tips and Techniques
By the editors of *Quilter's
Newsletter Magazine*
Rodale Books

Quilts, Quilts and More Quilts
By Diana McClun and Laura
Nownes
C&T Publishing

Speed Quilting
By Cheryl Fall
Sterling Publishing

The Thimbleberries Book of Quilts
By Lynette Jensen
Rodale Books

Ultimate Rotary Cutting Reference
By Judy Martin
Crosley-Griffth Publishers

Quilting Magazines to Inspire You!

Contact the magazines individually for subscription rates. Be sure to check
out the Web sites listed. Some sites have free patterns and things to print
out on your computer.

*American Patchwork and
Quilting*
1716 Locust Street
Des Moines, IA 50309
800-677-4876
Published bi-monthly
Web site: www.bhglive.com/
crafts/apq/apq.html

American Quilter
P.O. Box 3290
Paducah, KY 42002-3290
502-898-7903
Published quarterly

Creative Quilting
950 Third Avenue, 16th Floor
New York, NY 10022
212-888-1855
Published bi-monthly

McCall's Quilting
2 News Plaza,
P.O. Box 1790
Peoria, IL 61656
309-682-6626
Published bi-monthly
Web site: www.k3.com/media/
specialinterest/quilting.html

Quick and Easy Patchwork
243 Newton-Sparta Road
Newton, NJ 07860
973-383-8080
Published several times per year

Quick & Easy Quilting
306 East Parr Road
Berne, IN 46711
219-589-8741
Published bi-monthly

Quilt Magazine
1115 Broadway
New York, New York 10010
212-807-7100
Web site: www.quiltmag.com/
Published quarterly

Quilter's Newsletter Magazine
P.O. Box 59021
Boulder, CO 80322
800-477-6089
Published 10x/year
Web site:
www.quiltersnewsletter.com

Quiltmaker
P.O. Box 4101
Golden, CO 80401
800-477-6089
Published bi-monthly
Web site:
www.quiltmaker.com

Sew Many Quilts
22100 Lakeshore Drive
Birmingham, AL 35209
800-633-4910
Published bi-monthly

Traditional Quilter
243 Newton-Sparta Road
Newton, NJ 07860
973-383-8080
Published bi-monthly

Fun Reads Based on Quilting

Do you want to know more about the lives of quilters-past? Do you get hungry when you quilt? Maybe you just like a good "read." Here's a list of quilt-related titles I recommend.

New Recipes from Quilt Country: More Food & Folkways from the Amish & Mennonites
By Marcia Adams
Clarkson Potter

A Quilt of Words: Womens Diaries, Letters, and Original Accounts of Life in the Southwest, 1860-1960
By Sharon Niederman
Johnson Books

Silent Friends: A Quaker Quilt
By Margaret Lacey
Stormline Press

How to Make an American Quilt
By Whitney Otto
Ballantine Books

Twelve Golden Threads: Lessons for Successful Living from Grama's Quilt
By Aliske Webb
HarperCollins (paper)

Words & Quilts: A Selection of Quilt Poems
By Felicia Mitchell
Quilt Digest

Gatherings: America's Quilt Heritage
By Katy Christopherson,
Gerald E. Roy, Paul Pilgrim,
Kathryn F. Sullivan,
Kathlyn F. Sullivan
American Quilters Society

Elizabeth Roseberry Mitchell's Graveyard Quilt: An American Pioneer Saga
By Linda Otto Lipsett
Halstead & Meadows Pub

The Quilt & Other Stories
By Ismat Cughtai, Tahira
Nagyi, Syeda S. Hameed
Sheep Meadow Press

Quilt of Many Colors: A Collage of Prose and Poetry
By Grayce Confer
Beacon Hill Press

Sweet Clara and the Freedom Quilt (children's)
By Deborah Hopkinson,
James Ransome (Illustrator)
Demco Media

Dove in the Window
By Earlene Fowler
(One of a series of mysteries
with quilt block titles)
Berkley Publishing Group

The Persian Pickle Club
By Sandra Dallas
St. Martins Press

Death on the Drunkard's Path: An Iris House B&B Mystery
By Jean Hagar
Avon

A Piece of Justice: An Imogen Quy Mystery
By Jill Paton Walsh
St. Martins Press

Buried in Quilts
By Sara Hoskinson Frommer
Worldwide Publications

No Dragons on My Quilt (children's)
By Jean Ray Laury
Collector Books

World Wide Quilting Page

A good Web site with lots of information about quilting and lots of links to other good quilting information sites is the World Wide Quilting Page at `http://ttsw.com/MainQuiltingPage.html`.

Index

Notes

Notes

Notes

Notes

Playing games is really fun...
The Dummies Way™!

Pressman®
© 1998 Pressman Toy Corporation, New York, NY 10010

Crosswords For Dummies™ Game

You don't have to know how to spell to have a great time. Place a word strip on the board so that it overlaps another word or creates a new one. Special squares add to the fun. The first player to use up all their word strips wins!

For 2 to 4 players.

Trivia For Dummies™ Game

You're guaranteed to have an answer every time! Each player gets 10 cards that contain the answer to every question. Act quickly and be the first player to throw down the correct answer and move closer to the finish line!

For 3 or 4 players.

Charades For Dummies™ Game

Act out one-word charades: when other players guess them, they move ahead. The special cards keep the game full of surprises. The first player around the board wins.

For 3 or 4 players.

...For Dummies and The Dummies Way are trademarks or registered trademarks of IDG Books Worldwide, Inc.

IDG BOOKS WORLDWIDE
BOOK REGISTRATION

Register This Book and Win!

We want to hear from you!

Visit **http://my2cents.dummies.com** to register this book and tell us how you liked it!

- ✔ Get entered in our monthly prize giveaway.

- ✔ Give us feedback about this book — tell us what you like best, what you like least, or maybe what you'd like to ask the author and us to change!

- ✔ Let us know any other *For Dummies®* topics that interest you.

Your feedback helps us determine what books to publish, tells us what coverage to add as we revise our books, and lets us know whether we're meeting your needs as a *For Dummies* reader. You're our most valuable resource, and what you have to say is important to us!

Not on the Web yet? It's easy to get started with *Dummies 101®: The Internet For Windows® 98* or *The Internet For Dummies®* at local retailers everywhere.

Or let us know what you think by sending us a letter at the following address:

For Dummies Book Registration
Dummies Press
10475 Crosspoint Blvd.
Indianapolis, IN 46256

FOR DUMMIES™

BESTSELLING
BOOK SERIES